Feeling Beauty

Feeling Beauty

The Neuroscience of Aesthetic Experience

G. Gabrielle Starr

The MIT Press
Cambridge, Massachusetts
London, England

First MIT Press paperback edition, 2015

© 2013 Massachusetts Institute of Technology

All rights reserved. No part of this book may be reproduced in any form by any electronic or mechanical means (including photocopying, recording, or information storage and retrieval) without permission in writing from the publisher.

This book was set in Adobe Garamond and Gotham by the MIT Press. Printed and bound in the United States of America.

Library of Congress Cataloging-in-Publication Data
Starr, G. Gabrielle, 1974–
Feeling beauty : the neuroscience of aesthetic experience / G. Gabrielle Starr.
　pages　cm
Includes bibliographical references and index.
ISBN 978-0-262-01931-6 (hardcover : alk. paper)
1. Neurosciences and the arts. 2. Aesthetics. I. Title.
NX180.N48S73　2013
700.1′9—dc23
2012046928

10　9　8　7　6　5　4　3

For John, Always.

Contents

Figures ix

Preface xi

Acknowledgments xvii

Introduction: Aesthetics, Neuroaesthetics, and the Sister Arts 1

Pleasure and Emotion 4

Imagination and Imagery 7

Aesthetic Knowledge 11

What Holds Aesthetic Experiences Together? 17

Toward a Neuroaesthetic Model 21

1 Seen and Heard: A Model for the Sister Arts   33

Emotion and Variation   36

Pleasure, Comparison, and Reward   46

Conceiving of Difference and of Self   54

2 Aesthetics beyond the Mind's Eye: Imagery and the Sister Arts   69

The Imagery of Sense   72

Knowledge and Multisensory Imagery   76

Moving Pictures: Aesthetics and Imagery Networks   81

3 Toward a Dynamic Aesthetics: The Sister Arts and Beyond   101

Invisible Beauty: Keats and the Limits of the Senses   102

Dynamic Knowledge: Ovid, What Is New and What Is Not   118

Music and Temporality: Beethoven and Bluegrass   128

Endings and Rebirth: Van Gogh and Erasure   138

Conclusion: *Carmen Perpetuum*   144

Appendix: "The Brain on Art" (Excerpt)   151

Notes   159

Bibliography   221

Index   257

Figures

1. Jackson Pollock, *Shimmering Substance*
2. Elgin Marbles, Three Goddesses
3. Van Gogh, *Ravine*
4. X-ray of *Ravine*
5. Van Gogh, "Wild Vegetation"
6. Bernini, *Apollo and Daphne*
7. Bernini, *Apollo and Daphne,* detail
8. Theme, Diabelli's Waltz
9. Beethoven, *Diabelli Variations*, opus 120, Variation 31, mm. 1–7
10. Across-Observer Correlations
11. BOLD fMRI Pattern One

12. BOLD fMRI Pattern Two
13. BOLD fMRI Pattern Three
14. Isolation of Most Intense Responses
15. Emotional/Evaluative Factors
16. Awe and Pleasure Regressions
17. Individual Differences Regression
18. Mean Talairach Coordinates for All fMRI Activations
19. Kanizsa Triangle

Preface

Beauty matters in life and in art, but it also matters in the architecture of the brain itself. This book is born of my belief, as both a scholar of the humanities and a researcher in the neuroscience of aesthetics, that understanding the neural underpinnings of aesthetic experience—not just the experience of beauty or wonderment, but the other pleasures and displeasures of the arts and the natural world—can reshape our understanding of aesthetics and of the arts. A number of key questions about aesthetics can be fruitfully engaged with the tools of cognitive neuroscience. To what extent are the pleasures of poetry, painting, music, and the other arts parallel? How do the emotions of aesthetic experience relate to those of the rest of daily life? What role does imagery play across the arts? How do the differences that make us individuals shape aesthetic experience? What do aesthetic experiences say about how we think? What kind of knowledge might aesthetic experience bring? Answers to these questions can teach us more about aesthetics, but they have implications that go beyond aesthetic life. Inquiry into the neuroscience of aesthetics can give us insight into, and lead to new questions about, emotion, the adaptability of neural structures in different individuals, and the relations between complex neural systems ranging from those underpinning imagery to those supporting memory and identity.

Feeling Beauty attempts to answer some of the questions about aesthetic experience posed above. It explores not just how we feel aesthetic pleasures but how they matter. Employing the tools of cognitive neuroscience and humanist inquiry, and combining both our knowledge and our ways of knowing, this book offers a new perspective on aesthetics and aesthetic life, and a new vision of how the aesthetic fits into the broader picture of what we know—and have still to learn—about human cognition.

Aesthetics offers a particular challenge to both humanists and scientists. It might seem natural and simply logical to group under one banner all the things we might, for example, call "beautiful," just as it might seem natural to group together all of the arts. But the beautiful as a category of experience or objects has been dismissed from and restored to the Western canon repeatedly, and indeed, the very idea of beauty has been insufficient historically to describe how the world and the objects in it move us.[1] The pleasures of the senses more broadly have been both denigrated and exalted over time and across cultures, and the idea that there might be a set of refined pleasures of the imagination connecting different arts and experiences is of relatively recent (and conflicted) history. While art and discussions of its pleasures are ancient, the idea that there is a single autonomous domain in which we might discuss or reason about the visual arts, literature, music, imagination, beauty, the sublime, or even the vulgarly awful is an invention of the eighteenth century. There is yet more discontinuity, and even fragmentation: new, usually contested, arts emerge in cultures, from—roughly historically in the West—ballet to opera, photography, cinema, performance art, and beyond; as well, what members of particular cultures call art is not always readily or completely translatable, so that music or statuary might be of primarily religious importance in one culture, while in another, flower arranging or making and serving tea might be acts of high artistry and signify the virtues of a warrior.[2]

Such historical shifts and cultural differences in aesthetic ideas might mean that the only valid arguments about aesthetics are local, rooted in particular objects, places, or moments. It is possible, however, to offer a rigorous account of aesthetics in a different way. We can believe that what beauty is and what beauty does changes; we also can be clear that the terms we use to describe our pleasures and displeasures evolve, and in doing so reveal new ways of our encountering the world around us. I argue in the coming pages that exploring the neural underpinnings of aesthetic experiences helps us not only to understand the migrations of culture and even the temporal fluidity of aesthetic life (the changes in one's tastes over time, for example) but also to see that this fluidity is essential to the aesthetic.[3] Aesthetic experience changes, and understanding these changes may give us more insight not just into aesthetics but also into the dynamic interrelations of neural processes.

In turning to the tools and methods of cognitive neuroscience I am continuing, in new form, the fundamentally multidisciplinary inquiry that has obtained since the early years of modern aesthetics. As Alexander Baumgarten put it in his *Meditationes* of 1735 (the text that introduced the term *aesthetics* into the modern lexicon), aesthetic experience is a blend of sensation and knowledge such that we may almost feel thought itself ("scientiam sensitive quid cognoscendi").[4] Understanding that blend of sensation and cognition has, since Baumgarten, involved work that does not fit easily or neatly within any one of the modern divisions of knowledge. In eighteenth-century Britain, the moral sense theorists, thinkers like Anthony Cooper, Earl of Shaftesbury, and Francis Hutcheson, saw the investigation of beauty as a way to discover the basis of community standards and the bonds that link us together; and Adam Smith wrote a treatise on the imagination that established the moral principles that came to govern *The Wealth of Nations*. In Germany, Immanuel Kant saw in aesthetic judgment the answer to a fundamental schism between pure and practical reason; Johann Wolfgang von Goethe researched optics and light as a way to explore aesthetic power; and Hermann von Helmholtz explored mathematics and the brain to theorize the effects of music.[5] This arc has not ended: researchers continue to demonstrate that investigating aesthetic experience requires multidisciplinary inquiry, using cognitive approaches to brain and behavior as they study music, literature, creativity, visual art, dance, or film.[6] *Feeling Beauty* builds on some of this work and challenges some of it, and it takes up anew the cross-disciplinary principles that have been at the heart of aesthetic inquiry from its beginnings.

Centering on the Sister Arts of music, painting, and poetry, *Feeling Beauty* shows that neuroaesthetics, or the study of the neural bases of aesthetic experience, offers a model for understanding the dynamic and changing features of aesthetic life, for understanding the relationships between the arts, and for understanding how individual differences in aesthetic judgment shape the varieties of aesthetic experience. Neuroaesthetics also helps us to see how the emotions and the hedonic texture—the complex admixture of pleasures and displeasures—that help make up aesthetic experience set the stage for the creative expansion of knowledge through, in grand or subtle ways, changing the order by which we make sense of the world.

Aesthetic experience relies on a distributed neural architecture, a set of brain areas involved in emotion, perception, imagery, memory, and language. But more than this, aesthetic experience emerges from *networked* interactions, the workings of intricately connected and coordinated brain systems that, together, form a flexible architecture enabling us to develop new arts and to see the world around us differently. Systems for emotion and reward, along with the default mode network (an interconnected set of brain areas that contributes to our sense of self-identity, as well as to our ability to imagine other worlds and other people, among other functions), work to enact the necessarily dynamic, constantly reevaluative neural processes that underpin aesthetic life. Through this architecture, aesthetics fundamentally involves our ability to wrest pleasure from the unpredictable and to refine, continually, how we imagine the borders between the world of sense and our sense of self. The neural processes underlying aesthetics are complicated, and we are just beginning to understand them, but even with what we now know, it is possible not just to understand more about aesthetic experience and how it moves us, as well as more about the relationships between the arts, but even to begin to see more fully why it makes sense to speak of a domain of the aesthetic at all, and to see how that domain may shift and move. Let us begin, though, with the question of the Sister Arts.

Acknowledgments

Work across the disciplines requires collaboration. I must therefore thank, first, Ed Vessel and Nava Rubin, and Steve Quartz, who helped me navigate new disciplinary waters. My collaboration with Ed and Nava helped lay the foundation for this work. The research we produced on visual art was first published as "The Brain on Art" in *Frontiers in Human Neuroscience*; the interpretation and extension of those results here to other forms of art, however, are my own (as are any mistakes).

Collaboration does not end with writing, and I would like to thank the press reviewers of this work, who gave me extremely helpful feedback, and an editor who believed in the project and whose careful eye has improved it, Phil Laughlin.

The Andrew W. Mellon Foundation provided financial support in the form of a New Directions Fellowship, which enabled me to study neuroscience at the graduate level with some of the best faculty around. In particular, I thank Elizabeth Phelps, Chiye Aoki, Alex Reyes, Dan Sanes, Sam Feldman, and Paul Glimcher for their world-class instruction. At Caltech, I had the privilege of learning the mechanics of fMRI experimentation under the instruction of Geraint Rees and Jorge Jovicich; they have my thanks as well. The support of the leadership at New York University's Faculty of Arts and Science was crucial to my undertaking this work. Matthew Santirocco and Richard Foley gave early support in the form of an opportunity for collaborative teaching, and Jess Benhabib and Tom Carew offered material support as well as cheerful, searching questions about my work. Lauren Benton and Dan Stein supported this work directly with research and grant funding (in part through an NSF ADVANCE challenge grant). I was also very fortunate to work with departmental chairs who supported my forays into other disciplines: John Guillory, Una Chaudhuri, and Philip Brian Harper.

Colleagues at NYU and elsewhere offered disciplined criticism, profound intellectual engagement, and friendship: Amy King, Liz Phelps, Ernesto Gilman, Denis Donoghue, Lytle Shaw, Maureen McLane, Tom August, Elaine Freedgood, Mary Poovey, Sandra MacPherson, Kevis Goodman, Jeff Dolven, Oren Izenberg, Christopher R. Miller, and Lisa Zunshine. Collin Jennings and Alexander Denker were excellent interlocutors as well as great research assistants. Audiences at the Cold Spring Harbor Laboratories, the University of Chicago, the University of California–Berkeley, Yale, Princeton, the CUNY Graduate Center, the University of North Carolina–Charlotte, and the meetings of the American Society for Eighteenth-Century Studies contributed constructive, thoughtful criticism. The staff of the NYU Center for Brain Imaging is exceptional, and I thank Keith Sanzenbach, Jennifer Mangan, Joshua Dickinson, Souheil Inati (now at NIH), and Valerio Luccio. My friends on the ninth floor of the College deserve special thanks. Christina Ciambriello has given her critical eye and her sharp elbow cheerfully and expertly. But the ethos of hard work and high expectation that permeates the office in which I am privileged to work sets a daunting standard. Christina, Natalie Friedman, Karen Krahulik, Ken Kidd, Pamela McKelvin, Willie Long, Sally Sanderlin, Richard Kalb, Aaron DeLand, Amy Monaco, Cary Chan, and Brian Paquette are peerless. Sita Das has been a staunch supporter in more ways than I can count. Thank you.

My greatest debts, as always, are to family. My parents, G. Daviss and Barbara Starr, still provide a rock of support in all I do, as well as having given me the education and the enduring love of the life of the mind that move me forward. George Starr taught me the joys of competitive rigor, and the intense happiness that can come from a meeting of the minds.

My daughter is writing several books, too: she's five, and her unquenchable curiosity, love, and sparkling laughter make all things better. My son gives unfailing cheer, bright eyes, and love, and though he is only two, he is well on his way to conquering new worlds. Thank you to you both for helping your mommy, both by working with me and by making my life more meaningful.

My husband, John C. Harpole, deserves more than any acknowledgment in this form can ever deliver. He has read every draft; he has been a tough and fair critic; he has been a staunch supporter; he made room in our home and our lives for this work to be completed, and he has made every page and every day better. Thank you! Portions of this book appeared in different forms in other publications: "Poetic Subjects and Grecian Urns: Close Reading and the Tools of Cognitive Science," *Modern Philology* 105, no. 1 (2007): 48–61; "Ethics, Meaning and the Work of Beauty," *Eighteenth-Century Studies* 35, no. 3 (2002): 361–378; "The Brain on Art: Intense Aesthetic Experience Activates the Default Mode Network" (Edward A. Vessel, G. Gabrielle Starr, and Nava Rubin), *Frontiers in Human Neuroscience* 6, no. 66 (2012), doi:10.3389/fnhum.2012.00066; "Evolved Reading and the Science(s) of Literary Study," *Critical Inquiry,* Winter (2012): 418–425; and "Burney, Ovid, and the Value of the Beautiful," *Eighteenth-Century Fiction* 24, no. 1 (2011): 77–104. Finally, "Multi-Sensory Imagery" appeared in *Introduction to Cognitive Cultural Studies*, ed. Lisa Zunshine (Baltimore, MD: Johns Hopkins University Press, 2010), 275–291. © 2010 The Johns Hopkins University Press. Adapted and reprinted with permission of The Johns Hopkins University Press.

Introduction: Aesthetics, Neuroaesthetics, and the Sister Arts

> Thou still unravish'd bride of quietness
>   Thou foster-child of Silence and slow Time,
> Sylvan historian, who canst thus express
>   A flowery tale more sweetly than our rhyme:
> What leaf-fringed legend haunts about thy shape
>   Of deities or mortals, or of both,
>   In Tempe or the dales of Arcady?
>   What men or gods are these? What maidens loth?
> What mad pursuit? What struggle to escape?
>   What pipes and timbrels? What wild ecstasy?
>
> Heard melodies are sweet, but those unheard
>   Are sweeter; therefore, ye soft pipes, play on;
> Not to the sensual ear, but, more endear'd,
>   Pipe to the spirit ditties of no tone.
>
> —John Keats, "Ode on a Grecian Urn"

In *Pro Archia Poeta* (62 BCE), Cicero advanced a family metaphor: "All the arts of humankind share a common bond, almost as if linked by the bonds of blood."[1] The idea that there are Sister Arts whose differing modes might compete, be compared, and ultimately form a unified field offers an excellent route by which to approach the dynamic dimensions of aesthetic response and to explore the cognitive neuroscience of aesthetic experience. A number of arts have been called kin (Cicero links poetry, oratory, and historiography), but three Sisters, music, painting, and poetry, have been often taken up in ongoing comparison; these are the primary focus of this book as I build and test a neural model of aesthetic experience.

As I suggested in the preface, the very idea of the aesthetic poses a problem of cohesion. It is almost a riddle: how is a sonata like a sunset or a beloved face? The broader question of why we might call all these things beautiful, sublime, or heartbreaking has an analogous one in the domain of the arts: while many of us, specialists and amateurs alike, associate music, painting, poetry, and other kinds of creative works together, perhaps it ought to strike us as strange that we do. Why should works that address different senses, using differing means, seem to produce the same set or class of feelings? Why, in other words, should we feel beauty across the arts at all? The tradition of the Sister Arts does not suggest a single consistent answer but rather encompasses contests and conversations around the multiple ways in which painting, poetry, and music might be connected. Not only does exploring the problem of the Sister Arts through these avenues of potential connection allow me to model the problem of aesthetics in small but, because of the depth and longevity of its tradition, the theory of the Sisters also represents a powerful humanist strain of thought that can help direct neuroaesthetic inquiry and both test and be tested by it. Where these discourses meet in the following pages, I hope to produce a new and enlightening dialogue in which the history of the Sister Arts, of aesthetics, and of the science of perception, cognition, and emotion reciprocally advance and reflect on one another.

In this introductory chapter I briefly sketch the historical understanding of the connections between and among music, painting, and poetry in five areas: their subjects, their methods, the ways in which they move the emotions, the kinds of pleasure they give, and the question of their appeal to imagination. I do so not to give a full account of the history of these interconnections (for that has been done skillfully by other scholars) but rather to indicate the key areas of concern bearing on the question of why aesthetic experiences might cohere across artistic domains.[2] Each area of putative connection among the Sister Arts has been a focus of intense contests. The persistence of these debates certainly testifies to the strength with which scholars, artists, critics, and their audiences believe that the arts and our experience of them are coherently connected. However, it also suggests that the links between the Sister Arts are so extensive that even competing explanations may have the power to convince. Exploring the reasons why we might posit a kinship of the arts, then, not only illuminates areas of relation among them but also enables us to determine what aspects of the experience of the arts might be suited to the approaches of cognitive neuroscience. Further, it gives access to the question of the flexibility of our understanding of aesthetic experiences more broadly, including those experiences that come from what is made—dance, theater, film, sculpture, gardens; what is found—faces, uncultivated landscapes, the night sky; and even those pleasures not yet discovered but which may come from new arts awaiting human creative realization. Starting with questions of emotion and pleasure as they emerged historically in debates over the Sister Arts, I move on to discuss imagery and imagination, as well as the idea of aesthetic knowledge. I also introduce concepts from neuroscience that can help us model these relations differently. In closing, I give an overview of a neuroaesthetic model and consider how it differs from other cross-disciplinary models of aesthetic life.

Pleasure and Emotion

Most theories of the Sister Arts have focused resolutely and explicitly on the subjective dimensions of response. The affective potential of the Sister Arts has been primarily canvassed from a few key positions. Along with Horace in the *Ars Poetica*, some have argued that what unites the arts is that they *please* in the same way.[3] Such pleasures can be classified using special aesthetic terms, some more rarified than others (beautiful, grotesque, picturesque, sublime, interesting, elegant, graceful, and so on), but they may also be understood in reference to the supposedly unique dynamics surrounding them. The durability of the pleasures of art and the relative absence of surfeit (compared to other pleasures of sensation: we tire less quickly of art at one sitting than of most of the pleasures we physically consume) have been key differentiators for aesthetic pleasure.[4] The peculiar temporality of aesthetic pleasures is suggested by Horace in one of the more often quoted dicta linking the Sister Arts—*ut pictura poesis*, "as in painting, so in poetry." "A poem is like a picture: one strikes your fancy more, the nearer you stand; another the farther away. . . . This pleased but once; that, though ten times called for, will always please."[5] The effects of individual, perspectival difference and the peculiar time courses of appreciation might unite the arts in a system of taste (proponents of the idea of genius use that concept to contend that aesthetic pleasure might thus last eternally).[6] All aesthetic response is dynamic and individual, but as I show in the final chapter, the necessary differences involved in aesthetic experience mean that something does remain, even with the passage of time.

Now, beyond positing a particular kind of pleasure that is aesthetic, or a peculiar kind of temporality to aesthetic pleasures, there are other ways of thinking about the affective relations between arts. There is certainly a powerful strain of moral thought whereby our susceptibility to the emotions art can evoke unites the Sisters as potentially dangerous. Plato most famously would retain in his Republic the songs of praise of gods and heroes that stir youth to emulation, but he would exclude those stories and poems that raise false fears, inappropriate laughter, or lust. Music and the other rhythmic arts (poetry and dance), he argues, must also be disciplined in their tones and beat so that they encourage self-restraint and not excessive passion. On the other hand, the elegance, proper rhythm, and harmony of all the arts, from music, poetry, and painting to weaving, architecture, and decorative works, should be cultivated as ways of always keeping grace before our eyes, teaching us to love beauty, and purging negative emotion.[7]

It is thus that from Plato forward, philosophers, rhetoricians, critics, artists, and (eventually) scientists have been concerned with detailing the methods by which the arts could most effectively raise emotions for the purposes of the state, of social cohesion, or of art itself. Erasmus, for example, claimed that one of the ancient musical and poetic rhythms, the pyrrhic (paired unstressed or short beats), could rouse men to war, and that other rhythms, such as the spondee (paired stressed or long beats), could calm; the cathartic potential of music and tragedy to purge negative emotions (such as fear) was key to ancient theorists; and the potential for the arts to enhance sympathetic interaction was a tenet of much eighteenth-century European thought.[8]

There is also, however, a countertradition that either denies the very existence of emotional responses to works of art or denies that the affective responses art evokes are the same as the emotional responses of everyday life. Some theorists argue, for example, that in the absence of a valid belief that would motivate our responses to art or of a tendency toward real actions, it would be incorrect to call "anger" what we feel when we read about the murder of Hamlet's father, or to call it "fear" when we turn away from a masked, knife-wielding assassin on the big screen. Kendall Walton argues that such responses are themselves fictional, "as-if" or make-believe responses that do not fully meet the standard of emotion in daily life.[9] Other theorists argue that when it comes to art, what matters are not emotions such as fear or sorrow but rather a range of purely aesthetic affective responses, so that, for example, we are not saddened by songs but rather are "moved by the beauty or perfection of the music" itself.[10] However, there are ample reasons, as I discuss below, to hold that we do in fact have genuine emotional responses to art, and that all aesthetic experiences involve pleasure or displeasure and some degree of emotional response.[11]

It is essential to note here that this explanatory conflict is revealing: even when critics regard affective responses to the various forms of art as different from those of the matter-of-fact world, they still group those affective responses together as particularly belonging to a world of the aesthetic. Walton, for example, explicitly connects painting, plays, movies, sculpture, and novels, and Peter Kivy, beginning with music, uses the concept of beauty as the foundation of all aesthetic responses, regardless of artistic mode. I will return to these debates about emotion in the next chapter, where I marshal some of the empirical evidence on the subject in tandem with the theoretical concerns sketched here, as I offer a model for understanding the major emotional implications of the Sisters of poetry, painting, and music.

Imagination and Imagery

The debates around imagination and the internal representations or imagery that might be elicited by the Sister Arts are similar to those surrounding emotion. Plato believed that literature functions primarily if not exclusively by evoking images. These images he saw as a source of danger, for in their similarity to the images of perception and to the echoes of things as they are (the ideals, which we cannot directly perceive), the images of poetry can trick us with their simulation of truth.[12] The evocation of images then puts poets on a par with painters, as peddlers of falsity. However, from Aristotle through the Renaissance master of rhetoric Quintilian (and beyond to at least Hugh Blair in the eighteenth century), rhetoricians have seen the production of mental images as necessary to the evocation of emotion by artful language, and the vividness of the images the writer evokes have been understood as central to the arts of words and persuasion.[13] Two closely related terms of classical rhetoric, *energeia* and *enargeia*—imagery and the energy of particularly vivid imagery—indicate two persistently valued literary capacities; indeed, Elaine Scarry goes so far as to claim that the vivacity of images of motion is key for the aesthetic value of literature.[14] I will return to imagery and particularly the question of motion in chapters 2 and 3, where I argue that imagery offers a primary model for the ways aesthetic pleasure is enacted in the brain, and that the systems for creating imagery share core elements with the architecture of intense aesthetic experience.

Again, as with emotion, the contrasting positions of Plato and the rhetoricians with respect to imagery are indicative of a shared sense of the powerful connection between the arts based on how they change the way we think and feel. However, we also see that the idea that the arts have a special call on imagination establishes the benchmark not just for an individual work but for the reputation of a given art as paradigmatic. As W. J. T. Mitchell points out, the changing relationships and contests for ascendency between two of the Sister Arts, poetry and painting, have been underwritten by a dispute over images, over the relation between and the value of the images of perception, the visible images created by the visual artist, and the verbal and mental images of poetry.[15] On one hand, this can emerge as the valorization of different arts based on their production of actual images or of mental imagery. So, for example, painters might argue they are most suited to telling a story, for they could give the most vivid picture of action and emotion, one that "speaks" to the eye, not just to the mind's eye. Poets claim they can offer a "verbal icon" that, in seeming to bypass the external sense of vision (the "images" of the text are not the images made by reflected light on a page), can effectively speak directly to the mind or soul, and that the poet (often represented as a piper or a player of lyre, lute, or harp) employs his or her own kind of music, which enters, though subtly, by way of the senses and stirs reason and emotion together.[16] Musicians and music theorists have claimed that music, too, functions by producing images: these may involve narrative imagery that might explain the progress of the composition (the dancer who will be sacrificed in Stravinsky's *Rite of Spring*, for example), but musical imagery can also include motor imagery (imagined singing, playing an instrument, or keeping the beat), or the imagery of pitch and the seeming spatial dynamism of notes as music moves from high to low or swiftly and slowly.[17] However, arguing that the arts function by way of images need not mean that they are weak in comparison to the sensations of the rest of daily life. The ancient philosopher Epicurus, for example, saw mental images as no less real than those of external perception, for all images have a material existence in the brain that produces them.[18]

Curiously, if the capacity for imagery in the Sister Arts is valorized by some, there is an equally strong strain of iconoclasm that doesn't just demote imaginative activity but denies the very existence of images in the mind. Even this, however, can be used as a basis for comparisons between the arts. The eighteenth-century British philosopher and statesman Edmund Burke claimed that poetry does not rely on imagery for its effects. Poetry speaks directly to the mind and emotions for Burke, without needing the intervention of any mimicry of sight, or even sight at all (poetry can indeed be heard); hence its superiority to the plastic arts.[19] This debate has a long life; Zenon Pylyshyn and Stephen Kosslyn have been prime contenders in a contemporary discussion in cognitive psychology that focuses on the degree to which visual imagery and visual perception are homologous, and whether either is actually pictorial.[20] As I note below, the evidence supports the claim that the arts can indeed evoke imagery across the senses, that this imagery employs the neural machinery of perception with a difference, that imagery involves the networks for introspection, and that imagery is a key to aesthetic pleasures.

These are the primary areas of dispute that would seek to unite (and have historically united) the Sister Arts in one family, as well as ordering or ranking them at particular times and places.[21] The outlines of the debate matter not just for inquiry into aesthetics as a discipline but also for understanding individual works of art and how they affect us, so that, for example, the relations among the arts can even become the source of artistic pleasure, as with American choreographer George Balanchine's *Apollo*, in which the dancers evoke the muses of literature, music, and dance itself competing for the attention of the god who is patron of all art.[22] Such a peculiar competition is a major focus of this book: I seek to understand not just on what bases aesthetic experience might cohere but why aesthetic experiences are often understood to be in competition with each other.

Aesthetic Knowledge

Looking in some detail at a poem that explores artistic, aesthetic, and sensory competition across the Sisters is helpful in understanding the ways these competitions can produce aesthetic pleasures, and also why these competitive relations matter to the idea of the arts and to the problem of aesthetic knowledge. The poem from which I take the book's epigraph, John Keats's "Ode on a Grecian Urn," is a Romantic exemplar of the Sister Arts tradition and an ekphrasis (a verbal description of visual art) that helps focus some key questions about how aesthetic experience works across the arts, why the coherence of the arts might be founded in competition or comparison, and what knowledge aesthetic experience might bring. What the poet describes is an enigma—the incomplete, even evasive fragment of knowledge that he encounters in an ancient piece of pottery:

> Thou still unravish'd bride of quietness
>   Thou foster-child of Silence and slow Time,
> Sylvan historian, who canst thus express
>   A flowery tale more sweetly than our rhyme:
> What leaf-fringed legend haunts about thy shape
>   Of deities or mortals, or of both,
>   In Tempe or the dales of Arcady?
>   What men or gods are these? What maidens loth?
> What mad pursuit? What struggle to escape?
>   What pipes and timbrels? What wild ecstasy?[23]

The poem figures the art of the word in competition with what might be called the visual poetry of the urn, for while the urn can "express . . . more sweetly than . . . rhyme," poetry can evoke the visible surface of the urn as well as the internal response of a viewer—a sense of puzzlement at the urn's mysteries. Keats also gestures toward another Sister Art as he turns to the image of a piper, forever silent yet forever playing on the static curve of the urn:

> Heard melodies are sweet, but those unheard
>   Are sweeter; therefore, ye soft pipes, play on;
> Not to the sensual ear, but, more endear'd,
>   Pipe to the spirit ditties of no tone.

The pipe player in the pastoral tradition is a figure for the poet, and Keats thus neatly weaves the Sister Arts together (still claiming that poetry is first among equals). What unites the arts here is aesthetic experience—explicitly, experience of the beautiful—as well as some inner faculty (in "Ode on a Grecian Urn," "the spirit," but elsewhere in Keats, psyche or mind) to which beauty speaks its ditty of no tone:

> O Attic shape! fair attitude! with brede
>   Of marble men and maidens overwrought,
> With forest branches and the trodden weed;
>   Thou, silent form! dost tease us out of thought
> As doth eternity: Cold Pastoral!
>   When old age shall this generation waste,
>   Thou shalt remain, in midst of other woe
> Than ours, a friend to man, to whom thou say'st,
>   Beauty is truth, truth beauty,—that is all
>   Ye know on earth, and all ye need to know.

Keats closes his poem with another enigma at the heart of the emerging discipline of aesthetics: if aesthetic experience is at least in part about thought and about knowledge (*scientiam sensitive quid cognoscendi*), what kind of knowledge does it provide?[24]

In posing a question of aesthetic knowledge, Keats touches on a durable problem in aesthetic theory and theory of the Sister Arts. While the Sister Arts seem obviously distinct at the level of both form and content, some of the earliest links between the three were in fact on those bases. Plato argued that painting and poetry were kin in their content: he maintained that they imitate and represent the world around us (a world, to be sure, that was a diminished, surrogate reality, only an imitation of the world of ideals). For Aristotle as well—though without Plato's sense of condemnation—painting, poetry, and music (the last by extension, for poetry was generally accompanied by instruments and was itself sung) were linked because they were all imitative. Music, for example, was understood in ancient Greece to mimic the human voice, and thus to mimic emotional expressions.[25] Aristotle argued that while the tools of imitation differ in some of the arts (with painting and poetry it is color or line versus word, for example) and are the same in others (poetry and music share sound, rhythm, and meter), both form and content ultimately work to unite the arts, because we use the arts as extensions of and tools for our understanding of the world.[26]

This is an important point of contention in aesthetics and in culture: how can the arts help us to know or understand? The deck is stacked, in the history of philosophy, against such a possibility. For Plato, anything we think we understand because of art is necessarily mistaken. Art can offer no knowledge, as it is merely imitation of the world around us—truth and knowledge come from philosophy and from the pursuit of the ideals. Moreover, if, as Sir Philip Sidney claims in "The Defence of Poesy" (1583), "the poet . . . nothing affirms," one might argue that poetic fictions can give no propositional knowledge, for they have no referent in the world, no claim on truth, and no ability to give grounds for assessing the truth of anything they might represent.[27] Even if we grant, with Martha Nussbaum or Jenefer Robinson, that moral or emotional knowledge may come from art, with Denise Gigante that "pleasure is its own way of knowing," or with Berys Gaut or Gregory Currie that we can learn by imagining, by simulating problems and solutions, questions still remain.[28] Peter Lamarque argues that at best, art can produce generalizations about human nature, but little in the way of specific knowledge; Michael Tye points out that our phenomenal experience itself may give knowledge of experience, but not "knowledge of any new facts"; and as Susan Feagin claims, this means that our responses to art, as phenomenal experiences, need not give us any new factual knowledge either.[29] I hope to clarify one dimension of these debates here.[30]

I argue that the arts mediate our knowledge of the world around us by directing attention, shaping perceptions, and creating dissonance or harmony where none had been before, and that what aesthetics thus gives us is a restructuring of value. I discuss what I mean by value more fully in chapter 1, but here let me state that value, as I use the term, refers not primarily to something inherent in objects but to a feature of our experience of objects, perceptions, and ideas.

It also does not refer primarily to the restricted, institutional or cultural context that some versions of aesthetics began to propose in the eighteenth and nineteenth centuries. In thinking about value, I start with the hedonic signature of a given experience—that is, our phenomenal feelings of pleasure or displeasure. To use the terms of Peter de Bolla, I propose that "the aesthetic value of [a] work" maps onto "the quality of the [affective] response it generates."[31] Value in this sense is ductile, and aesthetic experience juxtaposes what had been valueless or incommensurable by giving perceptible, hedonic weight to thoughts and sensations. The restructuring of value such juxtapositions produce does not lead to new "facts" but rather sets the stage for new *configurations* of knowledge.[32]

How might this be? The first clue emerges when we acknowledge the materiality of aesthetic pleasures. Francis Hutcheson, one of the pivotal figures in the founding of modern aesthetics, argued that the effects of aesthetic perception are material:

> It is unquestionable, that we have a great number of perceptions, which one can scarcely reduce to any of the five senses, as they are commonly explained; such as either the ideas of grandeur, dignity, decency, beauty, harmony; or on the other hand, of meanness, baseness, indecency, deformity; and that we apply these ideas not only to material objects, but to characters, abilities, actions.[33]

It is possible that there is no such thing as beauty or baseness, that these are illusions corresponding to nothing that is real. But for Hutcheson, the proof of this reality is in the pleasures and displeasures we feel, and he takes the test case of laughter at the incongruent or ridiculous as his starting point: if we laugh, he suggests, at what we see, hear, or read, we cannot be mistaken in the perception that we have been pleased.[34] Laughter, for Hutcheson, means that we must recognize that we have given a value to something, and that this value is real.[35] As he goes on to explain in *An Inquiry into the Original of our Ideas of Beauty and Virtue*, published in 1725, our minds perceive beauty and virtue by the same route that we perceive incongruity, and it is not just laughter but our sense of beauty that is written on our bodies.[36] Ultimately, all aesthetic experience is the result not so much of perceiving the outside world as becoming aware of our own judgment of what matters to us.

The knowledge to which aesthetic experience can lead, I suggest, may emerge because aesthetic value is both thought and felt; it is something "cognitive," "sensory," and "emotional." It is subjective, contingent, experiential (and at a neural level computational). Aesthetic experience, in this view, is about ways of not only assigning perceptions a value but revealing a hierarchy and interrelation of values that goes beyond what we at first perceive.[37] I will explore Keats's "Ode on a Grecian Urn" as a figure—or object lesson—for this idea in the final chapter of this book. Aesthetic responses as Keats represents them involve the remarkable works of human creativity (from painted vase to poetry and music) and the forces and concerns of human culture (the historical changes in art and the conditions under which it is produced and consumed across cultures, the lost frameworks or changing stories that enable us to understand what we see). However, aesthetic responses also, necessarily, involve brain, body, thought, and behavior, and they happen with greatest power when one idea, image, or sensation is brought into surprising, revealing contact with another, when something we see somehow "pipes to the spirit ditties of no tone."

What Holds Aesthetic Experiences Together?

The theories of the Sister Arts reveal an intricate landscape of aesthetic possibilities. Untangling the multiple relations between and among the aspects of aesthetic life we have seen here is complicated, for no area exists in isolation. As an example, we may take the case of the emotions of aesthetic experience: we feel them in our bodies with the quickened heartbeat of watching a dancer execute a fall; we know them in our minds through our engagement with the fears or angers a tragic tale may provoke; our brains integrate our sensory and imaginative experiences as we look at black marks on a page and come to dread the arrival of the train that takes Anna Karenina's life; the cultures in which we live determine which arts are available to us, and help determine how we value the grace of a ballerina or the intricacies of kabuki.

In the pages that follow I seek to understand some of the relations between these threads, and I will return to Keats—and other poets, painters, and musicians—as I do, pursuing questions posed by their art. But let us first pursue the implications of what I submit as a basic principle of our engagement with all of the arts: the complex thoughts, sensations, actions, and feelings that make up aesthetic experience are best understood first as events. That is, we encounter an urn, and walk around it; a landscape, and we seek to dwell in it; a piper's melody, and we savor its movements; a poem, and we read and reread it; a dance, and we watch and then reimagine it. When we approach aesthetics thus in terms of events—and not primarily in terms of objects—we foreground dynamism and temporality, even at a minute level: for example, the emotions that help define aesthetic experience are far from static, having varying durations and changing intensities (a sweet song may not always bring tears—it may strike us a different time as manipulative or impersonal). Moreover, we recognize that variation is fundamental to many aesthetic evaluations: aesthetic value changes over time (what is beautiful now may not seem so always, what was understandable may now be incomprehensible), and aesthetic experiences may even create odd equations of value, whereby objects strangely diminish or increase in their pleasure and importance (an urn moves from funerary or religious object to take on the status of a paradigmatic sculpture; a urinal, with Duchamp, emerges as a work of art; or a single word, as in another poem by Keats, takes on an almost impossible weight: "'Forlorn!' The very word is like a bell / To toll me back from thee to my sole self").[38]

The events that make up aesthetic experiences are also constituted in part by a kind of layered perception, as Hutcheson's insight suggests. Aesthetic experience engages the senses (as well as sensory analogues in imagination), and we are not indifferent to that experience. Sensory perceptions are blended with emotions, and with sensations of pleasure and displeasure—but aesthetic experience also engages personal memories, prior knowledge, and evaluative judgments, and reaches out to touch the range of ideas and questions an experience of beauty or of wonderment can open.[39] It is a key feature of aesthetic experience that it may juxtapose thoughts and sensations that had been far, far distant, such as a woman turning into a laurel tree (a scene from Ovid's *Metamorphoses* to which I return later in this book—see Bernini's interpretation in *Apollo and Daphne* in figures 6 and 7). Encountering this figure in aesthetic terms is not just a matter of making sense of (im)possible worlds, for this concatenation of ideas and images should be felt as well as understood—felt as strange beauty, shock, pleasure, outrage, or even irritated disbelief.

It is reasonable to argue that the very emotional responses that help make up aesthetic experience are themselves judgments of a kind of value.[40] Frank Sibley contended that there is little, if any, distinction between evaluative and descriptive terminology in aesthetics because it is impossible to arrive at objectively descriptive terminology that exactly accounts for the aesthetic evaluation. If it were possible to do so, a description could stand in for the aesthetic object itself, but we must actually see, hear, or read the object in order to have an aesthetic experience of it.[41] Acknowledging that evaluation and description are interconnected might thus lead to the corollary that emotion and perception are themselves intertwined in the judgment. Indeed, David Hume and Jesse Prinz argue that evaluative judgments are fundamentally emotional because these judgments refer to the ability of objects or people to move us; even evidently dispassionate claims about art are intelligible to us only because we have first come to understand aesthetic responses as emotionally moving and potentially pleasurable.[42]

This dynamic, valenced interaction of emotion, ideas, and perception can work to restructure the hierarchies of value that motivate and map daily life. Scholars of the arts have long contended (perhaps most passionately, recently, Martha Nussbaum in *Love's Knowledge*) that works of art produce paradigm shifts in how we see, hear, or think: one might hear new tonal possibilities in music after the first encounter with an Indian raga; one might recognize different, painful implications of the theology of incarnation after encountering Damian Hirst's disconcerting, perhaps even awful flayed *Virgin Mother;* or one might newly understand the alienation of blackness after reading Ralph Ellison's *Invisible Man*. It is not just that ideas and perceptions, however, become newly linked in aesthetic experience but that the *hedonic value* assigned to those perceptions and ideas at a neural level enables powerful connections that had not existed before. Aesthetic experience thus makes possible the unexpected valuation of objects, ideas, and perceptions and enables new configurations of what is known, new frameworks for interpretation, and perhaps even a new willingness to entertain what is strange or to let the familiar and the novel live side by side. We may then acquire new knowledge, which enters into our lives differently—by showing us undiscovered similarities or contrasts, and opening new room for comparison and evaluation. It is an ongoing process: we encounter art and may be changed, and each re-encounter may leave us changed again. As I will show, intense aesthetic experience is marked by the integration of an internal hierarchy of pleasures and values, and by one's being simultaneously engaged in a world of perception and transfixed in a world that goes beyond what is heard or seen.[43]

Toward a Neuroaesthetic Model

A strong account of aesthetic life must be able to account for the ways in which such felt engagements of ideas and perceptions occur, and enable us to understand their dynamic interrelation. A neuroscientific account of aesthetic experience that invokes concepts of emotion, reward, and imagery can do this, helping to explain the relations among the Sister Arts and the idea of aesthetics as a coherent discipline; it also offers a way of understanding the interrelations of the ever-expanding world of aesthetic life.[44] Aesthetic experience involves not just universal principles of the human brain but also, as I will demonstrate below, highly individual and subjective processes. In the following chapters I will describe in some detail the ways in which this dynamic interaction is instantiated neurally through brain systems for emotion and reward, as well as through the default mode network. It is clear that aesthetic experience builds on emotional life as well as on our desires for beauty, awe, or wonder and for the pleasures they may bring, but it is also clear that aesthetic experience does not end there. Aesthetic experience juxtaposes what we know and feel (in both daily life and in our encounters with art) with what was previously valueless or incommensurable, and our experience of aesthetic pleasures gives perceptible, hedonic weight to thoughts and perceptions.

I discuss systems for emotion in more detail in chapter 1, but here let me state that current research has assembled evidence exploring emotion in a number of dimensions. Nicholas Frijda, Elizabeth Phelps, and others posit that emotions are "relevance detectors," affording swift appraisals of objects, people, events, and thoughts that represent their value for our own needs, desires, survival, sense of self, and sense of community. There are experiential somatic elements to emotions (such as a pounding heart or queasiness), cognitive elements (memories, thoughts, and beliefs), dispositional elements (mood or depression), and neural networks underpinning particular kinds of emotional responses (fear and fear learning have a highly localized cognitive architecture centered in the amygdala, disgust depends in part on the insula).[45] A number of researchers have contributed to the discovery of the "neural reference space" for emotion, the systems and subnetworks involved in the neural instantiation of emotional experience.[46] While the processes underlying emotions do not occur only in the brain, the neural reference space gives us a good starting point for understanding how the emotions of aesthetic experience relate to emotion more broadly, as well as for understanding one way in which the Sister Arts might in fact cohere.

A key element of the neural architecture of emotion involves the reward associated with a real or imagined object, which is the focus of emotional experience. A reward here, as defined by biology and the behavioral sciences, at base means some object or experience an organism desires and seeks to obtain, but in emotion research, reward has a more specific meaning. Brain-based reward is essential to human action and cognition. The human brain needs to be able not just to represent objects we encounter in the world but to represent the value, either positive or negative, of attaining (or avoiding) those objects. It is essential as well to much of our learned behavior: Will this plant help us or harm us? Is this water safe to drink or not? Our system of representing value must be dynamic, however, because reward value is not stable. Water is essential to life, but taking in too much too quickly will lead to intoxication and death. The systems that represent reward must also enable fast comparisons, both in valence (do I feel safe or not with this person or in this place?) and in kind (does this situation frighten or excite me?).[47]

A number of researchers have demonstrated that aesthetic response involves emotion systems as well as circuits in the brain that represent, evaluate, compare, and deliver reward.[48] However, not all emotions and not all rewards are aesthetic, and distinguishing aesthetic experience requires a broader look at brain and behavior. At New York University I worked with Nava Rubin (of the Center for Neural Science) and Edward Vessel (of the Center for Brain Imaging) to use functional magnetic resonance imaging (fMRI, a noninvasive tool for the indirect measurement of brain activity) to develop important new insights into the neural underpinnings of aesthetics.[49] Perhaps of most importance, this research on responses to visual art has shown the involvement of the default mode network (sometimes called the core network) in intense aesthetic experiences of paintings. The default mode network is a set of interconnected brain areas that are generally active in periods of waking rest but whose activity generally decreases with external stimulation. However, with intensely powerful aesthetic experience, parts of the default mode network are, surprisingly, engaged. As I explain in detail in the next chapter, this suggests that powerful aesthetic experience calls on the brain to integrate external perceptions with the inner senses, and ultimately, that imagery may be a key component of powerful aesthetic response.

All of this information enables us to begin to assemble the necessary components of a viable model of aesthetic experience, and I will further explore these components later in this book. Briefly, however, aesthetic experience starts with sensations or imagery, which we analyze perceptually and semantically and which engage processes of memory as well as of emotion; these sensations and images also have evolving reward value. The minute sequence of the neural events in aesthetic experience requires further experimental elaboration, but in general anatomical terms, neural activation moves from sensory cortex forward toward the basal ganglia (reward processes) and toward the hippocampus and amygdalae (memory and emotion—though these functions are not exclusively carried out in these structures). Activation in the orbitofrontal cortex follows, but there are interactive loops that reach between these frontal areas and the basal ganglia so that higher-order, complex processes of cognition, and emotional and reward processes, may continually feed into one another.

Much of the neural response to aesthetic experiences involves distributed increases in activity that correspond to subjective increases in the power of our aesthetic response, increases found across areas of the brain corresponding to perceptual and reward processing (see, for example, figures 11 and 12). There is a tipping point, however, at which appreciation or liking turns into a response that is both distinctly powerful and distinctly aesthetic (this response is not exclusively attributable to beauty), and reward value and emotional response both feed into the activation of something larger (see figures 13 and 14). That larger system, the default mode network, shares a good deal of its architecture with the systems that enable mental imagery, and this shared platform not only means that what drives imagery may help to drive aesthetic experience, it also suggests that intensely felt imagery (primarily multisensory imagery and imagery of motion) is one of the links that unites both the arts and our most intense experience of them.[50] And it is thus that the arts may have their own call on aesthetic experience. I am not saying that *only* art can drive powerful aesthetic experience; far from it. Rather, I believe that in their appeal to imagery, the multiple arts of human creativity enable swift access to what moves us, and thus may gain privileged status as heralds of—or standard bearers for—aesthetic life.

I also argue that while reward processing in general represents computational value—the weighted and comparative neural representation of the obtainability and desirability of an object or experience—aesthetic response enables the comparison and integration of *novel kinds of reward* in a process that makes these rewards particularly meaningful for inner life and opens up possibilities for new knowledge, or new ways of negotiating the world. The perceptions, images, and emotions we find through our experience of poetry, painting, and music put ideas and events into relation with one another that would rarely, if ever, be possible outside the arts. Thus, the pleasures, displeasures, and rewards of aesthetic experience are not always predictable a priori: for example, there is no reason we should find the transformation of a woman into a tree profoundly pleasing (rather than just frightening or simply incomprehensible nonsense) without the work of Ovid. Nor should we, of necessity, enjoy the vibrations of a hammer struck, in a given pattern, on twisted metal cords, or a unique, stylized weight of pigments layered thickly on a cloth. Indeed, the a priori unpredictability of aesthetic rewards and their dependence on continually changing experience are key.[51] The pleasures of Van Gogh, Ovid, or Beethoven may steal up on us, taking us by surprise with their loveliness. The a priori unpredictable yet powerful rewards that come with aesthetic experience point toward the kind of learning we have with aesthetic experience, in the brain can continually expand the context that maps emotions onto the world around us into previously uncharted territory.[52] What is thus gained has durable value.

The highly flexible, open-ended, and a priori unpredictable value of aesthetic rewards sets aesthetic experience apart from the rewards generally associated with evolutionary essentials: sex, food, water, and the like are so-called primary reinforcers, with clear survival value. These primary reinforcers are essential to learning. The human brain is adept at representing the rewards (and punishments) associated with our ability to obtain these reinforcers. Based on our experiences of success and failure, the brain predicts our ability to obtain goals, and as we either succeed or fail, we refine our strategies, insights, and methods. This occurs when parts of the brain (including the ventral striatum, orbitofrontal cortex, and amygdala) represent a prediction of success; other parts of the brain then step in to give a signal of error (lateral habenula, ventral tegmental area, and substantia nigra pars compacta). This elaborate cycle of prediction, reward, and memory is the foundation of reinforcement learning.[53] Such is the case for essential activities and primary reinforcers (and punishers such as pain), but what is the use of the kind of reward that is represented by the emotions of aesthetic experience? I believe that aesthetic experience helps us understand a world we cannot fully predict, helps us value things that are new and learn how to compare what seems, at first, incommensurable. This is true at a very small level, that of images that integrate multiple senses, and perhaps at a larger level, that of ideas and events beyond simple forms of representation.

In the model of aesthetic experience it advances, *Feeling Beauty* offers a challenge to many approaches to aesthetics that privilege evolutionary psychology.[54] Steven Pinker, for example (among others), has shown that evolutionary imperatives might lay the groundwork for the human appreciation of certain landscapes.[55] Lush environments have a clear survival value, for verdure promises food and water, as well as shelter and a temperate clime. But when we leave the world of landscape aesthetics and take the step to landscape painting, things change. While people tend to agree with great frequency as to the beauty of real-world scenes, there is a high degree of variability in taste for painted ones.[56] Most evolutionary approaches seem poorly equipped to deal with such variability, besides seeming, at times, to impoverish aesthetic experience by resolving complex emotions and objects to the level of crudely powerful drives.[57] They may also, in their search for long time (evolutionary or species time), ignore the (also) material demands of culture and history on the scale of nations and peoples. I do not contend that evolutionary forces have not ineluctably shaped our cognitive architecture and the aesthetic and literary experiences that architecture enables: of course they have.[58] Nor do I claim that aesthetic experience has no adaptive function (it might). Rather, I contend that the explanatory power of cognitive aesthetics does not lie in mapping the phenomena of aesthetic experience onto basic evolutionary drives.

Human experience has a felt richness that means attempts to resolve its variations into basic principles will always produce a significantly—perhaps fatally—underconstrained problem: however many evolutionary principles we grant explanatory power, it is hard to imagine enough such principles to account, convincingly or powerfully, for the combinations and diversity of human artistic production.[59] Say, for example, we identify five key naturally or sexually selected factors that arguably shape the production or experience of art. For how much of the complexity of (reading) Tolstoy can they account, and how might they differentiate (reading) Tolstoy from Dickens or Keats? How many factors would a rich explanatory model that could do this require? Ten thousand? A whole genome (23,000 genes and three billion base pairs of DNA)? Once you get to such numbers, you get more explanatory power about a work of fiction or poetry from criticism than from genetics—in part because criticism sews together a variety of disciplines, in part because it is focused not on genomes but on texts.[60]

Feeling Beauty takes a different approach. I ask what the basic workings of the human brain can tell us about how art changes human experience as it reorders our perceptions and engages our emotions.[61] As I will show, neuroscience can help us understand the areas of cognition and of feeling that aesthetic experience juxtaposes, and to understand not just how all human experience might be alike, but how the differences between us matter and how the difference between works of art matter too. Far from narrowly defining the feelings of aesthetic experience or defining the objects that produce them, *Feeling Beauty* offers a way of understanding the open-endedness of aesthetic life, and why that openness matters. Knowing more about how aesthetics shapes the human brain brings to our attention new features of our engagement with art, opening up new possibilities for understanding why art matters, and why aesthetic experience pervades so much of human life.

The key problem, however, is how we bridge the gaps between knowledge of matter (neurons, networks), experiences of works of art, and the works themselves. As Thomas Nagel noted in his seminal essay, "What Is It Like to Be a Bat?," conscious experience is always at least one step removed from the exploration of the mechanisms that (we theorize) enable it. While cognitive neuroscience does not describe subjective experience fully (and does not purport to do so), it can help to reinterpret it, and hence to build a more complete critical picture of experience.[62] I argue that the work of art is an active principle that can change how we think and how we feel; the neuroscientific framework I offer, in partnership with criticism, allows an integrative critical picture of how that happens. The experiences of art point toward a key mode in which we engage with and learn about the world. Aesthetic experience is about finding new value in the world in which we live, and *Feeling Beauty* seeks to show how art—both literally and figuratively—matters.

Any inquiry into subjective experience, whether based in neuroscience or in humanist critique, runs the risk of positing what Geoffrey Hartmann has called "benevolent normativeness."[63] In other words, scholars (particularly, for Hartman, those scholars schooled in traditions of formalist criticism and close reading) have tended to substitute one particular representation of interpretative practices for the sum of the experiences a work might produce. A single imaginative staging of a poem or novel comes to carry a coercive normativity, and we may mistakenly believe that because we know what a poem does for us, we know what it "does": how it makes meaning, how it shapes a reader's thought, how it evokes feelings and images.[64] Arguments about aesthetic response do not and need not commit such an argumentative fallacy; at its best, a cognitive approach to aesthetic experience is focused on the way cognitive architecture enables the *varieties* of such experience—the ways poems, paintings, and music are read or not read, heard or not heard, seen or not seen. Understanding the ways in which individuals experience art differently enhances our understanding of what art can do and why we care about it. An approach to neuroscience rooted in individual differences can help do this, and *Feeling Beauty,* both in terms of science and of the arts, attempts at all times to keep the variety of aesthetic responses always in play.

My aim in this book is to offer both testable hypotheses (in scientific terms) and a theory (in humanist terms) of experiences of art across multiple domains. I do so with my eye on the current moment—the early twenty-first century—but with a sense of a long history as well. The architecture of the human mind—an architecture made of brain, body, history (both personal and communal), and culture—is complex, but what makes us remarkable beings is that the physical bases of individual experience respond to what culture and world demand of it. I hope *Feeling Beauty* responds, in different ways, to both. Employing the methods and results of cognitive neuroscience alongside a more traditional humanist investigation of a wide range of literature, music, and visual art, *Feeling Beauty* investigates beauty both across the senses and in the imagination, and seeks to be true to our possibilities, complexities, differences, and even our limitations.

The model of aesthetic experience I describe enables us to see why and how the Sister Arts might function as they do, in complement as well as competition, always open to new kin, and the following chapters begin by asking how we both differentiate among and integrate the kinds of pleasure that come by way of different senses and from the different Sister Arts. In the first chapter I focus on the ways the neuroscience of emotion and reward show links between music and visual art, and explore both the route by which these arts may move us and the manner in which individual differences, in the enactment of emotion and reward processes as well as in the default mode network, are essential to aesthetic experience. This chapter is the one most focused on cognitive neuroscience, laying a broadly accessible foundation for the rest of the analysis to follow. Chapter 2 posits that the neuroscience of imagery can form a basis for understanding not just music and painting but also poetry, by integrating emotion and reward processes across the senses. As I show in this chapter, understanding the relationship of systems for mental imagery to the default mode network also enables us to understand how the Sister Arts are related and how they can move us. This chapter begins to explore, closely, particular works of art, to show how modeling the integrative potential of imagery can illuminate humanist criticism. The final chapter returns to the questions of dynamic, variable responses to art to explore key exemplars from each of the three Sisters. This chapter is most closely focused on individual works of art as I seek to offer a vision of aesthetics that speaks to the multiple ways in which we experience and describe aesthetic life, and to show how the cognitive dynamics of aesthetics matter to our understanding of the arts.

1

Seen and Heard: A Model for the Sister Arts

Powerful aesthetic experience not only hits at the heart of who we are (it is highly individual, perspectival, subjective), it also has implications for the processes that underlie self-conception. As I suggested in the introduction, subjective variations are fundamental to the structure of aesthetic experience. This chapter explores subjective variations in three dimensions: the variety of aesthetic objects. the variety of emotions associated with aesthetic experience, and the differing ways in which those emotions are processed. I also begin to describe what makes it possible to use what we know about visual and aural pleasures to create a model for aesthetics more broadly. Emotion is key to aesthetic experience, and as I show in the first section of this chapter, the emotions of aesthetic life exhibit characteristics that may subtly distinguish them from those of everyday life. Investigation of emotion and reward together shows us some of the ways the arts may be kin, and the second section explores the ways in which reward processes operate for the arts. Understanding the activity of the default mode network helps reveal how aesthetic experience is set apart from what surrounds it, and in the final section of this chapter I examine the function of the default mode network in detail, focusing on its potential to link aesthetic experience to processes underlying self-concept, social life, and a heightened sense of both the external world and its internal, subjective representation.

The first neuroscientists interested in aesthetics were primarily concerned with visual art, for vision, as the sense most accessible to behavioral evaluation, has been the most robustly understood area of perception. The initial wave of aesthetic inquiry sought to discover elements of art objects, which, qua visual features, were appealing to the brain—that is, features that are particularly well suited to components of neural processing.[1] The history of art, however, teaches that standards of beauty change; the more interesting questions, then, involve a search not for features of objects but for the characteristics of subjective experiences.[2] A neuroscientific approach might ask, even if people find different objects powerfully appealing and profoundly moving, is there something shared in that subjective experience of the aesthetic, something that can be identified and explored at the neural level?

One answer might be that the key to visual aesthetics lies primarily in the neural structures for processing visual information, and indeed, there is evidence that the brain structures enabling vision make us more likely to find certain kinds of visual input pleasing than others.[3] However, this is not the whole story. People disagree about the degree to which what they *see* is a dominant factor in an aesthetic evaluation. For example, something that is pleasing solely to the eye (a brightly colored wall seen in passing from a bus window) may be less moving than something in which the viewer finds profound meaning (the western rose windows of Chartres Cathedral, with their images of the Last Judgment), or something that is recognized to be a pivotal document in the history of art (David's *The Oath of the Horatii*), or something with which the viewer has a personal connection (a song that played on the radio the summer your child was born). Equally, a glimpse of a sun-burnt wall might link with the pleasures of the day to merge into a personal canon of joy and beauty. We might disagree with one another as to how much any of these judgments is "purely aesthetic" (indeed, in the Kantian sense, none of these judgments is properly aesthetic), but for nonspecialists and specialists alike, it is rare that we might attain such pure distinctions.[4] A variety of things may influence aesthetic evaluations and become part of aesthetic experience: mood, expertise, personal associations, cultural constraints or predilections, a desire to seem knowledgeable or fashionable, the perceptions of our peers, our own expectations, and so on. So vision—or any other perceptual mode—will get us only so far in seeking a core model for aesthetic evaluations and aesthetic experience, even for visual art. An investigation of emotion and of reward, however, will get us further, both for visual art and for its Sisters, in part because emotion and reward highlight the importance of individual and cultural differences in aesthetic experience, and in part because they help us approach the temporal dimensions of aesthetics.

Emotion and Variation

The cognitive neuroscience of emotion is rapidly evolving, and while a number of points of contention remain among emotion researchers, a consensus view is emerging that emotions serve to identify relationships that matter to us and give those relationships subjective, phenomenal shape. Emotions tell us when parts of the world around us or of our own worlds of thoughts and imaginings deserve our attention, and they tell us (in general, quickly and in broad if at times fallible strokes) how these objects of attention matter. In this view, feelings are a subset of the phenomena of emotions, and feelings themselves involve a variety of events and reactions. Part of the phenomenal shape of emotion involves the direction of our attention—a heightened awareness of parts of our environments or our own bodies, the cavalcade of somatic changes that we perceive—the tingling of hands, the heart racing, nausea, or shortened breath, which Jesse Prinz calls "gut reactions," as well as memories and the tendencies to take certain kinds of actions or to entertain certain kinds of thoughts (to give someone a good shove, say, or to imagine a caress).[5]

This latter distinction between what we might think and what we do has historically been key for those interested in aesthetics. In a debate going back to Aristotle, theorists of aesthetics have argued that it is unclear whether aesthetic responses involve events that are properly understood as emotional at all. In the most durable of these discussions, theorists have pointed out that the fear or anger of aesthetic life is not based on real beliefs about the world and rarely leads to the kind of action that fear or anger produces in the world at large; given the absence of such beliefs or action tendencies, a number of philosophers have classed aesthetic responses differently, even, in the case of Kendall Walton, calling these responses "fictional."[6] More recently, under the influence of cognitive science this question has evolved, for it is increasingly clear that everyday emotions, not just putatively aesthetic ones, do not always lead to action or require articulated or defensible beliefs, and it is probable that at least in some cases emotion even precedes belief.[7] Some emotions promote particular kinds of thoughts: feelings of sadness, for example, may lead to critical and more realistic evaluations of one's chances for success than feelings of happiness, and some psychologists, like Nico Frijda, argue that the "action tendency" component of emotion ought properly to include a tendency toward particular kinds of thought.[8]

While the absence of an action tendency (I don't run out to save Anna Karenina from a train) thus does not make responses to art something other than emotions, we ought not be hasty. It is not necessarily the case that what we call emotions in everyday parlance in fact denote the same class of events; they may involve different brain structures, as well as different kinds of affects, and different somatic components.[9] Amid this potential disunity (or even category error), aesthetic emotions might still distinguish a distinct subset of experiences, or might overlap with other responses we call, rightly or not, emotions. It is possible that aesthetic responses can be distinguished from everyday emotions in a variety of ways. For example, affective responses to artwork could be milder than those of everyday life, so one might feel a kind of mild fear in anticipating the worst for a beloved character, or be uneasy and disturbed in front of a painting of Armageddon. Such responses seem different from what belongs to walking down a dark street or fearing for someone else's safety in doing so, or thinking about what it would be like actually to confront the end of days, even leaving aside a tendency to act differently in the Metropolitan Museum of Art or in one's own easy chair.

Another way of approaching the potential distinctiveness of emotional responses to art is by evoking the concept of basic emotions. A number of emotion theorists (dating back to Descartes and Spinoza) identify what they call the basic emotions: primary, core emotions, which have relatively clear biological bases. There are competing sets of candidates for these emotions, but most often they include fear, anger, disgust, happiness, sadness, and surprise.[10] Some proponents of basic emotion theories tend to attribute these emotions to humans as well as to other animals, and then argue that combinations of these basic emotions underlie what they contend are more complex emotions (belonging peculiarly to humans and sometimes other primates).[11] However, not all researchers agree that the concept is a necessary or a fully defensible one, for it is not clear, for example, that something like nostalgia is properly understood as a combination of other emotions. Klaus Scherer argues that emotions are not discrete enough for any set number of them to be identified as basic. Because emotions are events, not states, and are distributed over a variety of physiological systems, "*the pattern of all synchronized changes in the different components over time constitutes the emotion* and even small differences in this pattern are expected to reflect real differences in the nature of the emotional state."[12]

While there may be debate over which, if any, emotions are basic, it is increasingly clear that the palette of emotions in aesthetic life is broader than what can be produced using basic emotions alone.[13] Aesthetic response is for many students of the aesthetic an emotional category. Burke's discussion of beauty and the sublime approaches them through the passions they induce (love and astonishment, respectively), and Hume argues that taste requires the proper operation of "those finer emotions of the mind . . . of a very tender and delicate nature."[14] Peter Kivy would resolve all emotional responses to music to the feeling of beauty, so that we are "moved by the beauty or perfection of the music" itself.[15] In the world of cognitive psychology, Scherer and his colleagues have claimed that aesthetic responses include what they identify as complex emotions, such as nostalgia or longing, as well as specifically aesthetic emotions, such as those belonging to beauty. In a series of studies designed to classify and study emotional responses to music, they began with forty-three emotion terms and used a factor analysis to produce nine terms that were able to capture most people's responses: wonder, transcendence, tenderness, nostalgia, peacefulness, power, joyful activation, tension.[16] It is noteworthy that "joyful activation" is a hybrid term that the authors (whose subjects were francophone) chose to accommodate the variety of descriptive terms (joyful, happy, radiant, elated, content, disinhibited, excited, active, agitated, energetic, and fiery) that fed into this category. We simply do not have a readymade terminology that can entirely map the emotions of aesthetic experience.[17]

Zentner, Grandjean, and Scherer argue that aesthetic responses belong to a class of emotions Frijda and Sundararajan called "refined"; such emotions "are more felt than acted upon and thus do not obviously manifest themselves in overt behaviors like attack, embrace, or flight; may not show pronounced physiological upset; are often about complex events or subtle event aspects; and are not done justice by common emotion labels."[18] What is key here is not Frijda and Sundararajan's terminology (I am hesitant to imply an evaluative trajectory or the kind of superiority hinted by the classifications of coarseness or refinement); rather, what matters is the recognition that there are important emotional responses that do not have major physiological output, are subtle, and go beyond the lexicon of the basic emotions. The emotional experience of art, in this view, may thus involve different dimensions and different tendencies: instead of our acting on emotions (though we might; I have known people to throw books in anger), we might have a tendency to savor these emotions in ways we don't in everyday life (especially with otherwise negative emotions such as sadness or fear).[19] What Frijda and Sundararajan imply is that there are good reasons to believe that the emotions attending experiences of art may be different, but that they are not entirely alien creatures when compared with the emotions of daily life; indeed, experimental psychology supports this view.

As we begin to understand the differentiability of aesthetic responses to art, we can refine our concepts of emotional response by focusing on the "neural reference space" for emotion—a set of brain areas through which emotion is neurally instantiated—which has been identified through a large number of imaging studies.[20] These areas are networked together and include structures implicated in memory, self-awareness, proprioception (the perception of the relative position of one's body in space), motion, arousal, attention, the analysis of meaning, the integration and association of data from the different senses, and reward, as well as structures that are more specialized for emotion (and sometimes particular emotions), including the amygdala and insula. In this reference space, there are brain areas that are more active for positive or negative emotions (though these areas generally do not serve either positive or negative affect exclusively), as well as for the perception of emotion as opposed to the experience of it.[21] The neural reference space of emotion thus helps model some components of aesthetic experience. Robert Blood and his collaborators were among the first to show significant overlap between areas of the neural reference space for emotion and responses to music, and similar results have come from experiments on visual art by Kawabata and Zeki, Vessel, Starr, and Rubin, and others.[22]

The evidence for a neural relation between everyday and aesthetic emotion is broad. Some studies of everyday emotion, for example, have suggested a tendency for a slight hemispheric bias, such that positive emotions are associated with greater activations left of midline in the basal forebrain and in the orbitofrontal cortex and negative emotions with greater activations to the right of midline (there is no hemispheric bias in the superior lateral cortex).[23] In many studies, musically induced emotions seem to show a similar pattern, as do emotional responses to painting; in my work with Vessel and Rubin we found a general lateralization of responses to visual art in the left hemisphere (see figure 18).[24] In addition, many of the somatic components of emotional experience can be produced in response to music.[25] When it comes to visual art, my collaborators and I also found differential sensitivity to emotional valence in particular regions of the brain for observers looking at visual art, so that the substantia nigra, striatum, and superior frontal gyrus were sensitive to positive emotions and the striatum, anterior medial prefrontal cortex, and inferior frontal gyrus were sensitive to negative emotions (see figure 15).[26] Such findings are in accord with research on emotion more broadly.[27] We might conclude that not only is the neurophysiological space of emotion similar for aesthetics and daily life but also that the way in which emotions are *evaluated* (as positive or negative) is similar (in terms of gross anatomical structures used in processing). The two need not cohere, but the coherence is good evidence for consanguinity.

While it is thus clear that music and painting produce effects in areas of the brain that are involved with emotion processing, and that the way in which aesthetic emotions are processed is similar to other emotion processing (especially in regard to emotional valence), it is still not clear that the neural activity associated with the emotions we feel in response to music or visual art is in fact the same as the neural activity associated with emotions elicited in daily life. This is intriguing: the relative degrees of spatial and temporal resolution of tools for discovering neural activity—electroencephalography (EEG), functional magnetic resonance imaging (fMRI), and positron emission tomography (PET)—do not preclude subtle differences in the timing of neural activity, or in very small localizations of that activity, so it is possible that adjacent areas might have different functional specificity, or that the sequence of neural activities might differ for different emotions or in aesthetic conditions.[28]

There is in fact further evidence of disjunction, both neurally and in somatic terms. Musical emotions may be more subject to cognitive control than everyday emotions, as in the case described by Antonio Damasio, in which monitoring of skin conductance showed that the pianist Maria João Pires was able to block some of the physiological expression of musical emotions (as measured by skin conductance) during performance.[29] My collaborators and I found that both positive and negative emotional responses to visual art were lateralized toward the left hemisphere, while other work has shown that the right hemisphere is more active for negative emotion than for positive and the left hemisphere is more active for positive emotion than for negative.[30] This may support the idea that while the emotions of aesthetic response can be nominally negative (we call sadness in general a negative emotion, for example), the neural evaluation of what we call a "negative" emotion may change in the context of a positive aesthetic response.

Saying that aesthetic emotions may be differentiable from those of daily life—especially that they may be subtle or subject to savoring—does not, however, mean they can't be powerful. There is a long history representing individual powerful emotional responses to works of art. Ovid's Pygmalion falls in love with a statue of his own making, and Augustine describes weeping passionately over the death of Virgil's Dido: "What is more pitiable than a wretch without pity for himself who weeps over the death of a Dido dying for love of Aeneas, but not weeping for himself."[31] Keats feels "a most dizzy pain" on encountering the ruined classical sculptures of the Elgin Marbles.[32] There is also evidence for a powerful aesthetic response outside the world of poetry, perhaps most clearly the well-documented psychology and psychophysiology of the "chills" effect of music, those moments when your body seems to thrill at a passage that seems exquisitely moving.[33] Moreover, music can produce some of the bodily responses that go along with emotions, and museumgoers show evidence of physiological arousal in response to artwork in line with emotional responses in daily life.[34]

If we can point to instances where we feel art strongly, we still ought to ask what it means to say that art is moving. In a study undertaken with Nava Rubin and Edward Vessel, we asked sixteen participants to imagine that they were helping a curator determine what paintings should be in the permanent collection of a museum, and used fMRI to investigate their brain responses to 109 images selected from museum collections. The images, taken from the CAMIO database (Catalogue of Museum Images Online), were not generally recognized by our participants, and were drawn from a number of different cultures and periods, from the fifteenth century to the twentieth. They were modified only by our setting a maximum size for their projection onto a screen for viewing.[35] Artworks vary in multiple ways, and even within the experimental framework, which is necessarily artificial in many dimensions, the experiment was designed to remain as true as possible to the variety of aesthetic objects and the variability of aesthetic experiences (more on this shortly; for a detailed account of data analysis procedures, see the appendix):

> Imagine that the images you see are of paintings that may be acquired by a museum of fine art. The curator needs to know which paintings are the most aesthetically pleasing based on how strongly you as an individual respond to them. Your job is to give your gut-level

response, based on how much you find the painting beautiful, compelling, or powerful. Note: The paintings may cover the entire range from "beautiful" to "strange" or even "ugly." Respond on the basis of how much this image "moves" you. What is most important is for you to indicate what works you find powerful, pleasing, or profound.

We asked subjects to indicate the strength of their responses ("How much does this image move you?") on a numerical scale (from 1 to 4), as well as to give a more detailed picture by using a numerical scale to indicate how much they felt a variety of emotional, evaluative, and aesthetic responses (awe, disgust, joy, sadness, pleasure, beauty, the sublime, fear, or confusion). Subjects also completed a questionnaire about their knowledge of art and art history, which also asked that they indicate any images they recognized; in addition, we administered an assessment of mood.[36] We aimed to get at a broad array of positive and negative evaluations that might contribute to the sense that art is experienced passionately. The results were in some ways surprising.

It would be perfectly reasonable to predict a kind of linearity to neural responses to art: some works one likes more and some less, and we might expect to find simple increases or decreases of neural activity accordingly. We indeed found such linear increases in some areas of the brain (see figures 11 and 12; see figure 18 for a complete table of activations). But another finding suggested that powerful aesthetic experience is in a class by itself. When viewers described their response to an artwork as extremely moving (assigning it the highest level on the four-point scale), components of the default mode network, an interlinked set of brain regions often implicated in self-assessment, forward planning, autobiographical memory, and ideas of self, were engaged (figure 14). I will discuss some of the implications of the involvement of the default mode network in aesthetics shortly; here I want to point out not only that aesthetic experience in response to visual art can be indeed powerfully moving but also that the most moving aesthetic experience may be categorically different from other aesthetic pleasures and other experiences of emotion. Being moved by art can mean something quite specific, and we can discern some keys to this difference through experimentation.

Pleasure, Comparison, and Reward

Responses to art may employ, with a difference, the machinery of emotion. However, while emotion gives us some access to what makes the aesthetic experience of music and painting distinct, another key area of investigation involves the question of reward. Reward in modern cognitive psychology is a key concept in understanding the motivations that orient our engagement with the world, and it has important connections to emotion. One way of approaching motivation is essentially behaviorist, defining reward and punishment according to observable actions: a reward is anything an organism will work to achieve, and punishment anything it works to avoid.[37] However, rewards and punishments have clear subjective components: they are certainly hedonic—either pleasurable or displeasurable, but not neutral; they also involve emotions, from frustration to fear, jealousy, joy, love, anxiety, nervousness, and beyond, as one achieves a reward, fails to find it, is robbed of it, or makes some kind of catastrophic mistake.[38]

The complex set of experiences, behaviors, and neural activity that make up emotion certainly reaches beyond a neural signal of reward. Indeed, emotions may even run counter to reward expectations, so that emotions continue even when we are punished for them (this is most certainly the case at times with anger and sadness).[39] On the other hand, reward may lead to an affect or action tendency without the felt complexity of emotions. So, for example, I like the fact that water slakes my thirst, and I am gratified in drinking it, but I don't have a picture of a glass of water on my desk alongside my family photos. However, in some cases, like those of addiction, the hedonic component of a reward can produce outsize or aberrant emotional effects, which emerge through the improper functioning of emotion systems.[40]

Reward and emotion involve interconnected neural components, and reward circuitry feeds into and is influenced by emotion processing more broadly.[41] The reward value of stimuli is represented in the brain in a manner that enables the comparison of reward values, and reward processing can represent both the longing and the satisfaction that frame our relationships to objects, ideas, and people (relations that emotion processing also represents and enacts). Reward processing also points toward the mechanics of learning, by enabling the neural calculation of the probability of success or failure and the assignment of hedonic value (a value experienced phenomenally, as, for example, pleasure or frustration) to particular outcomes: the bet and the payoff, so to speak. Studying reward processes in a number of domains, from classical conditioning to neuroeconomics, has begun to illuminate a variety of processes, including memory, decision making, and perceptions of risk.[42]

Aesthetic experience also involves reward processing, both for music and for visual art. Initial work in music showed some of the strongest findings, especially around the experience of chills.[43] Until recently, we had evidence only that roughly similar regions of brain activity were involved in the rewarding aspects of music and visual art, but Ishizu and Zeki have suggested that there is a significant region of overlap, which they describe as corresponding to the perceived "beauty" of both painting and music, in the medial orbitofrontal cortex (an area they designate A1).[44] The aesthetic pleasures, then, of these two Sisters in terms of reward processing may be unified in the brain. Whether or not identical neurons represent the rewards of music and visual art, however, the consistent involvement of reward processing in closely adjacent areas in anterior cortex indicates that we ought to begin to see the assessment of reward associated with music or painting—its "computational value" ("the mental representation of how [its] sensory properties . . . affect [us]")—as a generalizable basis for understanding the effects of multiple arts.[45]

The computational value that is brain-based reward, however, does not denote the same thing as concepts of aesthetic value. While the modern discourse of aesthetics has its roots in ancient discussions of beauty and in rhetoric, the concept of aesthetic value was a latecomer, largely an invention of the late eighteenth and nineteenth centuries, when it came to signify for some theorists an intrinsic form of value available only to art.[46] Such putative value is contested. Kant's insistence in the *Critique of Judgment* on the autonomy of the aesthetic *judgment* forms the basis for this conception of value, but there is not necessarily a reason to restrict the register of value for aesthetic *experiences* thus; art of course has social, economic, and even cognitive value. Adorno, for example, argues that the value of art comes through the testing of the belief systems and the social or ethical values of those who encounter it, Nussbaum that aesthetic experience provides access to sympathetic embodiment in a way that is morally educative.[47] The value that is represented through reward processing is both more abstract and more specific than what historically has been meant by aesthetic value. Reward systems can assign to and represent value for everything from money to water and beautiful faces, as well as a painting or a concerto. That flexibility is crucial for aesthetics.

In general, rewards are essential to much of what we learn: they represent both the motivation for and the payoff of success in exploring the world around us. The knowledge economy of human beings is thus linked to pleasures, and reward is its currency. Indeed, Irving Beiderman and Edward Vessel call human beings "infovores"—we are driven to know.[48] Accordingly, approaches to aesthetics influenced by evolutionary psychology—in particular, those concerned with landscape aesthetics or facial attractiveness—have taken the information value of reward to heart, and tend to approach aesthetic preferences as linked to, and even shorthand representations of, desirable characteristics belonging to what we perceive. Facial symmetry, in this view, signals reproductive health, and facial attractiveness is the felt consequence of the value of reproductive success; a sinuous line of trees in the distance signals a fresh watercourse, and so on.[49] The rewards these perceptions are understood to predict in these accounts are primary reinforcers, necessary to survival. Their value is, thus, essentially a priori predictable because these rewards have universal significance. As I have argued, however, with the Sister Arts, aesthetic rewards predict no such thing, and accordingly, people disagree about their value.

It is thus necessary to be quite specific about the value and reward that are part of aesthetic experience. If we define *aesthetic computational value* as the neural representation of noninstrumental, often mixed, pleasures and displeasures of the senses and of thought—rewards that do not correspond to primary reinforcers, and are thus a priori unpredictable in this sense—there are several potential consequences. One is that responses to faces and landscapes might be essentially and completely different from responses to the arts. I don't think this is true—portraiture, for example, builds on human beauty, and landscape painting and gardening similarly draw on and manipulate features of the natural world. While I suspect there are differences, I also suspect that the pleasures of landscapes and faces do not depend entirely on primary reinforcers. Intense aesthetic responses to painting engage not just reward but the default mode network; I believe not just that intense responses to human beauty and to landscape engage more than reward systems but also that there are appraisals and rewards of the environment and of the people in it that depend on more than what is evolutionarily essential to our survival. There is also no reason that multiple kinds of reward would not contribute to an integrated aesthetic experience. Further experimental work can help our understanding of aesthetics across these modes.

Another possibility is that the difference between primary and aesthetic rewards means that they behave differently in the brain, either in the way they engage reward systems or in the way that they are integrated in larger cognitive processes, or both. The finding that reward activations for painting straddles both the dorsal and ventral regions of the striatum (see figure 12) begins to support the possibility—and more experimentation can elucidate this further—that aesthetic rewards may be processed differently, for this finding seems to collapse the usual distinction that characterizes responses to most primary reinforcers, the distinction between reward prediction (often called "wanting," and represented in dorsal regions) and satisfaction ("liking," represented more ventrally).[50] There are also reasons to think, however, that not only is aesthetic reward processed differently, it is integrated differently, too.

Aesthetic experience seems to integrate reward signals to engage emotion processes, but also to engage significantly larger portions of the brain, as it calls on the default mode network as well as, at times, even engaging the broader body (as with the chills). Reward processing is essentially comparative, and with processes of memory, it binds experiences and perceptions in a web of associations. The engagement of the default mode network in intense aesthetic experience, however, may open wider horizons for such associations, reaching deep into one's sense of self and of social relations, as I describe in the next section. While aesthetic experience may bring new ideas (new moral quandaries or solutions, new perspectives, new categories of appreciation or understanding), in engaging reward processing in a broader neural context, it may also enable new epistemic possibilities as reward valences and strength produce new interconnections. The picture of reward we find with aesthetics offers a framework with particular epistemic implications, a way of perceiving relations between ideas and sensations, relations that hitherto had been not just absent but even unpredictably beyond the horizon of our knowledge.

Aesthetic experience can give the sense that we simply see the world differently, in part as an effect of changes in our mood or arousal: who knew I could feel this way (excited, compelled) about that (a urinal, a beat, a French horn, or a word)?[51] However, the dynamic framework of reward also gives us perspective on changes in how the arts may be valued. The rewards represented in the prefrontal cortex are, as I have said, not predetermined. Dollars, euros, or riyals are not hardwired into the brain; rather, the brain's wiring makes something as valuable to human life as money available for representation.[52] Equally, the complex interconnections of reward that, I argue, help make the Sister Arts sisters need not have always existed, or existed in the same way. There is no necessary reason that the kinds of pleasures we receive from painting or poetry were always proximal, or that their proximity was understood in the same ways as it is now.

If, for example, as in ancient Greece, drama was inseparable from music and dance, the pleasures of these forms might have been compared and linked entirely differently than they are now, and the pleasures of (the historical latecomer) painting might seem more estranged from, say, lyric poetry than they now do.[53] The comparative nature of reward processing means that the borders of aesthetic experience can be at times permeable. The unexpected similarity between the sensory reward of two different kinds of events or objects—hearing a musical instrument and hearing the bright din of a child's hammering, say—can make something new emerge into aesthetic space. (This is in some ways the essence of found objects in art.) However, it is also the case that some things might be forcibly or powerfully excluded from aesthetic experience. Imagine the case of a traveler who, on encountering the sounds of unfamiliar instruments played by unseen human hands, hears only the painful or frightening noise of strange animals, and not music at all. In such an event, the relations between rewards could be understood to be inhibiting: the hedonic value of the musical experiences previously known to the traveler is not comparable for him to the fearful and grating sounds he hears echoing through the rocks. In other words, these overlapping arenas of value may be weighed differently at different moments, resulting in a different landscape of pleasures or a different hierarchy of art. Still, we must remember that the dynamic nature of reward means there is in art an inherent potential for growth and expansion: like begets like, and new experiences can emerge into aesthetic space because we feel them similarly. We are hungry for comparisons and pleasures.[54] Aesthetics emerges at the points of contact between certain powerfully moving rewards. But which rewards count as aesthetic? Part of the answer lies below.

Conceiving of Difference and of Self

Thinking about the dynamic and potentially peculiar way that aesthetic reward functions should alert us not just to historical change but to individual differences. Thus far I have discussed ways in which human neural activity typically changes in response to visual art and to music. We can be reasonably certain that these arts speak to the neural reference spaces of emotion and reward. But there are ways that aesthetic experience is neurally enacted differently by different people, as one might expect—*à chacun son gout*—and this too gives crucial insight into the nature of aesthetic experience.

People disagree about much of what they find beautiful, ugly, or otherwise aesthetically moving. So while there are canons of literature, art, and music, these canons change. Shakespeare's creative force, famously, was not well recognized in Britain during much of the eighteenth century (he fared better in France): *King Lear* was given a happy ending for some hundred years. However, changes in canon and historical shifts in taste are not the only questions: research has shown that for contemporaries with similar levels of expertise, there is greater disagreement over abstract visual art than over representational works, but even with respect to the latter there is a significant level of disagreement.[55] Something similar is true of music, where research into the intensely pleasurable phenomenon of the "chills" depends on subjects' bringing in music of their own selection so that peak responses can be reliably evoked.[56] Such variability is not only a hallmark of aesthetic experience, it has benefits for experimental investigation, for it means that commonalities in responses are actually germane to the aesthetic response evoked, and not to the objects that evoke them.

Emotional responses to art tell an intriguing story. While people tend to agree on what emotions are *depicted* in a work of art (the evidence from music is particularly striking here),[57] the emotions *evoked* by artworks can vary significantly. Indeed, Vessel, Rubin, and I found that on average, observers did not agree about which paintings evoked particular emotions or aesthetic evaluations (our categories were pleasure, fear, disgust, sadness, confusion, awe, joy, sublime, and beauty).[58] Taste also matters: people who don't like heavy metal may feel angry when they hear it, or may think the music itself sounds angry, while lovers of metal simply feel joyful and energized by the music.[59] Emotional responses may also be more in conformity from person to person in some genres than others: tragedy as opposed to comedy, for example. The difference between emotion perceived and emotion experienced, however, points toward a variety of possibilities for aesthetic experience. The evaluation of aesthetic emotion calls on our ability to understand emotional behaviors—theory of mind. However, the predictability of others' reactions, as evidenced by the high degree of agreement in imputing emotion to art objects, is not matched by the predictability of our own experience.

This happens in part because we get everyday practice in interpreting the faces and body language of other people, and it is much less difficult to predict that a common emotional response might appear in someone else than to understand, based on our own experience, how a seemingly unprecedented emotion can emerge in ourselves. Our experience of self relies largely on a sensation of transparency, while our experience of others involves predictions premised on our penetrating opacity. However, our own surprise is necessarily opaque to us.[60] In essence, this begins to indicate one route by which aesthetic experiences are structured at the edges of predictability: while descriptions of the emotional dimensions of aesthetic objects are to some degree predictable, aesthetic experiences happen in the space between what is relatively predictable (our ability to identify others' emotions) and what is, perhaps strangely, not (the responses in ourselves we might never anticipate). There is a great deal of room here for empirical investigation.[61]

The variable power of emotion appears in other ways, too, and individual differences contribute not just to when and what emotions are produced but to *how* emotions function in a given aesthetic evaluation. Individuals weigh emotions differently. Some people privilege sadness, for example, as the feeling that contributes most to the experience of being overcome by a work of visual art, while others privilege beauty, joy, or awe.[62] There are in fact distinct neural signatures for the contribution of feelings of awe and pleasure to powerful aesthetic experience. For those for whom awe is a major driver of aesthetic response, an area in the pontine reticular formation (part of the midbrain) responds with increased activity, perhaps showing the degree to which the ability of an artwork to activate our system of arousal might motivate aesthetic evaluations for some people (but not others; see figure 16). Arousal is one of the key dimensions of the psychological study of emotion (the other is valence), and it identifies the degree to which we physically respond to a stimulus. The brain's arousal system helps drive consciousness and our awareness of the external world.

Some emotions, that is, are weakly (or negatively) arousing (such as contentment or nostalgia) and others are highly arousing (such as anger, joy, or fear). It isn't clear at this time why awe and arousal or pleasure matter more for the aesthetic experience of some people than for others'. Personality characteristics might make a difference (thrill seeking, for example), as might mood, or a learned taste for certain styles of artwork ("happy happiness," to slightly misquote Keats, may strike you as insipid). More research remains to be done, but it is important to realize that not all aesthetic experience is created the same, and being moved by a work of art means different things to different people. In part this reflects the variety of kinds of behavioral responses, neural processes, somatic sensations, subjective feelings, and evaluations that make up emotions, as well as the varying ways in which these are integrated into personal histories and cultural contexts.

Differences in the emotional signature for aesthetic pleasures are one neural finding that helps us understand the individuality of responses. But a shared neural response tells us something more compelling about how aesthetics can matter differently for different people. As I mentioned earlier, there is a categorical difference between what is neutral or moderately pleasing and the most powerful of aesthetic responses. In these cases—of only the most moving experience—the default mode network returns toward baseline function (figure 14).

The default mode network was discovered as researchers sought to answer a curious puzzle: how can we be sure that indirect measures of brain activity (such as PET or fMRI) are actually showing increases or decreases *specific* to a particular experimental paradigm—and thus functionally specific to the activity we want to investigate—and not the result of other general processes, default processes, which are being altered in some unknown way? In other words, are we measuring a particular response to a particular task (and hence we might properly judge that we see a neural substrate for the task), or is some part of what we are measuring the interaction of a particular task with more general, ongoing processes? How can we tell the difference? A number of studies have found that when people are asked to carry out an experimental task, something peculiar happens. One might predict that the brain's use of energy increases when asked to focus on any task, but while responses in an individual area might increase, overall metabolism remains constant.[63] So what is happening that takes all of that energy the rest of the time? What shuts off so that other things can turn on? When we are awake but not engaged in any particular task, the default mode or core network is continually engaged, and it has a variety of functions we are still coming to understand: it underpins our awareness of the world, our alertness to novelty and movement in our surroundings; it contributes to our ability to envision alternative states and futures, to imagine other people; and it helps shape our sense of self-awareness, both of our bodies and of our thoughts.[64]

Under most experimental conditions, when subjects are asked to carry out prescribed tasks, activity in the default mode network decreases. Indeed, such decreases were noted in response to almost all of the artworks in this experiment. However, key components of the default mode network approach baseline as part of the neural response to the most powerfully moving images. It is significant, however, not that individual components of the default mode network increase in activity but that they fire in the same pattern—a return toward baseline—a pattern that helps identify the default mode network as an interconnected system. It is not the case that engagement of the default mode network is the result simply of the introspection involved when subjects are asked to think about their own emotional states. If this were so, the default mode network would be active for all of the images in the Vessel, Starr, and Rubin study. It was only in the special case of intense aesthetic experience that components of the default mode network returned to a baseline level of function.

Why is this the case, and what might it tell us about how aesthetic experience matters? It is important to note that this finding helps ratify the idea that my collaborators and I were in fact evoking strong aesthetic responses in the (admittedly) strange environment of the bore of an MRI scanner, with its noise, vibrations, and isolation.[65] The presence of a response that was not just more of a particular process (a linear increase that one might just call "liking") but a categorical difference lends credence to the idea that, even under the constraints of an fMRI experiment, we were able to elicit something powerful (this was also confirmed by participants' written responses). It is part of our everyday experience of powerful aesthetic experience that it can take you by surprise, and distract—or even abstract—you from the rest of the world around you. This can be true even in an MRI study, as I will describe.

There is a categorical, quantitative—not just a qualitative—difference that distinguishes the most moving aesthetic experience, and the engagement of components of the default mode network in the most intensive response raises significant questions. Many accounts of the default mode network emphasize the importance of self and self-consciousness to its functions. So, for example, strong emotions that are personally relevant may (but do not always) engage the default mode network, while emotions involving other people generally do not.[66] Geday and Gjedde argue that one of the regions of the default mode network at stake in our own findings, the anterior medial prefrontal cortex, might compare information coming from different brain regions and give priority to what seems personally salient. A powerful aesthetic response may similarly affect activity in this region, so that the anterior medial prefrontal cortex gives weight to external sensations that have internal relevance. However, internal relevance is itself a complicated idea (what matters to us varies over time and includes potentially a huge array of possible classes of ideas and events), and there is also evidence that the default mode network is involved in social cognition, too. Two components of the default mode network, the temporoparietal junction and the medial prefrontal cortex, are involved in theory of mind—the simulation of others' consciousness and the imputation of inner life to them.[67]

The anterior medial prefrontal cortex forms part of a subsystem in the default mode network that involves actions and experiences that include daydreaming, making judgments about oneself, and assigning oneself personality traits.[68] The ability to assign oneself traits ("I am funny," "I don't like opera") is a crucial part of self-concept, but it relies on social knowledge, as well as on memory and self-experience.[69] We need to know how others define these traits and what it means for others to perceive them in us in order to understand what it means for us to have them, as well as to understand their value. That is to say, while the default mode network does subserve concepts and experience of the self, it is not a self in isolation, a self unmoored from the social world, especially the social world that is other minds (that is, we are not bound to a post-Renaissance, Western construct of subjectivity-in-isolation).[70]

The return to baseline in the anterior medial prefrontal cortex in our experiment was not the only thing distinguishing the most intense aesthetic experience. Areas in the posterior cingulate cortex, the substantia nigra, and the hippocampus showed similar rebounds toward baseline (see figure 14). The substantia nigra is largely composed of neurons that respond to and produce dopamine, a neurotransmitter essential (among other things) for reward processing; it probably acts (in part) to set a threshold for triggering emotional components of reward (which in turn are implemented through other systems).[71] The substantia nigra, along with other structures that make up a set of brain areas known as the basal ganglia (including the striatum and the caudate, where there are reward-related linear increases in activation), is part of a major center for the reward processing that underpins both basic and complex behaviors and experiences, from the social to the perceptual.[72] The posterior cingulate cortex is, like the anterior medial prefrontal cortex, an important part of the default mode network, and it is also involved in memory processing (like the hippocampus), as well as in self-monitoring. In the default mode network the posterior cingulate cortex and anterior medial prefrontal cortex interact to create a "neuronal platform for" reflection on self and surroundings, as well as for "internal mentation."[73]

The rebound in posterior cingulate cortex function, while not a full return to baseline, thus still offers strong evidence for the involvement of the default mode network in intense aesthetic experience. Because the posterior cingulate cortex has the most active connections to the rest of the default mode network (excluding the medial temporal lobes, which form a separate subsystem),[74] it has been called a central node of the network, subserving systems involving episodic memory and forward planning, but also interfacing with the system dominated by the anterior medial prefrontal cortex, which is engaged in self-referential thought. In addition, the posterior cingulate cortex, with its connections to sensory areas, is probably (as Raichle and colleagues suspected), "a tonically active region of the brain that may continually gather information about the world around, and . . . within us" (2001, 681).

The default mode network in fact seems to be particularly integrative, so, as Buckner and Carroll propose, "default modes of cognition [may be] characterized by a shift from perceiving the external world to internal modes of cognition that simulate worlds that are separate from the one being directly experienced."[75] That is, default modes of cognition bring us into worlds other than what we directly perceive, and they bring the two worlds, of inside and outside, into contact. (Default modes of cognition may thus reveal the condistinction of internal worlds—other minds may be represented using parts of the same network we use to represent ourselves to ourselves.)[76] Components of the default mode network are also crucial to processes of memory (and, as we will see in the next chapter, imagination); while we need to know more in order to understand the mechanisms of interrelation, the functionality of the default mode network suggests that intense aesthetic pleasure may indeed have far-reaching effects.[77] The rebound to baseline in the anterior medial prefrontal cortex, combined with the shift back toward baseline in the posterior cingulate cortex and similar activations in the substantia nigra and hippocampus, indicates that the default mode network is important to aesthetic experience in its ability to mediate the interconnectivity of the internal and external worlds, an interconnectivity lit up by pleasures and reward.

The activity of the default mode network can be aesthetic, and it enables us to say, perhaps surprisingly, that works of art are "transporting"—to use the term commonly employed to describe the peculiar feeling of intense aesthetic involvement. We can become so absorbed, so enrapt in the experience of reading, listening, or looking, that the world of perception seems far away; but this happens only because we were so intensely drawn by part of that world of perception to begin with. Even in the noisy confines of an fMRI scanner, art could so grab the attention that auditory processes were suppressed (see figure 11), and inner life began to take over.[78] The default mode network contributes to the integration of the social, perceptual, and exterior with the emotional, evaluative, and interior as both pleasure and its opposite, as well as in the delicate and expansive texture of emotional response.[79]

Understanding that integration for aesthetics means looking at the brain broadly. The peculiar pattern of response in the default mode network in the Vessel, Starr, and Rubin experiment—a plateau for everything but the most powerful of experiences—was also apparent in a set of brain regions that may provide a gateway to the default mode network: areas of the frontal cortex involved in emotional processing and a subcortical region involved in reward (figure 13). Elsewhere, the activation levels in areas involved in reward (and arousal) were linear (figure 12), as we have seen. Something additional kicks in, however, in some brain regions, suggesting a threshold has been reached that engages an additional process for intense aesthetic experience. In other words, reward itself is not enough to distinguish aesthetic response, nor is it enough to identify what is different about arresting experience. Rather, reward must be made available to us as a particular kind of resonant experience, and either the default mode network may integrate computational reward into a complex experience of emotions and intense aesthetic feeling or, perhaps more likely, its engagement may signify that such an integration has taken place.[80]

This connection awaits further scientific explorations, but we now have begun to see that visual art might strike a person so strongly that it engages this system of integration between different worlds of experience. Philosophers of aesthetics have long argued that aesthetic experience sits on or helps us negotiate the borders of what we perceive through the senses and the world of subjectivity. Kant makes one of the most consequential claims for this when in the *Critique of Judgment* he argues that beauty is the name for what happens when the imagination is able to engage in "free play"— the harmonious, pleasurable recognition of the suitability of our minds to perceive and to engage the world around us.[81] Kant argues, however, that the most powerful aesthetic experience—that of sublimity—comes home differently yet may take hold of us more fully. For Kant, objects whose size dwarfs our ability to grasp them fully in imagination or whose force threatens our physical being may call from us a sense of the power of human mental and moral capacities. Thus, while there is no picture that the imagination can draw that could adequately encapsulate the infinite universe, we can use equations that describe it and even predict its behavior; and while we cannot physically survive the power of a volcanic eruption, we can understand it, build machines that can withstand it, and call on our humanity to aid those devastated by it.[82] Our thrilled recognition of what it means to be human as we confront the infinite, the great, and the terrible—our realization that we, as Blaise Pascal suggested, may be only grassy reeds compared to the might of the universe, but we are thinking reeds—is what some forms of powerful aesthetic experience can bring us.[83]

The idea, then, that some objects of thought can call on and even intensify our sense of being who we are—even if they are something short of sublime—is deeply rooted in aesthetic thought. Before Kant, Baruch Spinoza argued for what he called the *conatus*, an assertion of life and life-affirming activity that is the essence of the connection between body and mind: "Whatsoever increases or diminishes, assists or checks, the power of the activity of our body, the idea of the said thing increases or diminishes, assists or checks the power of thought of our mind. . . . The mind, as far as it can, endeavors to think of those things that increase or assist the body's power of activity."[84] Such a concept is what for Kant is at the root of our ability to make judgments of what pleases us: what we find aesthetically pleasing emerges only when an object is "presented," via imagination, "to the . . . feeling of life."[85] Aesthetic experience in this sense may be what the mind strives to think, because it vivifies our sense of being and of being in the world,[86] and, as Peter de Bolla writes, "intense moments of *aesthetic* experience feel as if they are in the orbit of knowing, as if something has been barely whispered yet somehow heard. . . . These experiences often may help me to identify what it is I already know but have yet to figure to myself as knowledge."[87]

Powerful aesthetic experiences integrate a variety of ways of knowing an object—sensory perceptions as well as the emotions, sensations of pleasure, and the cascade of thoughts we have about what we see—but they also involve representation of multiple kinds of reward in the brain, and the involvement of the default mode network indeed suggests that aesthetic emotions make us newly aware of being ourselves and being in the world. Aesthetic experience works to produce new value in what we see and what we feel. The reward and emotional systems help make that value available to compare with a range of other kinds of knowledge, from the knowledge of experts (kinds of artwork, histories, or brain functions) to that of all of us (of our lives, what a song or painting meant that summer day, what we like, what our communities and cultures value). Being moved by art means all of this, but it also means more. Neurally speaking, art moves us by harnessing a key system with extraordinary resources, a system that not only helps make us who we are but also helps us be aware of who we are. Powerful aesthetic experience makes us return to that state of watchful waiting characteristic of core consciousness, but carrying an awareness of the pleasure of looking at an object and contemplating its worth: perhaps powerful aesthetic experience unites what we didn't predict with what we are always waiting for. In the next chapter I will begin to show how understanding aesthetic response in terms of reward, emotion, and the default mode network may help us integrate our knowledge of visual art, music, and the verbal arts, too.

2

Aesthetics beyond the Mind's Eye: Imagery and the Sister Arts

The cognitive architecture of aesthetics I have sketched so far allows for a reinterpretation of the relations among visual art, music, and literature. Historically, as W.J.T. Mitchell points out, the relation of two of the Sisters, poetry and painting, has in part been mapped through a contest between two sides: iconologists propose that both arts are fundamentally arts of sight, privileging the power of either visual images (painting, sculpture, and so on) or visual imagery (literature and rhetoric); iconoclasts assert that visual images are inherently inferior to the concepts of language, or even that imagery as such doesn't exist.[1] However, sight is not the only mode for imagery, and as I argue below, the sensory variety and functional power of imagery make it crucial to understanding aesthetics across the Sister Arts, and beyond. At first glance, imagery might seem the natural province of the literary, for literature subordinates actual perception, marks on a page, to imagined perception, what those marks can evoke. Accordingly, I begin this chapter with the visual imagery associated with words, but move beyond it, exploring in a second section not just multisensory imagery but the way in which imagery has both epistemic and reward functions. In the third and final section of this chapter, I propose that imagery moves us across the arts, and that it does so in part because of its relation to default modes of cognition.

I start with vision because theorists of imagery historically have focused overwhelmingly on the mind's eye; this has caused problems for both imagery and aesthetics.[2] It is easy to see that painting and poetry might be kin analogically: much as painting might be said to produce images on paper or canvas for the eye to see, poetry may take life as imagery in mind and brain. There is also a strong, perhaps counterintuitive claim, however, made by proponents of the Sister Arts: the more properly visual arts may produce imagery as well. Thus, in 1712 Joseph Addison described what he called "pleasures of the imagination," "such as arise from visible Objects, either when we have them actually in our View, or when we call up their Ideas into our Minds by Paintings, Statues, Descriptions, or any the like Occasion."[3] He linked the Sister Arts of vision and word by suggesting two things: that imagination is itself involved in vision, and that the imagination is the faculty by which all perceptions and all the arts come into our lives as pleasure.

This is a somewhat curious claim, connecting pleasures of actual perception to particular, extraperceptual mental activity, but Addison is not the only person to make it, and it has a long afterlife in Romantic ideology as well as in perceptual psychology. William Hogarth, Addison's near contemporary, gives the idea a new dimension for visual art, however, and suggests different ways in which the imaginative components of vision provide a basis for aesthetic experience. In *The Analysis of Beauty* (a manual for painters and viewers aspiring to expert knowledge), Hogarth recommends that one practice a special kind of sight if she or he wishes to understand what artists see:

> Let every object under our consideration, be imagined to have its inward contents scoop'd out so nicely, as to have nothing of it left but a thin shell, exactly corresponding both in its inner and outer surface, to the shape of the object itself: and let us likewise suppose this thin shell to be made up of very fine threads, closely connected together, and equally perceptible, whether the eye is supposed to observe them from without, or within; and we shall find the ideas of the two surfaces of this shell will naturally coincide.[4]

As we practice this method, "the imagination will naturally enter into the vacant space within this shell, and there at once, as from a center, view the whole from within, and mark the opposite corresponding parts so strongly, as to retain the idea of the whole, and make us masters of the meaning of every view of the object, as we walk round it, and view it from without."[5] This vision, impossible with the eye alone, combines mental imagery with actual sight as the basis of artistic production. Mastering this sight is the foundation of the ability to see beauty where others might miss it. Imagined perception, in this view, is important to vision as more than its internal echo; what Hogarth is implying is that taste, not just perception but evaluative, aesthetic perception, involves more than sight. It involves a projection of self, and a dismantling and reintegration of the senses; this process depends on the motion of the eye and body. Evaluative perception produces a kind of knowledge (of the hidden contours of what we see, in the example above) that is pleasurable and enables us to judge the perfection of form. This is a kind of learned vision, where the reward is found in a new mode of sight that gives access to beauty. The idea that imagery—especially dynamic imagery—can thus be a learned focus of our delight or distress offers a powerful model for thinking about poetry, painting, and music in the framework of reward and emotion.

The Imagery of Sense

We experience the imagery of sense when we have the subjective experience of sensation without having corresponding sensory input: closing your eyes and imagining your mother's face, or constantly rehearsing (and being perhaps annoyed by) a repeated musical phrase you just can't get out of your head. In this sense, mental imagery is heavily reliant on memory and its mechanics, both short term and long, as much as it is reliant on propositions about the world. Some imagery can be prompted by instruction, and some is spontaneous. Images also vary in vividity.[6] The power and strength of mental images, as well as their ability to be controlled and manipulated by the person experiencing them, vary from person to person, from time to time, and also by sensory mode. Visual images for most people are stronger and more controllable than any other kind of imagery.

Auditory images can be quite strong as well as controllable, but images of smell and taste are generally neither strong nor particularly subject to individual control (think of Proust with his madeleine, trying, waiting for an image of the past, then suddenly being surprised by it). Some forms of imagery, as well, can be almost hallucinatory; and most people experience almost all of the forms of mental imagery, in varying degrees, in dreams.[7]

Cognitive neuroscientists carried out a debate about the nature of visual imagery from the 1980s into the twenty-first century.[8] There were two central questions. The first was whether images—"seeing" with the mind's eye, "hearing" with the mind's ear, and so forth—should be understood as propositional or analogical.[9] That is to say, when we close our eyes and imagine a lion, do we "see" a cat in some way analogous to actual sight, or do we keep track of semantic propositions about such an animal (it's large, it has a mane, whiskers, and fur)? The second was about the form of the mental representations behind both sight and imagery. In a classic example of the tension between iconology and iconoclasm, while some neuroscientists argued not just that imagery involves pictorial representations in the brain but that perception does so, too, others argued that neither imagery nor perception involves pictorial depiction.[10] There seems to be contradictory evidence in the imagery debate.

One key part of the debate surrounding visual imagery has to do with the proximity of imagery to perception. Some investigators argue that much of what we attribute to "images" could be ascribed to propositions that denote "greenness" or "roundness," say, rather than to any phenomenon of "seeing" a green ball in the mind's eye.[11] In this view, any seemingly pictorial features of mental imagery can be explained by an individual's use of descriptive data to create an intelligible simulation that is not necessarily pictorial at all. In some cases this is true: incorrect beliefs about how visual events occur can lead to faulty predictions and reported imagery when actual perception would tell a different story. Zenon Pylyshyn describes one such experiment in which subjects were asked to imagine what happens when a blue filter and yellow filter for light are superimposed. One might predict green light, but in actuality the filter would not allow any light to penetrate, and the result would be blackness.[12] In other cases, imagery seems to diverge from description: experiments suggest that even imagined olfaction and taste—the senses most difficult to imagine—may produce effects that are more likely with "images" than with propositions, and that seem to exclude the possibility of explicit propositional knowledge. Most of us are familiar with the experience of expecting a drink to be one thing (say, iced tea, cola, or red wine); picking up the glass without looking, we may be surprised at the taste of water. In such a case, we are surprised not only to find ourselves not drinking water but also that the water seems to taste strangely unpleasant, not like water at all. Something similar has been demonstrated with imagined odors, which may interfere with or alter our perception of actually present tastes.[13] A series of investigations has also shown that the experience of imagined taste and odor combinations corresponds better to actual experience than to subjects' beliefs about these combinations.[14] Perhaps even more compelling is evidence that actually perceived color is in part determined by what people think they are seeing: people see achromatic images (uncolored, gray-scale pixels) of fruits and vegetables as slightly tinted in their natural color, and this slight tint can be measured objectively. Olkonnen and colleagues theorize this is one basis for the phenomenon known as color constancy (in which we see objects as the same color in a variety of different lighting conditions; such differing conditions affect the wavelength of reflected light, and hence *should* effect perceptual differences, but they generally do not).[15] Perception and imagery may thus in some ways go hand in hand.

In part, this is true because perception and imagery employ some of the same brain architecture.[16] With the advent of functional brain imaging (technologies and techniques that reveal not just neuroanatomical features but features of brain metabolism, electrical activity, and, more recently, connectivity), investigations of imagery began to produce very good evidence that across sensory modes, when people experience perceptual imagery, areas of the brain involved in actual perception are active, and function in similar patterns for imagined sensation as during actual perception.[17] For example, neural activation associated with motor imagery has been found to prime the brain cortex for actual motor activity, so that less signal is needed to produce movement using transcranial magnetic stimulation; motor facilitation can also be produced in muscles themselves via imagery.[18] However, it is not just localizable activity that connects imagery to perception. For example, while auditory images use much of the same areas of the brain as does actual audition, they also use many of the same processes and principles of organization as well: auditory images are organized temporally (as opposed to visual and haptic images, which tend to be organized to reflect spatial detail and relations).[19]

Knowledge and Multisensory Imagery

Samuel Moulton and Stephen Kosslyn argue that imagery functions epistemically: it is aimed at "mak[ing] available or generat[ing] knowledge," and it enables us "to predict the imminent or distant future, but also to consider many possible futures—or even many possible worlds."[20] However, imagery can in fact model what is not properly predictable at all. For example, to return to Ovid, what would it look like if a woman became a tree? Why might this transformation be beautiful and not simply horrifying or, in the worst sense, simply dehumanizing? In George Sandys's canonical translation:

> a numbnesse all her limbs possest;
> And slender filmes her softer sides invest.
> Haire into leaves, her Armes to branches grow:
> And late swift feet, now rootes, are lesse than slow.
> Her gracefull head a leafy top sustaines:
> One beauty throughout all her form remaines.
> Still Phoebus loves. He handles the new Plant;
> And feeles her Heart within the barks to pant.
> Imbrac't the bole, as he would her have done;
> And kist the boughs: the boughs his kisses shun.[21]

I will return to the peculiarity of this passage and to questions of translation, but here let me point out that the impossibility of Sandys's Ovidian imagery, with its mixture of sounds of panting from the heaving breast of bark, the trembling skin of something part arboreal, part woman, can make sense to us in part because of the ways in which imagery and perception diverge.

This is true across sensory modes, and part of the artistic use of imagery is to exploit such divergences. Though we may rarely notice it, images of sound, for example, only occasionally employ features that are indispensable for our experience of actual sound, like loudness. In this case, even though imagery gives us something less than perception, that less can be exploited for more. This scene plays with the ambiguity of volume for imagined sounds when Sandys evokes the impossibly faint pant of skin (half bark, half flesh) moving with the breath of fear; Keats does this too in "The Eve of St. Agnes": "The music, yearning like a god in pain, / She scarcely heard. . . . She sighs / Amid the timbrels."[22] Madeline is so absorbed in her inner world that she sees and hears nothing, but our seeing and hearing are different: these lines are able to make "sense" because of the sonoral characteristics of mental imagery.

Imagery can work to model existing knowledge and point toward emergent possibilities because people use different strategies to make "sense" of imagined sensory experience. Some people are very good at evoking perceptually vivid images in their minds; some are not, reporting very little in the way of images that seem to mime perceptual experience. In addition, even under the best of conditions, some forms of imagery are very difficult to evoke, especially images of smell and taste (it is hard for most people to think of a potato and to get a strong image of its taste). If images of taste and smell are difficult to evoke volitionally and linguistically, then, it might make sense to think about what help readers are given in making such evocations, modeling the world they are given. Keats's "Eve of St. Agnes" offers one path of resolution: "Into her dream he melted, as the rose / Blendeth its odour with the violet, — / Solution sweet" (ll. 321–22). Keats may be evoking potentially well-known scents, perhaps that of a common English posy or of contemporary eaux de toilette.[23] However, he also makes odor fugitive, one scent blending into another so that the resolution is primarily semantic: a sweet mixture. Indeed, there is considerable debate as to whether olfactory imagery is primarily perceptual or semantic: do we imaginatively perceive a smell, or do we instead frame our thoughts based on meaning and associations? The fact that most people have problems evoking olfactory imagery on command makes it probable that people use a variety of strategies for making "sense" of imagined olfaction, including focusing on associations or categories like "sweet" or "foul."[24] Keats's evocation of a solution sweet is a semantic-sensory metaphor not just for modeling difficult-to-imagine sensations but also for the blending of one consciousness into another, as Porphyro's voice and lute influence Madeleine's dreams. These examples point toward the complex ways in which mental images fundamentally can serve to integrate a variety of information and expand our ways of knowing.

The complexity of this integration comes in part because most imagery is, de facto, not just multidimensional but multisensory.[25] For example, there are at least four categories of auditory imagery: imagery involving music, imagery involving speech, imagery involving metrical speech, and general images of sound (some more semantically clear: dogs barking, trucks passing; some less: clicks or bangs).[26] Auditory imagery may behave differently if it carries semantic information (words, certainly, but, to take one example, dogs don't just sound, they signify, and the may signify differently to different people) and also if it combines categories (mental imagery involving music with lyrics involves different parts of the brain than imagery for music without words). So auditory imagery integrates a variety of kinds of information, only some of which we typically think of as aural: semantic information, while drawing on sensory information, generally goes beyond the data of a single sense. Moreover, part of the multisensory dimension of auditory imagery is linked to the complexity of what we think of primarily as auditory experience: in a crowded, noisy room, we may think what we are doing is primarily *listening* to the person across the dinner table, but our understanding depends a great deal on being able to see her as she speaks, too.[27] Ovid, again, in Sandys's translation, toys with the multisensory nature of imagery, with the "pant" of bark and flesh as Daphne changes: the multiple sensory implications of breath, both the halting sound and the sight of heaving, brittle skin, contribute to the estrangement of this scene of transformation.

It is not just that aural imagery can also be visual. Other kinds of imagery are inherently multisensory, in ways that go beyond commonly used concepts of synesthesia.[28] Smell and taste are closely related (they are the two chemical senses, involving receptors specialized for particular substances), and the imagery of each of the two modes also tends to overlap.[29] The imagery of touch draws on representations of texture, temperature, and movement, as well as sight. Haptic activity is almost essential to human survival: the networks enabling it are complex, recruiting sensations of touch, motor processes, and visual systems to enable robust and detailed imagery.[30] Vision and touch are closely related for most people; imagined reaching and grasping or the sensations of texture involve both visual and haptic representations. Some investigators argue we have common forms of representation, which are used for imagining objects visually as well as in terms of touch and the motions of grasping.[31] Significantly, motion is often at the heart of the multisensory nature of imagery, so that, for example, visual imagery can call on motor activity by evoking the gaze, such that the frontal eye fields, areas in the brain employed for planning and executing eye movements, are active in some imagery tasks, and in the case of navigation, even routine tasks, such as planning a path through toys littering the living room floor or threading our way through a crowd, may call on proprioceptive and motor imagery.[32]

Fundamentally, thus, visual imagery and vision may feed into or build on motor imagery because vision allows for (and in sighted persons is preparatory to) motion: to use the term invented by James J. Gibson, the visual world allows affordances—action possibilities.[33] What one sees affords possibilities for motion, such as grasping a handle, turning a page, or finding one's way through divergent paths. These possibilities for action are one way we make *sense* of the world and are determined not just by instinct but also by experience and capacity. Indeed, as Alva Noë and Kevin O'Regan argue, our conscious experience of sight does not involve an essentially visual representation at all, but rather the mastery of the relation between sense and motion. Vision is itself an "exploratory activity," rooted in our navigation of the world around us.[34] Translated into aesthetic terms, objects of vision may draw us in to explore the world in reality and imagination, and to engage with both inner and outer world as made to move us, to meet us as we grasp them.

Moving Pictures: Aesthetics and Imagery Networks

Indeed, I believe imagery of motion to be at the heart of our capacities for both simulation and aesthetic experience. Let us return again to Hogarth to think about these questions. The imagined projection of one's own body into three-dimensional space in Hogarth's wire-line vision of an invisible, interior construction blends perception with imagery as he searches for a model for the apprehension of beauty. We are to enter inside a three-dimensional "thin shell" that will give us a "perfect" idea of every side of the object—even its notional inner contour:

> Let every object under our consideration, be imagined to have its inward contents scoop'd out so nicely, as to have nothing of it left but a thin shell, exactly corresponding both in its inner and outer surface, to the shape of the object itself: and let us likewise suppose this thin shell to be made up of very fine threads, closely connected together, and equally perceptible, whether the eye is supposed to observe them from without, or within; and we shall find the ideas of the two surfaces of this shell will naturally coincide.

Imagery of motion and of proprioception are present in Hogarth's model of the pursuit of visual aesthetic pleasures; Hogarth says that to see beauty fully, we must learn to engage what we see as subject to mental motion and to a complete, ideal form of vision. I want to explore with some care the reasons this might in fact be a powerful model for the active experience of beauty and its kin.

Motor imagery is, I believe, a better paradigmatic case for imagery than is visual imagery: the mind's body is more encompassing than the mind's eye. Indeed, if multisensory imagery is the norm rather than the exception across sensory modes, this is nowhere clearer than in imagery of motion. Generally, people imagine motion along with sight—the experience of moving one's body is, for sighted persons, both visual and kinetic. Of note, however, when we imagine other people moving, we usually, and preferentially, employ visual images: imagine, for example, your mother walking across a room. On the other hand, when we imagine ourselves moving—clapping our hands, reaching for the stars, sticking out our tongues—we may use visual images, but unlike in the case of an imagined other, we also imagine the sensations of movement for ourselves—what it would be like *if we actually were to do what we are thinking*. Instead of using solely or primarily parts of the brain that correspond to vision and imagined vision, we use areas normally employed in planning our own movements.[35]

Motor imagery also holds a peculiar importance for human development and social cognition. We learn to move in part by imitation: we watch others move, and then slowly come to imitate those motions by associating our own planned movements with our actual ones.[36] Such a process may involve mirror neurons, specialized cells, which become active not just when we are in motion but when we perceive motion in others.[37] While a number of researchers have questioned whether there are in fact neurons specialized to carry out imitative functions in humans (mirror neurons were discovered in macaques), it is clear there are complex, distributed motor systems in the brain that underpin many phenomena of embodiment.[38] These motor systems are crucial to a variety of perceptual and imagined experiences.

Some critics suggest motor systems may be fundamentally important for art because of the involvement of imagined action not just in mimesis but also in empathy.[39] The classic examples linking the perception of action to imagination and our own mirrored emotions are Adam Smith's:

> When we see a stroke aimed and just ready to fall upon the leg or arm of another person, we naturally shrink and draw back our own leg or our own arm; and when it does fall, we feel it in some measure, and are hurt by it as well as the sufferer. The mob, when they are gazing at a dancer on the slack rope, naturally writhe and twist and balance their own bodies, as they see him do, and as they feel that they themselves must do if in his situation.[40]

Smith argues that the imaginative process he calls sympathy (the term empathy is a creation of the nineteenth century) happens from the inside out, when we place ourselves imaginatively in the situations of others. Because sympathy starts from within, and with imagery, external perceptions aren't in fact necessary; at times, he argues, literary images work even better than the exterior world to create images of others, which are also then written on our own bodies.[41]

Recent critics have followed Smith's lead and argued that mental simulation through imagery of motion is an important element of a number of phenomenologically full experiences of art. Elaine Scarry led the way with *Dreaming by the Book* as she explored methods for evoking imagery and argued that motion is the key to vivid imaginative experience (indeed, I borrow the subtitle of this section from her). John Sitter, from a different perspective, contends that we move from disgust to identification with the frail body of the prostitute in Swift's "A Beautiful Young Nymph Going to Bed" as we focus on sensations of touch and the movements that she makes, in pain, as she prepares for sleep without rest.[42] However, the importance of motor imagery goes beyond the representation of motion through the description of bodies, and even beyond the machinery of empathy, where we imagine others' actions and use those imaginings for simulations of others' identities. Remarkably, motor imagery can be produced even when motion is not represented in the arts that elicit it—it can attend music or static visual representations.

With Hogarth's method of trained artistic vision (the scoop'd-out shell), he made the claim for the necessity of motor imagery for seeing the totality of visual form and attaining the pleasures of visual beauty. We in imagination "naturally enter into the vacant space within this shell, and there at once, as from a center, view the whole from within, and mark the opposite corresponding parts so strongly, as to retain the idea of the whole, and make us masters of the meaning of every view of the object, as we walk round it, and view it from without."[43] Hogarth's representation of the imaginative component of artistic vision requires that we learn to capitalize on a peculiar feature of sight—its three-dimensional navigability and completeness, even encompassing what is beyond immediate visual experience, "the world behind the head."[44] We would take this kind of super-perception along with our sense of inhabited space into the imagined shell.

Hogarth describes the interpenetration of sight and motion in an ideal form of vision, but there is initial evidence that visual art can evoke motor imagery more regularly. Freedberg and Gallese argue that for visual art, motor imagery mediates between the actions of the artist, the artwork itself, and the body of the viewer.[45] The physical traces of brush, scalpel, and file may evoke motor imagery as viewers imagine the gestures that produced it; one might thus encounter the arcs of a Jackson Pollock painting as gesture and not just lines of paint. It is also possible that with representational arts, motor imagery can attend our response to the bodies we see, either in painting, as Freedberg and Gallese argue, or, as di Dio, Macaluso, and Rizzolati find, with sculpture as well.[46] These intriguing findings deserve further elaboration and replication.

It is, however, neither necessary to imagine the hand that made a work nor to enact a neural simulation of a body in a work in order to engage the imagery of motion. In Pollock's 1946 *Shimmering Substance* (figure 1), the yellow spiral or circle that seems to dominate the painting doesn't actually exist on the surface of the canvas: there is no yellow line, only the illusion of a yellow line, which can be constructed around the interruptions of white, blue, green, and pink pigment. The circular image is produced by the sweep of the eye as it follows an imagined curve and by the standard embroidery of vision (whereby we assume unbroken forms even where they do not exist, as with the illusion of the Kanizsa triangle [figure 19]), and it is strengthened by the suggestive echoes of loops throughout the canvas. The vibrancy of the painting—its "shimmering"—comes through our own visual and imagined engagement, the sense of motion that comes from the eyes and from the filling in of the golden curve as it draws the viewer on and in to the painting's perceptual and formal logic.

Motor imagery can come thus with static art, but not only thus; indeed, motor imagery is prevalent across responses to all the Sisters. When we experience musical imagery, some of us participate in "covert" singing or humming, and part of the experience of imagined music can involve remembering movements (especially for musicians). Pleasant music may elicit activity in sensorimotor areas used for vocalization,[47] but, more than this, many of us know how much sound may physically "move" us, even discovering this anew every time we sit in a jazz club and can't seem to help tapping, moving, nodding. Indeed, the expectation that, as a sign of aesthetic appreciation, an audience should remain still and quiet during a secular musical performance is relatively recent, and the practice is certainly not universal across genres or cultures today; it is more likely that individuals respond to music by moving than by remaining still both in the past and the present.[48] This is true of genres linked to dance (such as reel, minuet, gavotte, house, waltz, merengue, or salsa), but also of many forms more often encountered (at least now) in the relative stillness of an auditorium (such as avant-garde jazz), because rhythmic sound has motive power. As Levitin argues, "music activates . . . motor sequences and our sympathetic nervous system"; it has thoroughgoing effects, and "increases our alertness through modulation of norepinephrine and epinephrine and taps into our motor response system through cortisol production."[49]

Some theorists argue that motion, as much as sound, should be understood as a foundational component of music. For musicians, music *is* movement, the flying fingers, bowing arms, drumming hand, and swelling breast and belly of song.[50] For many people music seems to have motor foundations in other ways: the experience of pitch, for example, is often described using dynamic terms (moving from high to low); technical components of music as well as compositional elements are described using motor terms ("runs" or a "movement"), and a number of scholars and neuroscientists argue that the basis of the emotional power of music involves a connection to motion.[51] Malcolm Budd argues that music's evocativeness cannot be dependent on a merely metaphorical notion of musical movement.[52] However, music moves us not just metaphorically or analogically but also physically and imagistically, and its evocation of motion and the imagery of motion places music beyond the frame of sound and the world of audition.

Charles Nussbaum points out that music can also provide affordances—propensities or opportunities for action—that are in part based on the ways we make music and the ways we perceive it, from the facts of vocalization to the organization of music into rhythmic sections: "musical experience is based on bodily experience," but music transcends "the possibilities of physical motion that constrain the . . . human body" because the imagined world of musical movement involves other voices, and feats of perfect skill of which few are capable.[53] Part of the importance of motion for music, however, also has to do with musical temporality.

Ethnomusicologists have explored musical dynamics by building on findings surrounding the phenomenon of entrainment, the mutually dependent synchronization of otherwise autonomous rhythmic behaviors or processes either across individuals, or within the brain, or between the brain and the rest of the body. Entrainment is originally a concept from mechanics, but it has a broad reach. Ethnomusicologists have noted that social relations and identification can follow from entrainment, as people come to share rhythms situationally or socially (for example, dancing, marching, or clapping together).[54] In terms of individual psychology and physiology, however, a number of processes can become entrained, so that, for example, gross bodily motion (moving one's arms and legs in synchrony) can be linked to breathing and heart rates, to patterns of motor imagery, and to firing rates of neurons. These processes can synchronize in motor activity and motor imagery around music, and processes of entrainment may be one route by which music evokes emotions.[55]

If motion and imagined motion are central to music, they are also key to poetry, and for similar reasons. Poetry, like music, is metrical, involving temporal regularity as well as moments of surprise. The processing of timing in the brain is complex, involving a variety of regions, including the basal ganglia and cerebellum.[56] Neurons in the cerebellum coordinate perceptual imagery and motor output. Such activity must always involve temporal coordination: we need to know not just what we are doing but when we're doing it, in order to be able to run without falling or catch a cup as it tumbles to the floor. The cerebellum is important not just for coordinating our actions in the outside world but also for silently humming a tune.[57] In the case of poetry, metrical writing can evoke not only auditory imagery but the imagery of motion; as we time the words that we "hear," motor centers of the brain, including the cerebellum, are also active, perhaps in helping us catch the beat, and what enables the timing of action also enables us to understand and produce metrical speech.[58] As Empson put it, reading poetry involves getting its "muscular image."[59]

Given that parts of the brain's architecture that coordinate motion are recruited by metrical writing, it makes all the more sense that poems, like music, may make us wish to keep time, to move and to imagine motion, as one might find in reading Gerard Manley Hopkins's "The Woodlark":

> The blue wheat-acre is underneath
> And the corn is corded and shoulders its sheath,
> The ear in milk, lush the sash,
> And crush-silk poppies aflash,
> The blood-gush blade-gash
> Flame-rash rudred
> Bud shelling or broad-shed
> Tatter-tangled and dingle-a-dangled
> Dandy-hung dainty head.[60]

The bird's motion may be an effect not just of mental vision but of the motor imagery associated with meter. Visual images are fractured in the poem; the poet draws attention first to, then away from, color, and toward a graphical, alliterative index of words and indices of sound. The potential motion of poppy-heads swaying in a field here is ultimately subject less to imagined vision than to the texture of words:

The blùe whèat-àcre is ùndernèath
And the còrn is còrded and shòulders its shèath,
The eàr in mìlk, lùsh the sàsh,
And crùsh-sìlk pòppies aflàsh,
The boòd-gùsh blàde-gàsh
Flàme-ràsh rùdrèd
Bùd shèlling or bròad-shèd
Tàtter-tànglèd and dìngle-a-dànglèd
Dàndy-hùng daìnty heàd.

The rapidly moving beats, redistributed in changing form and changing feet from line to line, are meter in motion; there is less a repeated pattern than an evolving landscape of intensified sound. Horace recommends writer or reader use "fingers and ear . . . [to] catch the lawful rhythm" of poetry; if he and modern cognitive science are right, this changing beat can have physiological effects, and the way that motor imagery may accompany meter and music may, literally physically, matter.[61] Imagined motion can have very real physical effects: Decety and colleagues show that heart rates and breathing increase when we imagine lifting heavy loads or doing complicated tasks.[62] In the case of Hopkins, however, our pulses may quicken not just with the swiftness of imagined flight but with the swiftness of meter. Poems may evoke sound inside our heads—the rise and fall of meter, the symmetry of rhyme. This, too, is aural imagery: the "voice" in our mind that says, "Glory be to God for dappled things, / For skies of couple-color as a brinded cow," and the "ear" in our mind that "hears" smooth assonance and the beat of sprung rhythm.[63] Poetry, then, from the moments our minds "hear" what our eyes see, is multisensory, and I strongly suspect that part of the process of learning to love poetry is learning to enact the motor imagery of meter—learning to feel the beat.[64]

The evocation of motor imagery and motor response with visual art, music, and poetry, should give pause. Motor imagery both integrates a variety of sensory information and is at the heart of a variety of kinds of sensory imagery. This is crucial, for as I will show, the integrative potential of imagery, and especially of motor imagery, is key to its aesthetic potential. Elaine Scarry suggests powerfully in *Dreaming by the Book* that imagined motion is at the heart of the way writers can engage readers' most vivid imaginative experiences. Indeed, imagery of motion may be the most aesthetically consequential kind, and it is at the heart of a variety of modes of imagery that don't appear to be visual at all.

Multisensory imagery, especially the multisensory imagery of motion, is centrally important to a variety of aesthetic pleasures in part because it gives us access not to the "real" complexity of experience but to certain powerfully connected aspects of the ways our minds *internally represent* experiences and objects.[65] Colin Martindale has proposed that much of our experience of beauty comes from the ways our brains represent the world to us.[66] He hypothesizes that hedonic pleasure and displeasure correspond to the degree to which particular parts of our cognitive architecture are stimulated. Some representations promote these pleasures better than others because of the way they are constructed:

> Cognitive units are connected in several ways. [Some] connections are excitatory. On the other hand, cognitive units are hypothetically connected in a[n] . . .

inhibitory fashion [neurons are certainly thus connected]. Units inhibit neighboring units in proportion to their distance. Given the principle of arrangement, this means that the more similar two units are, the more they will inhibit one another. There are also indirect excitatory . . . connections. (60)

This means, for instance, we find that key element of classical concepts of beauty, uniformity amid variety, pleasing because the uniformity (similarity and proximity) excites connections—speeds them up, reinforces them—while the variety (the distance between elements, physical and representational, in our mental worlds) ensures that inhibition—slowing down, contradiction, counterbalancing—will be minimal, and this comes together as a powerful and pleasing experience (67–68).

Mental images bring together a range of kinds and modes of information, from sensations to memories of and propositions about the world; they also are not necessarily neutral to us; they may be pleasurable or displeasurable, and may evoke strong emotional responses.[67] In Martindale's model, the integrative potential of imagery is key to its pleasures, or more accurately to its *potential* for pleasure when it is enacted in brain and mind. Imagery sits at an important nexus, bringing together sensory information, emotional experience, and semantic data, and points toward the way in which powerful aesthetic experience integrates information and sensation to redefine and revalue what we feel and know.[68]

Crucially, imagery taps into mechanisms of reward. In addition to recruiting responses both in body and in mind, emotional imagery can recruit motor imagery and reward circuitry, and these effects are enhanced by emotional content.[69] It is worth pointing out that imagery can be used to modify and even induce responses in classical conditioning, which offers reliable evidence of both the emotional power of imagery and the connections between and among imagery, reward, memory, and learned behaviors.[70]

Even for those who experience imagery without vividity, however, imagistic language is emotionally evocative, with a difference: the emotion is felt more in body than in mind. Somatic responses (what we might think of as visceral responses associated with emotion, from increased sweating to trembling, blushing, and so on) are *reduced* with more vivid imagery; conversely, people who experience more vivid images may feel the emotional punch more in their minds than in their bodies.[71] Such individual differences support rather than detract from the extraordinary ability of images to enable or focus connections between disparate modes of being and knowing, and, in connecting them, to create value—as emotion, as beauty, as delight—where there had been nothing before.

Findings from music and painting support the aesthetic significance of motor imagery across the Sisters. Juslin and colleagues have posited seven neural routes through which music might produce emotion: a brain stem "reflex" (the term is used loosely) based on acoustical features that are coded as influencing arousal or valence, rhythmic entrainment, evaluative conditioning (based on the pairing of music with rewarding events), contagion (a quasi-sympathetic response to perceived emotional qualities of music), visual imagery (imagining scenes attending the music), episodic memory (of experiences accompanying music or of other moments), and expectation (based on knowledge of musical structures). Five of these categories (all but the purported relatively automatic brain stem responses and evaluative conditioning) may draw on imagery networks, and motor imagery may be involved in all five. For example, musical expectancy can involve subvocal humming of the next note or the motor processes of timing or tapping in waiting for a beat; contagion, as Juslin and colleagues propose, may involve the motor processes linked to empathy. In suggestive research with visual art, Battaglia, Lisanby, and Freedberg contend that what they call aesthetic "quality" is linked to motor imagery. In comparing Renaissance paintings to photographs of individuals in similar poses, they found that a single painting, alone among the images they studied, evoked motor potentials.[72] This single painting was Michelangelo's *Expulsion from Paradise,* and they hypothesize that the reason one might call that painting aesthetically powerful is because it *moves* us both neurally and imaginatively.

Motor imagery and motor processes thus may have significant reach in aesthetic pleasures; Hogarth was on to something when he promised new, learned pleasures with his scoop'd-out shell. Literature to some extent offers itself as externalized imagery—as Scarry suggests in her title, literature gives us the instructions for dreams. Turning to a poem, then, one that takes as its focus the manipulation of sensory imagery under the sign of motion, may help realize some of the consequences of the cognitive architecture I have been discussing. The potential for imagery to reorder sensation in line with emerging nuances of pleasure and reward is strikingly clear in Elizabeth Bishop's "At the

Fishhouses," and I close this chapter by exploring this poem.[73] "At the Fishhouses" depends on the ability of imagery to enable strong representations, allowing sometimes surprising connections between ostensibly disparate ideas and effects. Not only may the strength of the image produce pleasure of its own, the evolving relations illuminated by the images as they are felt can be powerful, too. The poem opens at the limits of the visual:

> Although it is a cold evening,
> down by one of the fishhouses
> an old man sits netting,
> his net, in the gloaming almost invisible,
> a dark purple-brown. (ll. 1–5)

Bishop subsequently evokes all the senses, and one comes into play as another recedes: "the air smells so strong of codfish / it makes one's nose run and one's eyes water" (ll. 7–8). Smell almost wipes out sight, reducing it to light filtered through tears, giving little clarity. Though the sky it shows is almost dark, the rest of the poem is full of striking, almost dazzling moments of reflection, in which herring scales appear like "creamy iridescent coats of mail" and "the sparse bright sprinkle of grass" flashes next to "long bleached handles." Sight is on the edge of failure as darkness falls in the far north, and at the heart of the poem are images that evoke other senses and other modes: not just the strong smell of cod, but images of movement, touch, sound, and taste.

Bishop sketches a seal listening to the sounds of hymns, at the edge of a water that teases vision without satisfying it. The sea is "cold, dark, deep, and absolutely clear":

> If you should dip your hand in,
> your wrist would ache immediately,
> your bones would begin to ache and your hand would burn
> as if the water were a transmutation of fire
> that feeds on stones and burns with a dark gray flame.
> If you tasted it, it would first taste bitter,
> then briny, then surely burn your tongue. (ll. 73–79)

Bishop moves through a range of sensory modes: visual, olfactory, haptic, and gustatory imagery are all sewn together through the imagery of a hand in motion, scooping water to the mouth.

By the end of the poem, however, the ocean takes over as the central object of perception and imagination. Bishop has twice described it as "cold, dark, deep, and absolutely clear"; but it evolves in the final lines:

> It is like what we imagine knowledge to be:
> dark, salt, clear, moving, utterly free,
> drawn from the cold hard mouth
> of the world, derived from the rocky breasts
> forever, flowing and drawn, and since
> our knowledge is historical, flowing, and flown. (ll. 78–83)

The sense-strewn landscape of the poem's images ultimately melds onto a world of words, words that gesture toward what we could not ever properly sense. That thing which we "imagine knowledge to be"—something beyond perception—is counter, original, spare, strange (to borrow terms from Hopkins's "Pied Beauty"); but the poem's doublings and returns back through the layers of sensory imagery, from sight (dark) to taste (salt), touch (cold), and motion and sound (with poetry itself), matter. Bishop recalls, in new combinations, the sensory images we have been given, but she surprises by intensifying the proximity of these images, so that the (oxymoronic) dark clarity becomes anew a briny burn, in a mouth other than ours. The quick shifts through sensory modalities offer challenges to realizing any of them fully and brightly; the "image" of knowledge is on one level fractured and distanced from realistic perception. But the sensory combinations we have seen before in the poem leave traces; briny-burn layers with salt dark. Ultimately, vision, taste, and touch all blend into the imagery of motion, which, "drawn . . . forever, flowing and drawn, . . . flowing and flown," unites the sensory modes together, from audition to vision, taste, and touch. Motion can thus emerge not just as denoted or described but as felt, making the lawful rhythm of the poem in mind, or hands, or tongue. The pleasures of interconnection are organized around imagined movement and are distributed in a variety of images that call on the broad variety of modes through which imagery may come to life.

I have argued that motor imagery may be the proper prototype for the epistemic, emotional, hedonic, and integrative potential of imagery. The connection of imagery processes to aesthetic experience has broad repercussions, for the network of brain areas that produces imagery is to a significant extent coextensive with the default mode network.[74] Drawing on Buckner and Carroll, as well as on work by Hassanbis and colleagues, Moulton and Kosslyn argue that the default mode network and the neural space of imagery are largely coincident because they both involve the interaction of what we remember with what we project, and they provide the ability to create knowledge-based and knowledge-generating simulations about the self in the world.[75] Imagery does not always do this, but it is perhaps uniquely well situated to bring self and world intimately together.

Self-generated, complex fictional imagery recruits parts of the distributed network of the default mode, including, prominently, the medial prefrontal cortex, a large swath of which is implicated, as we have seen, in intense aesthetic experience.[76] However, the relationship among default modes of brain activity, imagination, and aesthetics does not involve simply an overlap of brain areas but may involve similar of patterns of activity and connectivity, too, in a distributed, interactive network.[77] Exploring this relationship requires further experimental amplification, but the initial findings are noteworthy. Powerful aesthetic experience involves the engagement of multiple components of the default mode network; it is possible that imagery may provide a gateway to this engagement, recruiting a large portion of the brain in a networked way. The undergirding of aesthetic engagement is broad indeed, and recruits massive (metabolic) resources.

The examples we have seen from Hogarth and Bishop emphasize something important about the aesthetics of imagery—its pleasures are something for which readers and viewers must work, and which many of us may have to learn. This is the classic definition of a reward—we work to attain it. Aesthetic pleasures do not strike us all equally all the time. For example, most people in the industrialized world are surrounded by music, even bombarded by it, but we do not always feel transported while shopping at a mall or grocery store.[78] Aesthetic pleasures may sometimes seem to grab us, but often we must work to meet them halfway, and the work and the experience are highly individual.

It is here that the particular networks of imagery matter again. Powerful aesthetic experience can draw on the capacity of the default mode network to situate us newly in the world of sensation with visual art. The interrelation of the default mode network and the space of imagery suggests one way in which the world of internal sensation—of imagery and imagination—may be integrated with self and pleasure in the architecture of aesthetic experience.[79] Imagery can in fact underpin aesthetic responses even where we might not think images matter. The imagery of the written word can go beyond practices of depiction, music can evoke motor imagery, and even visual art can have motor implications, as I have shown. Motor imagery points toward the integration of the broader family of the arts: evidence shows that when viewers enjoy watching dance—another Sister—it evokes motor imagery in its viewers, and temporal processes in dance involve motor system coordination and even entrainment; we might expect similar results with drama and film.[80]

Imagery integrates and remakes knowledge, and, enacted in the brain and in the mind, it can take powerful hold of the self. This is what Wolfgang Iser suggests when he emphasizes the active role readers play in imaginatively constructing and completing the worlds that texts offer us, and what Ernst Gombrich argued for when he described "the beholder's share."[81] By creating our own imagery, we build the affective world of the arts around us. We do not feel this activity, in the default mode network and elsewhere, as a neural construct, of course—neural activity is not conscious or available to consciousness as such. But imagery is itself experiential, and in framing our conscious experience of art, it becomes available to both humanistic and neuroscientific analysis, as I have shown here. The imagery that contributes to aesthetic experience is not always powerfully moving, but its integrative and hedonic potential helps us understand how intense aesthetic experience can take shape, and the fragmented yet curiously whole knowledge that is beauty—invisible, flowing, cold as it passes us—can thus be understood in part through the architecture of the imagery of the senses. The cognitive framework I advance enables us to rethink the connections among the Sister Arts of poetry, painting, and music by showing how the pleasures we experience in all three may rely on the integration of kinds of knowledge not just as data but as knowledge that has been given a value. The brain makes us aware of words on a page, sounds in silence, or daubs of paint not just as words, tones, or light and colors but as the pleasures that come with interconnection.

3

Toward a Dynamic Aesthetics: The Sister Arts and Beyond

In this final chapter I turn to the history of aesthetics and to particular exemplars of each of the Sister Arts as I pursue the explanatory and interpretative power of a dynamic and cognitive concept of aesthetic experience. I have proposed that motor imagery offers a promising route for modeling the aesthetic pleasures of poetry, music, and visual art, and the clearest case for understanding the complex ways in which imagery more broadly can enable the integration of and comparison between new areas of knowledge and experience. But this model raises questions, both around imagery and concerning the dynamic character that I posit is at the heart of these processes. As we saw in the last chapter, Elizabeth Bishop's "At the Fishhouses" connects a dizzying array of sensory modes in images of sensory failure, with one sense taking over at the limits of another to create a kind of knowledge that is "utterly free, historical, flowing, and flown." It is reasonable to ask, however, what happens when aesthetic experience itself is what is flown? After all, images are hard to create and keep in mind; vision is necessarily discontinuous and fades away; and emotion and reward are both finite and dynamic. All aesthetic experience thus must of necessity sometimes be left behind. I propose, however, that something new remains.

If arts change, if tastes change, and if these dynamics are neurally encoded in the ways I suggest, what are the implications for art and for humanist criticism? In seeking answers to this question, the first section of this chapter focuses on poetry and on the way in which limiting sensation can help reveal the roles of both sensory competition and valenced comparisons in aesthetic experience. The second and third sections examine the questions of novelty, repetition, and predictability in poetry, visual art, and music. The fourth section explores the closure of aesthetic experience, focusing on visual art and erasure, and in the last section of this book, I take up the question of how aesthetic experience might have an afterlife.

Invisible Beauty: Keats and the Limits of the Senses

Let us first return to the poem with which this book began. Keats's "Ode on a Grecian Urn" draws attention to the dynamics of perception as part of the essential underpinning of aesthetic experience. Here I will address the role of aesthetic perception by approaching the poem through the most vivid of its imagery. The close reading that I offer later in this chapter, however, is framed by the knowledge of the necessary role individual differences play in the cognitive model of aesthetic experience I have been laying out.[1] Not everyone, as I mentioned in the previous chapter, enacts imagery vividly (the pyrotechnics of close reading as an interpretative tool at times rely on exploiting the extraordinary imaginative strength of some readers). But as I hope to show, "Ode on a Grecian Urn" forecloses even the most vivid imagining as a seeming precondition for engaging with a particular aesthetic effect—what Keats calls "beauty."[2] At the same time that the poem explores the adequacy of perceptual experience to explain powerful aesthetic experience, it also points toward something more—and not simply something ineffable. The urn, a fragment of ancient beauty, is distant because of the vagaries of time, but it is also distant because of the way that aesthetic experience comes to life in the ode.

Keats's engagement with a mute and mysterious relic is a canonical Romantic engagement with evolving ideas of the past; it is also, with its meditation on beauty and truth, an engagement with the (then recent) history of aesthetic thought.[3] Indeed, the two domains are related.[4] In the formative years of modern aesthetics, Baumgarten's turn to a Greek concept, *aesthesis,* as he sought a word to describe the kind of knowledge that comes with sensation was emblematic of the blending of classical thought and empirical investigation that became essential to aesthetics. Indeed, seventeenth- and eighteenth-century aesthetic thought continually reconfigured the relationships between new knowledge and that of the classical past; empiricism came to challenge (though not immediately fully to displace) Aristotelian forms of knowledge.[5] While eighteenth-century aesthetics thus tended to approach the subject in terms of a posteriori sensory experience and not as categorical, a priori knowledge, the persistence of Platonic ideas of beauty meant that early aesthetics consistently involved a blending of Hellenic thought and modern empiricism.[6]

It is in the context of this blending of epistemological and historical approaches that, in 1755, when Johann Winckelmann wrote an essay that became crucially important to debates about aesthetics in Germany and Britain well into the Romantic period, he recommended his readers turn to Greek antiquity.[7] The modern world, he claimed, had lost both the standard and the reality of what was to him the paradigmatic aesthetic experience, beauty. In his essay he confronts two problems of aesthetic experience: the irrevocable loss of the past as a material presence (time gone by, damage done to objects), and the question of how we experience and perceive what is left to us. It is important that one of the key early documents of modern aesthetics thus engages aesthetic pleasure in terms of what is empirically observable as well as in terms of what is lost and attainable only in ideal.

It is indeed remarkable, especially for an essay about the visual arts, that "On the Imitation of the Painting and Sculpture of the Greeks" focuses more on imaginative than on sensual perceptions—or, as Winckelmann calls them, "brain-born images."[8] In one of the most famous of these images, Winckelmann takes his readers to the ancient gymnasium, where he describes Phidias, most acclaimed of the classical Greek sculptors, seeking models for his art by studying "the outlines of fair forms . . . the contour left by the young wrestler on the sand."[9] Such a haunting contour for Winckelmann indicates a standard of ideal beauty, a beauty more powerful than anything the senses might offer directly. The return to the ancients was part of the neoclassical engagement of history and tradition, certainly, but at the dawn of modern theories of the aesthetic, attention was not turned just to the position of authority or the possibility of progress, that Enlightenment ideal. Barbara Maria Stafford argues that what matters most for Winckelmann is a kind of invisible beauty, something beyond sight itself. This was a concern with perception and subjectivity: it is not just "by the observation of the individual . . . components that make up nature [that] the artist can determine what is correct; . . . he must bear within himself an image of the whole."[10] This "image" is *imagery*—wholly invisible to perception. At the limits of what is actually visible, Winckelmann evoked imagined presence multiply: for the reader, who is asked to "see" the story in the mind's eye; for Phidias, searching for beauty in the traces left by a perfectly sculpted young body, a body remembered or imagined; again, for Phidias, in his version of the outlined form that will in the future be embodied in a sculpture; and ultimately in a statue, which if it existed for Winckelmann at all was a scarred remnant of what it once was.[11]

Winckelmann's idealization of a lost past through imagination and imagery was underscored by a series of discoveries of ancient art, especially the excavations of Herculaneum in 1738 and Pompeii ten years later, and the recovery of lost works, most notably that of the Elgin Marbles—fragments of the Parthenon brought to Britain by Thomas Bruce, Lord Elgin, in the early years of the nineteenth century. Galileo's discovery of craters on the moon had, famously, struck a powerful blow to the Platonic and Aristotelian idea of the perfect, unchanging beauty of the heavens; the scarred antiquities that began to surface in the eighteenth and nineteenth centuries had an equally revolutionary effect.[12] The sculptures on the pediments and frieze of the Parthenon had become synonymous with the greatest of classical achievements throughout the years of the Grand Tour, primarily by word of mouth and in terms, like those of Winckelmann, which emphasized imagined engagement rather than visual detail. But when the sculptures were unveiled to the British public in 1816 at the British Museum, they produced a revolution in aesthetics.[13] If there was artistic perfection to be found in the marbles, it could not lie in the material perfection of their surface form, for that had been pockmarked and broken over a millennium and a half of exposure to the elements.[14]

The sculptures remain incredibly lovely; even with the passing of thousands of years, one can trace in them something beyond moving and exquisite (figure 2). Yet it is not without meaning that an art form built on the manipulation of surfaces and solid form had its outermost skin so badly damaged (we know now that on their arrival in England it was not just a question of pitting or fragmentation, as the marbles originally were colorfully painted; after attempts in the 1930s to further whiten them, they have been irretrievably scarred).[15] As Jonah Siegel puts it, "the Marbles were notably unsettling"; before their appearance, "lovers of antiquity were accustomed to the smooth finish and complete form of restored statues. . . . [So,] even when the relatively well preserved metopes and frieze were admired, the pitted surfaces and ravaged forms of the pedimental statues were often felt to be intolerable" to their viewers. They were not just fragments but "mutilated fragments."[16]

The conception of beauty as ideal, and hence necessarily estranged perfection, had belonged to a historically durable Platonic tradition—one alive well into the Romantic period and beyond—that argued true beauty was spiritual or intellectual, what Percy Bysshe Shelley in his 1816 "Hymn to Intellectual Beauty" described as an "unseen Power," which

> Floats though unseen among us,—visiting
> This various world with as inconstant wing
> . . .
> It visits with inconstant glance
> Each human heart and countenance;
> Like hues and harmonies of evening,—
> Like clouds in starlight widely spread,—
> Like memory of music fled. . . .[17]

However, even Shelley's strongly neo-Platonist version of beauty—ideal, perfect, and inaccessible to the senses and to mimetic art—does not escape entirely from the world of creation or of matter.[18] As ideal beauty becomes the object of mourning in this poem, beauty flees, crossing the boundaries of the natural, of the individual arts, and even of the senses, into the world of landscapes, of faces, and of lost music. Indeed, especially after the exhibition of the fragments of beauty that were the Elgin Marbles, early nineteenth-century discussions of fragile, remembered, imagined, or even invisible beauty increasingly tempered idealism with materialism in their awareness of the ravages of history (an example is Shelley's own "Ozymandias," with its ruined fragments).[19] Too, Shelley is not alone in the way in which the tension surrounding a beauty that seems doomed to fade extended into concerns for the relative status of the arts, for the status of perception, and for the history of the aesthetic.[20]

Keats's ode concentrates this tension to a breaking point, and in weaving these questions together, the poem suggests something important about the dynamics of aesthetic experience, both in its material, physical implications—in body and in art—and in its imagined ones. If we follow the sensory landscape of the poem as might a vivid reader—one with a keen facility to enact verbal imagery—we can see how the poem figures aesthetic pleasures as reliant on dynamic, unstable experience at the edges of imagined sensation. The poem also, in such a reading, can help clarify why the Sister Arts thrive at the junctures of the senses, and what we might learn from an aesthetic experience at sensory limits. Let's return, then, to the opening two stanzas.

The poem opens in a void of meaning. The sense of vision seems clear, while meaning is not: "What men or gods are these?" (l. 8). However, Keats describes an experience that takes the senses to their limits: "Heard melodies are sweet, but those unheard / Are sweeter; therefore ye soft pipes, play on; / Not to the sensual ear, but, more endear'd / Pipe to the spirit ditties of no tone" (ll. 11–14). The songs we cannot hear contrast with a maiden so visible she "cannot fade" (l. 19). Imagined sight—or at least visual description—rules the initial encounter with the poem's urn. In contrast to the silent song of the piper, the "ditt[y] of no tone," objects of vision—the painted figures on the urn—may seem stable in Keats's opening scene, but as it turns out, the urn is an object calculated to evoke visual instability, too.[21] An urn is a tricky thing. We cannot see its entirety at once, if we stand, ourselves alone, and without (let's say, a mirror's) aid. The images the urn carries fade away with the curve of its surface, the swell of its skin. To get a sense of its entire form, we must turn it or walk around it, and each moment, if we look closely, may reveal to us the loss of vision as well as the gaining of it.

Vision is supreme in Keats's initial descriptions of the urn, and with the silent music, vision is paired with a relatively deficient sense of sound. Still, both of these senses are eventually revealed to be unstable and even ineffectual: neither sound nor sight prevails. Keats finally finishes describing the visual dimensions of the painted urn when he reaches the most peripheral of the urn's decorative features, the brede (the woven design border), and the grass and branches at the bottom and top. In the final stanza, he thus indicates that we have arrived at some version of the fullness of the urn's form (the fantasy that we can perceive not just the whole urn but everything, even the meaning and context lost to time), and something important happens:

> O Attic shape! Fair attitude! With brede
>   Of marble men and maidens overwrought,
> With forest branches and the trodden weed;
>   Thou, silent form, dost tease us out of thought
> As doth eternity: Cold Pastoral! (ll. 41–45)

The full, "silent form," the urn's "fair attitude," comes with the frame of decoration that surrounds it—the parergon—of brede, branches, weed.[22] But the completion of the urn's form, the closure and culmination of its variations into a whole, also seems to "tease us out of thought," and the urn's form comes to completion several lines earlier than does the poem.[23]

The ending of the ode is thus (famously) odd. The poem is an ekphrasis—a description of a work of visual art—and it might naturally end once the work of description is done.[24] But Keats carries on to a somewhat enigmatic, and for many an unsatisfying, conclusion:

> When old age shall this generation waste,
>   Thou shalt remain, in midst of other woe
> Than ours, a friend to man, to whom thou say'st,
> Beauty is truth, truth beauty,—that is all
>   Ye know on earth, and all ye need to know. (ll. 46–50)

When Barbara Herrnstein Smith examined this poem in her broader analysis of poetic closure—what makes a poem seem a complete form—she went beyond the framework offered by literary tradition (for example, a sonnet is complete with fourteen lines) to explore Gestalt rules of perceptual psychology. Gestalt psychology argues that there are rules that enable us to perceive something as a whole—as a "figure" distinct from "ground."[25] These rules began with a visual model, positing ideas of proximity, common fate (the idea that components of a perception that seem to move together are understood to be related or part of a single object), similarity of size, and so on as bases for distinguishing complete, consistent objects. Poetic closure offered a different puzzle, and Smith argued that one could find analogous rules, determined by convention, perception, and the progress of an individual work, that would similarly signal aesthetically satisfactory closure. The problem with

Keats's ode, in her view, is that the final lines for many readers seem too final, and bring the poem to an abrupt end—is that really "all we need to know"?[26]

I argue, however, that "Ode on a Grecian Urn" figures a Gestalt of form that reveals incompletion as much as completion. The form of the urn is finished, but the poem does not end. A Gestalt reading of the concluding stanza of this poem would suggest that with the closure of completed form, new room has opened up in a reader's mental world—we are "teased out of thought." But for Keats, there is a void here, as much as a completed form. It is a void that a vivid reader might recognize from the stunted sensations that have contributed to the "fair" though "silent form." The flat lines of Shaftesburian wisdom, which close the poem, do not entirely fill the space the completed form has opened up.

If a vivid reader were to follow the scene Keats lays out, she or he might find that at this moment the interplay of intensity and contradiction—the elevation of the visual, reinforced by a series of detailed, beautiful, and puzzling imagined pictures—combines with a delicate play of the aural imagination. In other words, at the same time that a reader vividly enacting the sensory landscape of the poem is being surrounded by, carried along with, a pattern of rhythm and meter that "sounds" within imagination, she or he is being told that the world is one of silence, infused with "ditties of no tone." Imagined vision is privileged in the illusion of the mute world of the urn: to accept the "silence" of the silent form, a reader would have to demote what is actually experienced in the form of the aural imagery of poetry, read "silently"—without vocalization, but "heard" inside the head.

The final effect of the poem, however, depends on blacking out imagined vision, and here we return to the *question* of vivid reading (not to an enactment of it). Not every reader of this poem reads in Technicolor, or even slowly enough (or with the desire) to follow the swell of the urn's skin or the sounds of its illusory silence. As I described in the preceding chapter, while just about everyone with intact sensory capacity is also capable of mental imagery (most people experience almost every form of imagery in dreams), individual facility with images differs greatly. It is thus remarkable that in blacking out inner vision, even for those most willing to "see," and in covering over sound, even for those most willing and able to "hear," Keats's poem revises its own sensory strategy, suggesting that intense aesthetic experience happens at the limits of the senses.[27]

Even the strongest imagined vision can go no further at the end of the poem—the point of "truth" and "beauty"—for there is nothing left to see: there is no *picture* here, only poetry. If new cognitive room opens up with the finished visual Gestalt of the urn, to take Smith's point, what fills this room is the rebounding presence of sound and language; a vivid reader's attention may be cast back onto the baseline of poetic sound that includes meter and rhyme—words heard, imaginatively.[28] The poem offers a version of vision that is commingled with sound. However, the imagery of sound itself is impure. As I described above, the experience of reading metrical speech, insofar as it is perceived as metrical, involves not just imagery of sound but imagery of motion. Keats is manipulating "impure" or mixed sensory imagery for his vivid readers, creating an illusion of stability—of pure vision—that is ruptured by the return of something repressed or covered over, the aural.

One way of understanding the interaction of vivid sensory imagery is by understanding that units of our cognitive architecture compete, and this competition is basic to cognitive function; attention may select for or against a sight or sound, one image or sound may overwrite another, and one word may interfere with the ability to recall another.[29] Much of this competition goes unnoticed or unremarked in daily life, but, as Colin Martindale has observed, such moments of interference may have hedonic effects.[30] When one word effaces another similar one, when one tune grips the mind and precludes another, when the memory of one lost face eats at the joy of a beloved melody, the landscape of our pleasures is altered. In Martindale's model, with such give and take of sensations and thoughts, the displeasures of interference and competition may resolve into pleasure because of the competition itself. As Edmund Burke held, displeasure and pain may have an aesthetic resolution.[31] However, as in the case with the beauty of uniformity amid variety, one doesn't need felt pain for the resolution of competition or tension to be pleasurable. The pleasures of thought and of perception may be felt for vivid readers because of the competition between ideas, emotions, and sensations.[32]

One simplistic example of such pleasures of competition comes with the phenomenon known as disinhibition. Disinhibition occurs when two related stimuli are mutually inhibiting. If one of the pair of sensations is experienced repeatedly, the other is restrained: this is the case with the colors red and green. But if one stimulus is repeated until it results in fatigue; the second in the pair may simply activate, immediately. This happens with the colors paired in the retina: "Prolonged staring at a patch of red produces fatiguing of the sensory units coding red and a disinhibition of units coding green. A green color after-effect then results. However, if a green stimulus is actually presented and 'superimposed' on the after-effect, hedonic tone is influenced: one sees a supersaturated green that is 'spectacular.'"[33] This simple example suggests that very basic sensory perceptions, like color disassociated from form, have hedonic potential that emerges from their neural coding (in this case, the opposition of red and green). What is essential to note is that the pleasure, if we feel it, comes not simply because of that coding but because we have *manipulated* our sensory architecture so that the loss of visual stimulus (the removal of the red patch) and the production of imagery in exchange for sensation (the illusory greenness) combine with a new sensation (a new green object) *to produce pleasure where imagery and perception come together.* Such is the case for a simple trick of color. But what about works of art? There is evidence that complex perceptions, coming from complex aesthetic objects, produce pleasures that play out through sensory competition. For visual art, increasing aesthetic power can be indexed to increasing suppression of the auditory cortex—aesthetic power tips the sensory balance to inhibit one sense in favor of another, so that even in a noisy MRI machine, hearing is increasingly suppressed as aesthetic experience emerging from vision increasingly takes hold (figure 11, lower right panel).

The fact that, both for simple and complex perceptions, sensory competition can be linked to pleasure offers a new route for thinking about Keats. The aesthetic effects of the exchange of one sensation for another, I believe, are part of the payoff of a vivid reading of "Ode on a Grecian Urn." Language and sound reopen on the space left by foreclosed vision, with an effect that can be in some ways "spectacular" and in some ways deeply disturbing. The shift from imagined vision to darkness and silence, suddenly being "teased out of thought," can hit strongly when the description of the urn is completed. The metrical irregularity here—"Cóld Pástoral"—draws attention to imagined sound and the motor imagery of rhythm. The evacuation of visual content by the shift from an elaborately described visual scene to the abstraction of a generic category is equally sudden; and this has implications for vivid readers and for those who are not. This moment, for a vivid reader, has the potential to light up the edges of one mode of mental experience, one that had so taken up the view as to seem all of thought. When imaginative sight is shut down, sound is reasserted, together with what is primarily of semantic or verbal significance—pastoral is here primarily a generic term, not a visually or aurally descriptive one—and we are in a different world.

I have sketched what an intensely vivid form of imaginative engagement might produce in reading this poem, but Keats at this point offers an equalizer. The poem closes out vivid sensation, and even in the absence of vivid imagination of the visual or auditory content of the poem it relies on reading as "hearing" the words and keeping their beat—a baseline facility with rhythm—to interrupt and reshape readers' experiences of the poem at this point. That is, you don't have to see or hear the poem's images to be drawn up short by, to move with the beat of, the interruptive force of these words: "Cold Pastoral" throws up a sensory as well as a conceptual wall and is the precursor to the near evacuation of imagined sensation that is essential to the final lines, the change of discursive register from description to gnomic wisdom, from direct address to muted quotation.

Keats recreates for vivid readers a competition among the senses in imaginative space; there are always limits on the ability to attend to detail, and those limits may be even stronger for mental images than for sensory perceptions.[34] We are creating everything to which we attend, and this is a demanding task that imposes large constraints on what we can see and hear, as Descartes so well knew. Imagined scenes are subject to their own limits—imagined sound, after all, only occasionally makes use of something so basic to physical sound as loudness; "ditties of no tone" may be "soft," but how loud, after all, is anything that strikes the mental rather than "the sensual ear" (ll. 14, 12, 13)?[35] But Keats manipulates the limits of imagined sense: at some point every reader can see no more, and amid the silence and the illusion of visual clarity and completion, Keats suddenly calls attention to the bizarrely incomplete silence that is both imagined sound and the silent reading of poetry.[36]

In other words, understanding poetry as altered, imagined perception can be revealing but also limited, for aesthetic experience happens at sensory limits, whether the limits of vivid reading or the limits of the capacity (and competing strengths) of readers whose experience of poetry does not rely on vivid perceptual imagery. This was part of the case I made for the workings of imagined motion across the arts, but it also matters here, in a canonical example of both the poetry of sense and the Sister Arts. Aesthetic experience happens at the points where sensation abuts something else—imagery, often—because it is less *sensation* that drives aesthetics than the *valenced relations* between what we experience—sensations and images, yes, but also ideas and events—and how those valenced relations come to mind. This is, in some ways, what we "need to know."[37]

Keats plays at the limits of imagined sensation as he seeks to bring something into the world that can restore the loss of one kind of aesthetic pleasure, one he names the beautiful. As I discussed at the start of this book, aesthetic terms have a history. Beauty (*kallos* for Plato and Aristotle) was the term of choice in the Platonic tradition, but there have been others, and in the period between Winckelmann and Keats, "beauty" loses ground to the "sublime," in part because of the way that the ideal beauty of neoclassicism becomes associated with its own erasure, its devastating loss to the powers of darkness and time.[38] Such power—and the evocative power of the ruin—comes to dominate aesthetics into the early nineteenth century.[39] A number of scholars have traced this shift, one in which a feminine beauty is displaced by a masculine sublime, feeling by cognition, and moral lassitude by moral superiority.[40] I give some account of these historical changes in the course of this chapter because it is a necessary correlate of my argument that such shifts are part and parcel of the deep structure of aesthetic experience: aesthetic experience is predicated on the dynamic interplay not just of senses but of values, and of knowledge.

I have argued that the experience of aesthetics is in part built on the perceived pleasures of newly discovered relations. Beauty, along with its kin, in this sense is necessarily about comparison, contrast, integration, and competition, and it is always going to bring the haunting possibility of loss. But

Keats seems to be asking if we might produce yet more beauty in the space marked out by those comparisons, between the weights of different senses, times, forms, or arts. When we suspect that beauty evolves from relations between objects and sensations, we start to seek strange and new relations. Beauty can come then from shutting down the very routes by which we gain initial access to it. Hence Keats, in "Ode on a Grecian Urn," offers an exemplary Sister Arts poem by trying to find beauty where the senses to which the Sister Arts peculiarly appeal fail.

Dynamic Knowledge: Ovid, What Is New and What Is Not

Aesthetic experience produces new relations of value, relations that could not be predicted a priori. But do such experiences have to be entirely novel? As I suggested above, there is no reason that one should find the image of a woman being transformed into a tree to be anything other than strange, confusing, or frightening. Yet Daphne's transformation in the *Metamorphoses* is hauntingly beautiful, disturbing, and even comical:

> when her feet she found
> Benumb'd with cold, and fasten'd to the ground:
> A filmy rind about her body grows;
> Her hair to leaves, her arms extend to boughs:
> The nymph is all into a lawrel gone;
> The smoothness of her skin remains alone.
> Yet Phoebus loves her still, and casting round
> Her bole, his arms, some little warmth he found.

> The tree still panted in th' unfinish'd part:
> Not wholly vegetive, and heav'd her heart.
> He fixt his lips upon the trembling rind;
> It swerv'd aside, and his embrace declin'd.[41]

Dryden's translation (echoing that of Sandys, from which I quoted above) wonderfully captures the oddity of Ovid's image (if not his erudite wordplay, in which Daphne's newly born wood, *ligno,* becomes ready to combust, *lignum*: "oscula dat ligno; refugit tamen oscula lignum"). As if such a sight of radical transformation were not strange enough, the bark of the newborn tree moves, politely ("declin'd") and comically, every time Apollo tries to kiss it. Indeed, it is a hallmark of Ovid's *Metamorphoses* that the poems blend novelty with beauty and cruelty with humor, and thus seem an odd aesthetic (and moral) mixture.[42]

Given that I maintain the centrality of unpredictable knowledge in aesthetic experience, it might seem that I have been primarily describing responses to the kind of art that, like Ovid's, privileges novelty. One might then ask, what happens when we have already seen, heard, or read it all before? The experimental record concerning novelty and pleasure is increasingly well developed. In 1968, Robert Zajonc claimed an effect on preferences of "mere exposure," showing that people are more likely to find objects (words, music, pictures) pleasing the more they have been exposed to them.[43] But there is competing evidence that complex stimuli have differing effects, and Daniel Berlyne claimed that "the hedonic value of complex stimuli tends to rise as they become less novel while the opposite holds true for simple stimuli."[44] This dual, even competing function of novelty in aesthetics is mediated neurally in multiple ways. Responses to the sensory components of aesthetic experience may happen relatively quickly, and it is probable that novelty assessment may happen at this stage, while responses based on evaluations of varying forms of complexity (such as semantic or emotional) happen in more anterior regions of the brain and more slowly; they also may involve the kinds of self-assessment and integration that are mediated by the default mode network.[45]

I would submit that all powerful aesthetic experiences involve an element of the unexpected, but this does not mean that aesthetic experience expires with novelty: there are pleasures to repetition, as Zajonc and others have shown. The durable potential of complex aesthetic experience, however, emerges because it allows us to integrate unexpected or evolving knowledge in new ways, and ultimately to build on that evolving knowledge in a dynamic form of learning (one that also employs a dynamic neural representation). It is thus that we might value multiple translations or reimaginings of the same poem, so that Ovid's revision by Sandys, and the further revision of both by Dryden, each bring different pleasures. However, there is a more general principle at stake. Part of the evolving web of value that makes aesthetic experience powerful is created by the ways in which aesthetic pleasures tend to be *mixed*. We encountered such mixtures empirically in the research described in the first chapter of this book, where multiple positive and negative emotional factors combine in aesthetic responses (figure 15), and single emotions, such as awe, may be valenced in both directions. This kind of mixed response happens differently for different artistic media.

A reader who has had a powerful response to Daphne's transformation might emerge with new juxtapositions of kinds of value, kinds of value that had before seemed incongruous: anger at Apollo's rapacious pursuit of Daphne might combine with disturbed wonder at her transformation; with a poignant sense of sadness that her humanity seems not lost entirely but rather trapped in the still warm bark of a tree; with laughter at the absurdity of the polite squirming of flesh-turned-wood; distress that laughter intrudes in the midst of suffering and threatened rape; transfixion at the beauty of the description; sober knowledge that perhaps it is true that civilization and barbarism, to quote Benjamin, are in fact too tightly linked.[46] Not all of these sentiments or responses need occur, and perhaps none of them might, but if Ovid does not leave you coldly uninterested, something similar to this—a rush of an at times impure pleasure at the ideas, images, beat, words, or associations that do occur to you—happens, and it gives *value* to these lines.

The unpredictability of such mixed pleasures has nothing necessarily to do with Ovid's novelty (while for Addison, Ovid exemplifies the novel, his work is two thousand years old, after all); rather, unpredictability enters first because there is no necessity that anything Ovid imagined be pleasing to anyone, and this includes no necessity born of neural architecture, cultural heritage, or education. We may take as an example the shock of approaching the face of Daphne in Bernini's sculpture (figure 7). The fear, the passion, one might feel in approaching the newly formed emptiness of her eyes as her humanity leaves her do not require a response for an object carved in stone; but they can be deeply moving. The emergent, emotionally and hedonically weighted web of emotions, ideas, and perceptions that can come with reading Ovid or his translators, or in looking at Bernini's Daphne (whatever that web might be for any individual), is what is at stake when I propose that interrelations of value themselves create new structures of knowledge.

These emotions, ideas, and perceptions have a neural value, a reward value, that helps produce the structure of aesthetic experience. Such reward values, as I have described above, of necessity exist in comparison (for that is what reward value does, enabling us to compare choices, experiences, desires, and outcomes), so that pleasures, displeasures, and uneasiness combine in dynamic play. Any such configuration (laughter, discomfort, awe, longing, pleasure) is a unique one. And once made, it is not fixed but can decay over time or newly evolve, becoming available for new configurations and new evaluations. From the perspective of neural circuitry this occurs through communication between reward regions (such as the nucleus accumbens) and the frontal cortex.[47] We see this operating from the perspective of conscious aesthetic life as well. For example, on rereading the passage above, we might notice a different feature of the text that retrospectively revalues what has already been thought and felt: the way, say, that Daphne's body is benumbed with cold implies she is not just turning into a living tree but into something hardened, no longer truly alive.

The "filmy rind" that covers Daphne is both bark and an echo of the "cold" "numb[ing]" frost from the preceding line; the nearest analogue (besides death) for such a hardened, frozen, immobile human form is sculpture. Such an interpretation of Dryden's linguistic play has historical weight. England was becoming increasingly fascinated by

Baroque sculpture as young men took to the continent to explore European art in the wake of the Restoration, and in evoking the coldness of Daphne's hardening body, Dryden here is likely alluding to Bernini's *Apollo and Daphne,* which was one of the most famous sculptures on the European tour (figure 6).[48] Bernini explores the wonder of the moment of transformation, and it seems truly as if an instant has been frozen in time, with branches and leaves sprouting from fingertips whose warmth has only just faded. Bernini's fame in the seventeenth century, largely emerging from the reputation of this sculpture, was precisely rooted in the sense that the stone was just on the other side of life, that he had somehow made marble almost flesh.[49] As Andrea Bolland argues, the power of this statue comes from the way in which Bernini is able simultaneously to evoke the tactile qualities of flesh and stone and to convey the idea that all sensory access to Daphne's beauty, whether by sight or by touch, is on the verge of failure.[50] Such a paradox—that beauty written in stone might at the same time fade away—keeps one gazing at, even transfixed by, Bernini's almost impossibly beautiful work.

Dryden's evocation of a hard white frost covering the living body of Daphne would certainly refer many of his contemporary readers to this startlingly beautiful object. Similar allusions to the plastic arts were common in late seventeenth- and eighteenth-century British poetry, where the Sister Arts were never far away; these allusions are rooted in an increasing conviction that these arts offered a set of pleasures that naturally cohered.[51] This cohesion, however, far from being natural, was in part produced by the historical practices of allusion, which verified and even cross-checked aesthetic pleasures by establishing their likeness to one another (again, we see the dynamic interconnections of reward). Beauty encountered in one mode, say Dryden's version of Ovid, then became more truly beautiful in this cultural frame when a viewer or reader was able to recognize in it an echo of another beautiful object. Augustan poetry as a whole is best understood by recognizing the degree to which translation and imitation—across arts, languages, or historical moments—were prized by poets and their readers.[52] But the sense of interconnectedness I am describing here is fundamentally aesthetic; the web of value and valuation that links ideas and works of art together is not simply rooted in an Augustan ideal. Indeed, one can argue that part of what makes a poem artful—and even recognizable as poetry—is its relationship to other poetry, to other sensations, to something outside itself.

Alice Fulton's 1994 version of Ovid, "Give: Daphne and Apollo," makes this point powerfully, weaving together the voices of other victims of transformation in the *Metamorphoses* with the Latin of Ovid and the English of Keats:

> Her sonar let her see right through opacities: read
> the entrails
> coiled inside the trees.
> . . .
>   While Apollo hardened with love for her,
> Daphne stripped the euphemism from the pith. *Love*
> was nothing
> but a suite
> of polished steel: mirrors breeding mirrors in successions
> of forever, his

FIGURE 1

Jackson Pollock, *Shimmering Substance*, oil on canvas, 1946. 30⅛ × 24¼ inches (76.3 × 61.6 cm). © Artists Rights Society, New York. Mr. and Mrs. Albert Lewin and Mrs. Sam A. Lewisohn Funds. © Pollock-Krasner Foundation / Artists Rights Society, New York. Digital Image © The Museum of Modern Art/Licensed by SCALA / Art Resource, New York, The Museum of Modern Art, New York.

FIGURE 2
Elgin Marbles, Three Goddesses. © The Trustees of the British Museum.

FIGURE 3
Vincent Van Gogh, *Ravine*, oil on canvas, 1889. Photograph © 2013 Museum of Fine Arts, Boston.

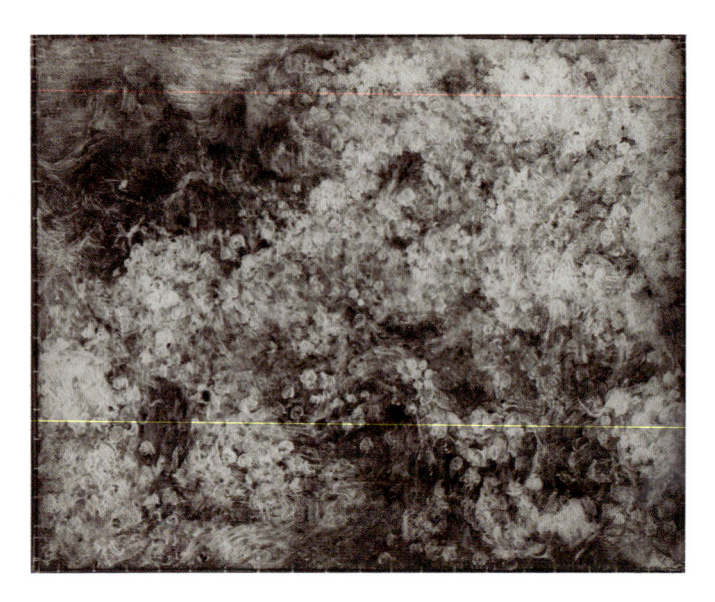

FIGURE 4
X-ray of *Ravine*. Photograph © 2013 Museum of Fine Arts, Boston.

FIGURE 5
Vincent Van Gogh, "Wild Vegetation," pen and ink, 1889. Photograph © Stichting Van Gogh Museum.

FIGURE 6
Gian Lorenzo Bernini, *Apollo and Daphne*, 1622–1625. © Andrea Jemolo / Scal / Art Resource, New York

FIGURE 7
Gian Lorenzo Bernini, *Apollo and Daphne*, detail. ©Mauro Magliani for Alinari, 1997 / Art Resource, New York

FIGURE 8
Theme, Diabelli's Waltz

FIGURE 9
Ludwig van Beethoven, 33 Variations on a Waltz by Anton Diabelli (*Diabelli Variations*), 1819–1823, Opus 120, Variation 31 mm. 1–7

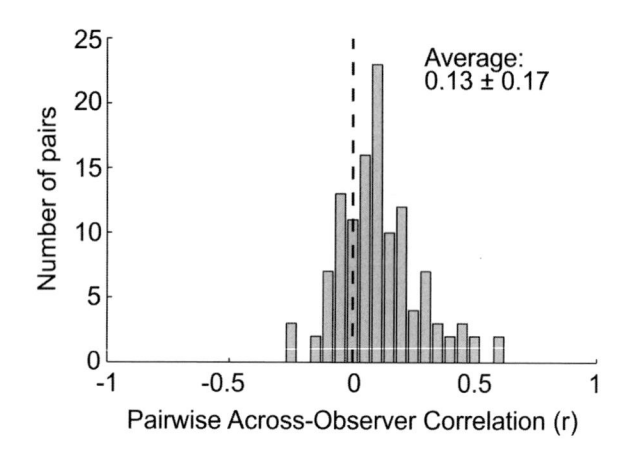

FIGURE 10
Across-Observer Correlations. Analysis of which images were most powerfully moving showed low agreement across observers. Each observer's recommendations were correlated with every other observer's recommendations, taken in pairs. This histogram shows the distribution of all the correlation coefficients.
Source: Adapted with permission from Edward A. Vessel, G. Gabrielle Starr, and Nava Rubin, "The Brain on Art: Intense Aesthetic Experience Activates the Default Mode Network," *Frontiers in Human Neuroscience* 6, no. 66 (2012). doi:10.3389/fnhum.2012.00066.

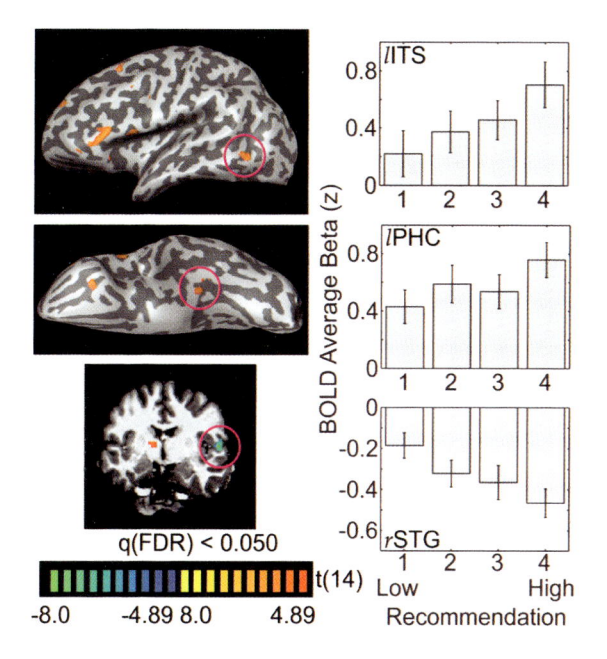

FIGURE 11

BOLD fMRI Pattern One. Posterior occipitotemporal regions of cortex show linear deflections from baseline with increasing recommendation. The whole-brain images illustrate the t-statistic for the 4-vs.-1 contrast. Panels on the right illustrate the average beta weight (as a z score) for each recommendation level, averaged across fifteen observers (lITS = left inferotemporal sulcus, lPHC = left parahippocampal cortex, rSTG = right superior temporal sulcus). Error bars are standard errors of the mean across observers.

Source: Adapted with permission from Edward A. Vessel, G. Gabrielle Starr, and Nava Rubin, "The Brain on Art: Intense Aesthetic Experience Activates the Default Mode Network," *Frontiers in Human Neuroscience* 6, no. 66 (2012). doi:10.3389/fnhum.2012.00066.

FIGURE 12
BOLD fMRI Pattern Two. Linear activation straddling baseline tracks increasing recommendation in some brain areas. The whole-brain images illustrate the *t*-statistic for the 4-vs.-1 contrast. Panels on the right illustrate the average beta weight (as a z score) for each recommendation level, averaged across fifteen observers (*l*STR = left striatum, PRF = pontine reticular formation). Error bars are standard errors of the mean across observers.

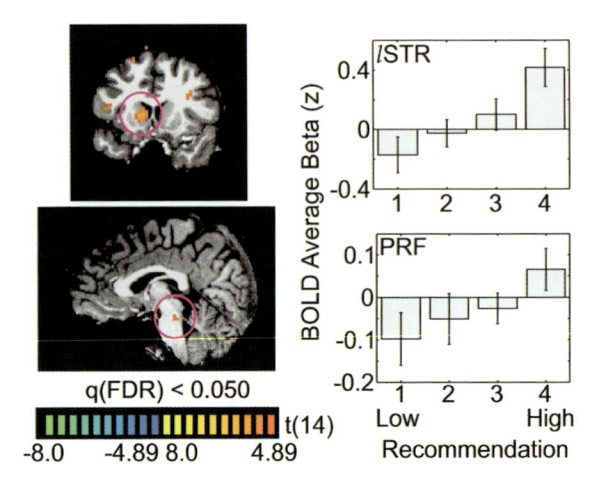

Source: Adapted with permission from Edward A. Vessel, G. Gabrielle Starr, and Nava Rubin, "The Brain on Art: Intense Aesthetic Experience Activates the Default Mode Network," *Frontiers in Human Neuroscience* 6, no. 66 (2012). doi:10.3389/fnhum.2012.00066.

FIGURE 13
BOLD fMRI Pattern Three. What distinguishes the strongest responses? The whole-brain images illustrate the *t*-statistic for the 4-vs.-1 contrast. Panels on the right illustrate the average beta weight (as a z score) for each recommendation level, averaged across fifteen observers (*l*SFG = left superior frontal gyrus, lIFGt = left inferior frontal gyrus, pars triangularis, lLOFC = left lateral orbitofrontal cortex, lmdThal = left mediodorsal thalamus). Error bars are standard errors of the mean across observers.
Source: Adapted with permission from Edward A. Vessel, G. Gabrielle Starr, and Nava Rubin, "The Brain on Art: Intense Aesthetic Experience Activates the Default Mode Network," *Frontiers in Human Neuroscience* 6, no. 66 (2012). doi:10.3389/fnhum.2012.00066.

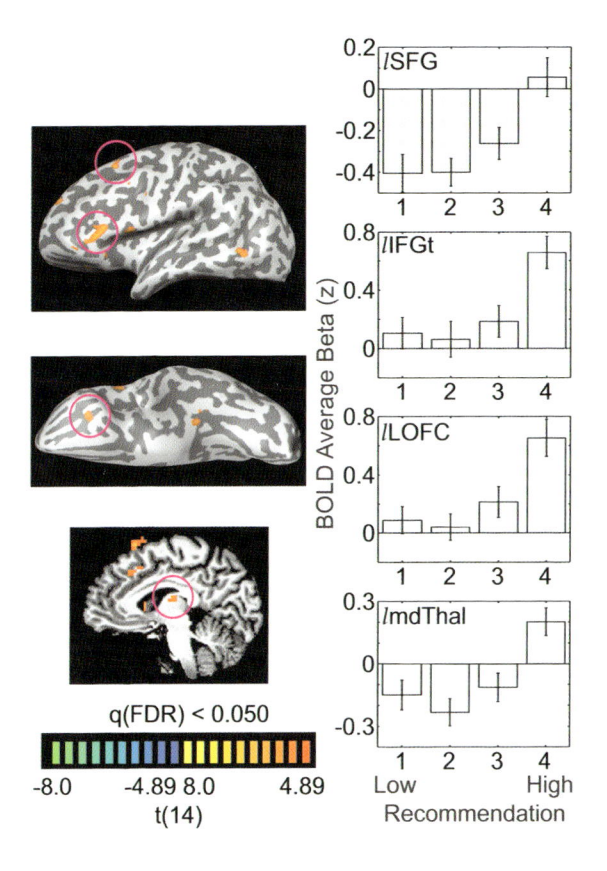

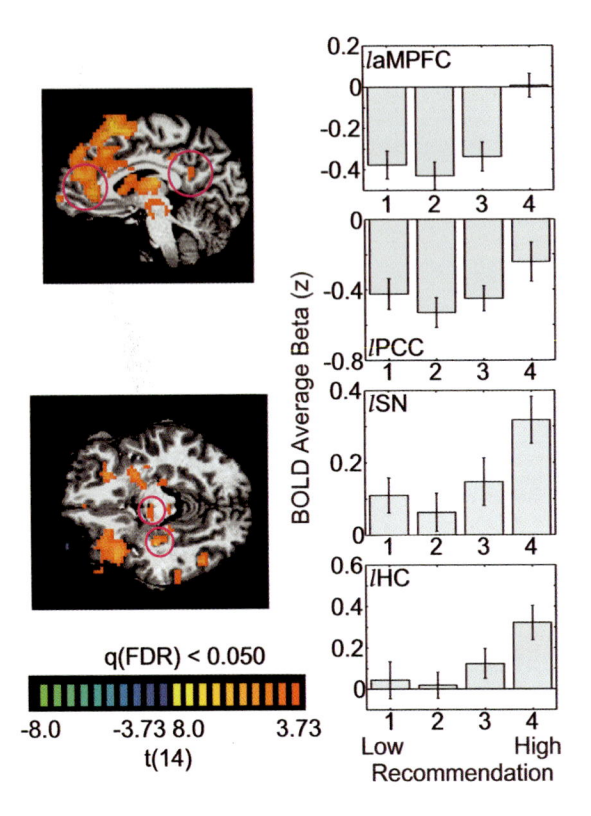

FIGURE 14

Isolation of Most Intense Responses. The default mode network and several subcortical regions show increased activation for only the most aesthetically pleasing images. The whole-brain images illustrate the *t*-statistic for the 4-vs.-321 contrast. Panels on the right illustrate the average beta weight (as a z score) for each recommendation level, averaged across fifteen observers (*l*aMPFC = left anterior medial prefrontal cortex, *l*PCC = left posterior cingulate cortex, *l*SN = left substantia nigra, *l*HC = left hippocampus). Error bars are standard errors of the mean across observers.

Source: Adapted with permission from Edward A. Vessel, G. Gabrielle Starr, and Nava Rubin, "The Brain on Art: Intense Aesthetic Experience Activates the Default Mode Network," *Frontiers in Human Neuroscience* 6, no. 66 (2012). doi:10.3389/fnhum.2012.00066.

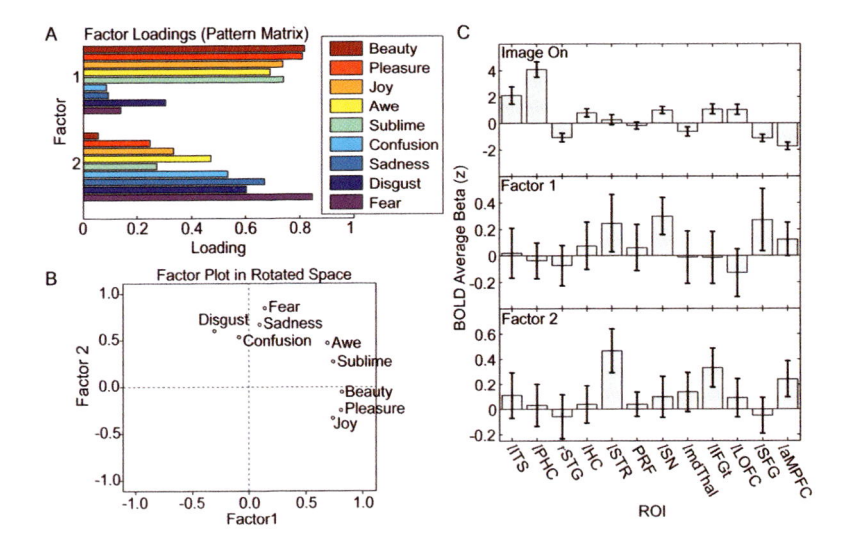

FIGURE 15

Emotional/Evaluative Factors. Factor analysis of the nine-item questionnaire reveals two major group-level factors that are reflected in the activation of frontal and subcortical regions. (A) Loadings for the two factors on each of the nine items. (B) A plot of the nine items in the two-factor solution reveals a cluster that groups high on Factor 1, a second cluster that groups high on Factor 2, with Awe and Sublime being partway between the two clusters. (C) BOLD predictors constructed from scores on Factor 1 and Factor 2 reveal a set of regions that respond to image onset, responsivity to Factor 1 in *l*SN and weakly in *l*STR and *l*SFG, and responsivity to Factor 2 in *l*STR and *l*IFGt and weakly in *l*aMPFC. Error bars are standard errors of the mean, computed across observers.

Source: Adapted with permission from Edward A. Vessel, G. Gabrielle Starr, and Nava Rubin, "The Brain on Art: Intense Aesthetic Experience Activates the Default Mode Network," *Frontiers in Human Neuroscience* 6, no. 66 (2012). doi:10.3389/fnhum.2012.00066.

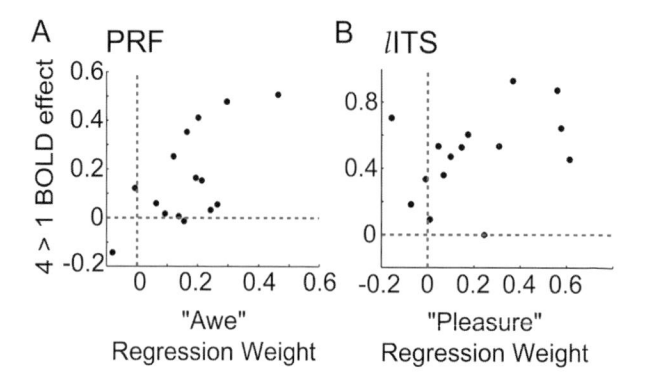

FIGURE 16

Awe and Pleasure Regressions: Two Cases for Individual Differences. Individual differences in the importance of different feelings when making aesthetic recommendations are correlated with the size of the BOLD effect in two ROIs. (A) Observers for whom "awe" is an important predictor of aesthetic recommendation show a larger 4-vs.-1 BOLD effect size in PRF (R^2 = 0.70; "awe" beta weight = 1.22, $t(8)$= 2.88, P = .021). (B) Observers for whom "pleasure" is an important predictor of aesthetic recommendation show a larger 4-vs.-1 BOLD effect size in left ITS (R^2 = 0.62; "pleasure" beta weight 1.72, $t(8)$ = 2.96, P = .018).

Source: Adapted with permission from Edward A. Vessel, G. Gabrielle Starr, and Nava Rubin, "The Brain on Art: Intense Aesthetic Experience Activates the Default Mode Network." *Frontiers in Human Neuroscience* 6, no. 66 (2012). doi:10.3389/fnhum.2012.00066.

						Standardized Beta Coefficient			
R^2	F	p	resVar	Beauty	Awe	Fear	Pleasure	Sadness	Disgust
0.50	17.1	1.4×10^{-13}	0.53	0.34	0.22	0.11	0.29	0.06	-0.02
0.30	7.2	1.9×10^{-05}	0.74	0.52	0.14	0.00	0.01	0.03	-0.08
0.47	15.4	1.8×10^{-12}	0.56	0.22	0.24	0.30	-0.07	0.15	0.11
0.35	9.3	4.1×10^{-08}	0.68	0.42	-0.08	0.02	0.24	-0.10	0.05
0.65	31.0	6.3×10^{-21}	0.38	0.66	0.16	0.08	0.07	-0.21	-0.04
0.41	8.8	3.3×10^{-07}	0.63	0.33	0.21	0.41	-0.16	0.08	0.01
0.53	19.3	6.7×10^{-15}	0.50	0.43	0.27	0.21	-0.01	0.09	0.33
0.66	33.1	7.1×10^{-22}	0.36	0.56	0.09	0.08	0.17	0.09	-0.02
0.78	58.8	9.1×10^{-31}	0.24	0.21	0.30	0.05	0.37	0.09	-0.07
0.73	33.6	3.0×10^{-19}	0.29	0.47	0.12	0.24	0.05	0.15	0.12
0.60	25.9	1.6×10^{-18}	0.42	0.53	0.20	-0.13	0.15	-0.11	0.10
0.65	30.3	1.8×10^{-20}	0.38	0.18	-0.01	0.12	0.58	0.07	-0.04
0.65	31.5	3.7×10^{-21}	0.37	0.00	0.19	-0.05	0.61	-0.05	0.32
0.57	22.5	9.4×10^{-17}	0.46	0.18	0.06	0.06	0.56	0.04	0.09
0.38	9.8	2.5×10^{-08}	0.66	0.38	0.17	-0.22	0.31	0.16	0.25
0.62	28.3	1.1×10^{-19}	0.40	0.22	0.46	0.11	0.10	0.04	-0.12
Average									
0.55	23.9	1.2×10^{-06}	0.48	0.35	0.17	0.09	0.20	0.04	0.06

FIGURE 17

Results of the Individual Differences Regression. Each observer's recommendations were predicted from the reduced set of six emotional terms. The reported F-statistic has 6,102 degrees of freedom (resVar = residual variance in recommendation not accounted for by the regression).
Source: Adapted with permission from Edward A. Vessel, G. Gabrielle Starr, and Nava Rubin, "The Brain on Art: Intense Aesthetic Experience Activates the Default Mode Network," *Frontiers in Human Neuroscience* 6, no. 66. (2012). doi:10.3389/fnhum.2012.00066.

Anatomical Region	BA		X	Y	Z	SD X	SD Y	SD Z	Vol (mm³)	Avg t
4 > 1										
Occipitotemporal Ctx										
Inf Temporal Sulc (ITS)	37	L	-49	-61	-2	4.2	2.7	4.1	1053	5.48
Parahippocampal Ctx (PHC)	36	L	-31	-32	-15	2.3	2.3	2.3	405	5.44
Superior Temporal Sulc (STS)	22	R	44	-48	4	2.5	2.1	2.2	351	5.61
Fusiform Gyr	37	R	42	-40	-14	1.4	2.9	1.6	162	5.40
Frontal Ctx										
Inf Frontal Gyr p triangularis (IFGt)	45/46	L	-50	32	12	3.7	7.5	5.7	2727	5.57
Lateral Orbitofrontal Ctx (LOFC)	47	L	-35	24	-4	6.7	3.6	3.7	918	5.18
Superior Frontal Sulc (SFS)	6	L	-24	16	50	3.4	3.0	3.6	810	5.55
Superior Frontal Sulc (SFS)	8	L	-19	32	51	2.4	3.1	2.2	594	5.61
Superior Frontal Sulc (SFS)	9	L	-18	47	31	2.3	2.8	2.9	351	5.63
Superior Frontal Gyr (SFG)	6	L	-5	19	62	2.1	3.9	4.4	729	5.51
Inf Frontal Gyr p orbitalis (IFGo)	44	L	-44	7	15	2.0	2.8	2.6	378	5.53
Dorsolateral Prefrontal Ctx (dlPFC)	9	L	-44	5	37	2.0	2.3	1.7	297	5.27
Precentral Sulc	9	R	34	9	25	1.7	1.5	2.4	135	5.19
Cingulate Sulc	32	L	-7	22	38	1.4	2.6	1.6	162	5.23
Precentral Gyr	6	L	-33	-13	65	1.6	1.6	1.7	162	5.27
Subcortical Regions										
Striatum (Str)	-	L	-12	10	6	2.8	2.3	2.9	702	5.43
Pontine Reticular Formation (PRF)	-		0	-28	-17	2.5	1.7	1.5	135	5.03
MedioDorsal Thalamus (mdThal)	-	L	-6	-18	12	1.7	2.1	2.8	243	5.26
Thalamus	-	L	-12	-9	8	2.4	1.4	1.6	162	5.11
1 > 4										
Superior Temporal Gyr (STG)	42/22	R	52	-10	7	4.5	2.7	3.2	702	-6.06

FIGURE 18
Mean Talairach Coordinates. Mean Talairach coordinates for all fMRI activations found in the 4-vs.-1 whole-brain contrast (BA = Brodmann's area, SD = spatial standard deviation, Vol = volume, Avg t = average *t* statistic, Ctx = cortex, Sulc = Sulcus, Gyr = Gyrus, Inf = Inferior, p = pars). *Source*: Adapted with permission from Edward A. Vessel, G. Gabrielle Starr, and Nava Rubin, "The Brain on Art: Intense Aesthetic Experience Activates the Default Mode Network," *Frontiers in Human Neuroscience* 6, no. 66 (2012). doi:10.3389/fnhum2012.00066.

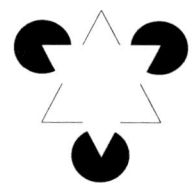

FIGURE 19
Kanizsa Triangle. There is no white triangle here, only thee "circles" missing a quadrant and three black outlines of "triangles" with missing sides

> name amplified through sons of sons and coats of arms, her limbs
> spidering, her mind changed to moss and symbol, a trousseau of fumed wood
> the scent of perforations as his relief rose above her smoky field.[53]

With hints of Echo (sonar), Narcissus (mirrors), and Arachne (spidering), Fulton's poem reveals with clear-sighted horror the threatened violation of nymph by god, while balancing the exquisite beauty of the lines above with discord: "My first emotion happened to be revulsion: an ungreen, sour / cramp / as Daphne shrank—'oh, baby,' he kept saying—from Apollo's colonizing kiss. / Of course, he liked her better as a tree" (50).

Fulton richly reimagines Daphne as collateral damage in a competition between two pop music icons, Apollo and Cupid, each bent on turning his album gold. Cupid strikes Apollo and Daphne, as in Ovid, with bolts that lead to unrequited love. Fulton thus mixes fidelity to the Latin (above, Daphne shrinking from Apollo's kiss) with startling, even estranging modernity. The poem opens by taking its readers, themselves listeners in a newly digital era (the early 1990s), back to a time when music was made by a "stylus" that "vibrated, shaking a crystal in its head"—a needle on a vinyl record, grooved like the bole of a tree. The sometimes jarring clash between a comically distant golden age of gods and an already obsolete (yet nostalgically beloved) modern technology, however, sets the stage for a meditation on novelty and the unexpected as well as for the true melding of old and new: "Since the truly new," she writes, "looks truly wrong at first, / / it gives the sublime and grotesque, hoping you'll receive them kindly, / hoping for the best—newness being not so much a truth / / as it is an emotion." The poem asks us if we can "receive the hybridized and recombined?" (28–29).

It is not just that Fulton blends Ovid with the (then) recent past, however, for she echoes Keats's "Ode on a Grecian Urn" and Yeats's "Leda and the Swan" in the middle of her "Daphne." In a short vignette, a young woman awaits her wedding, playing out a ritual of reluctance:

> A parade formed to take her
>
> >   to his house.
>
> What festive obscenities.
>
> >   She listened.
>
> Pipes and timbrels.
>
> >   Venereal hymns.
>
> Thigh or breast?
>
> >   What wild X is seized? (36)

Fulton turns to a mysterious scene of silent music—to Keats and his urn: "What men or gods are these? What maidens loth? / What mad pursuit? What struggle to escape? / What pipes and timbrels? What wild ecstasy?" (ll. 8–10). But in the midst of this echo of Keats's solemnity, ecstasy is turned, with disturbing comedy, into an illicit drug, into the thing, the "X," which is female genitalia, and into a simple play on words: ecstasy is x-is-seized.

In rewriting Keats thus, Fulton is embroidering on a theme that runs throughout the *Metamorphoses.* Transformation is essentially connected to aesthetic experience: Daphne's "beauty was mutable" (33). Beauty, comedy, pleasure and our experience of them come from somewhere—they have origins, they are not stable—and the web of value created by aesthetic experience is ever expanding, taking in not just what is similar to what we already know, but even creating links to strange, unsettling, and disturbing places. Alice Fulton, Bernini, Dryden, and Sandys before them, with their recycling and revivifications of Ovid, offer us a way of seeing that aesthetic life exists in temporal flow. In dwelling on the fluid borders of aesthetic experiences—how they link one sense to another, one poem or form or body to the next—they encourage our recognition that aesthetic experience implies a tension between novelty and repetition. In broad strokes, this is the world of literary history, but on a different scale, such a fluidity plays out in the dynamic experience of aesthetic engagement. As Fulton writes:

> There are holes—
> have you noticed—
> where the seams don't quite close? Daphne peers
>   through
> those gaps. (55)

As we encounter arts that move us, nothing stands still, and with Fulton, we might find ourselves listening to a song long gone, at "the end . . . / when everybody is left . . . / And the record turns and turns into the night" (58). Aesthetic life, in giving us new configurations of value, can send us into the past and memory in search of what we have already known, but it can also leave us waiting, expectantly, to see what new sensations or ideas will suddenly make sense—will appear, out of nothingness, now to have meaning.

Music and Temporality: Beethoven and Bluegrass

Fulton's exploitation of the traditional kinship between poetry and music points explicitly to essentially blended, impure, or competing emotions in aesthetic experience. However, blended sensation and the dynamic character of aesthetic experience appear everywhere in aesthetic life, even in the space between an initial confrontation with a person, object, or event that compels attention and the desire to prolong enjoyment in the expectation of a loss, disappearance, or silence. This dynamic of change and mixture also matters for how we are able to assimilate new aesthetic objects and new aesthetic emotions into our world. Perhaps the problem of dynamic experience is nowhere clearer than in music, where timing is everything and the tension between what is new and what is expected is ever present. Music works, in the model given by David Huron, by teaching expectations, not only over the course of an individual piece but across the lives of listeners. We learn to listen to music, beginning even before birth, as sounds travel across the fluid that surrounds us. The scales and tonal progressions (patterns of movement from one chord or note to another) are in fact learned, and not a priori predictable, varying across cultures and time periods. The pleasures of music, thus, may come when a neural reward signals the coincidence of our learned expectations—a note here, a beat there—with actual experience. The pleasures of satisfied prediction are complemented, however, by the dynamics of surprise, when musicians manipulate our expectations to delay satisfaction (producing tension that is pleasurably resolved), or to lead us to expect one kind of experience while substituting another, more pleasurable one.[54] Musical novelty is not an oxymoron, but in Huron's argument, true novelty requires something else before it can be translated into pleasure.

Huron models the translation of novelty into pleasure using the idea of contrastive valence. Generally, surprises have a negative reward value: all creatures want to be able to predict the outcomes of behaviors and situations and reward accurate predictions. Surprises involve a failure to predict what will happen next. But we often like them. This paradox matters to aesthetic experience.[55] While reward systems may enact a punishment for surprise in survival contexts, these are relatively quick responses; they have to be. But at times, the quick response elicited by a reward evaluation may be in contrast with a slower, more considered appraisal. As Huron points out, in aesthetic circumstances, our responses cannot just sum over the negative value of failed prediction by adding that negative value to an unexpectedly pleasurable event, but they can benefit from the contrasting power of the pleasure, so that if we expect something unpleasant (the tension of expectation, let's say, or the apprehension of a building phrase in a movie score), the pleasurable conclusion that we didn't predict resounds all the more powerfully. Again, the neural payoffs of survival get us only so far in understanding aesthetics because survival is ultimately about what we can reliably predict.

With musical aesthetics, rewards exist in dynamic interplay, and that dynamism involves the additive, learned evaluation of pleasures and displeasures. One way of seeing how repetition thus may be a platform for delight is by thinking about technical virtuosity. Bluegrass music offers a prime example of these dynamics. The easily identifiable sound of a bluegrass run or flourish is certainly no impediment to pleasure for someone who loves the genre; rather, it signals the pleasure to come. One can learn the idiom of the music easily; indeed, the opening bars of bluegrass tunes, with their intensive rhythmic cycle, quickly inculcate the beat, but a virtuoso display within that idiom can surpass any deadening that might come with mere repetition. With this folk (revival) form, a repeated banjo line is an invitation to engage in the rhythmic cycle of tapping the toes or of dancing, but with a superb performance there is something else.[56] The breathtaking speed at which Eric Weissberg or Ralph Stanley executes a well-known progression in a canonical folk song like "Little Maggie" or "Arkansas Traveler" is itself delightful—a listener's jolt of elation may attend the completion of an intricate or exceptionally difficult phrase. Bluegrass is a genre of both improvisation and canon, so that individual artists' interpretations of standards and favorites become the hallmark of bluegrass performance. Thus, a phrase may be a familiar one (either culturally or because of the repetition within the song itself), but the changing complexity of a given execution of the phrase makes each hearing unfold so that while the concluding notes themselves are not a surprise, their intricately timed appearance may still evoke wonder: the level of technical skill can leave you breathless, disbelieving that someone can be so exquisitely talented, as you follow the motion in mind and keep the beat as it flashes forward and away.[57]

This movement forward in bluegrass is often called "drive," and it depends primarily on the intricate, rolling right-hand finger movements of the banjo player. Bluegrass is most identifiable, at one level, by this rolling motion as much as the timbre of its instruments.[58] At times, bluegrass drive as both motion and rhythmic fluidity seems to escape regular time signatures, and in particular, the subgenre of the "backstep" involves the interruption of the pulses that make up the rhythm. Bluegrass generally involves layered beats, with a combination of vocals, banjo, mandolin, or fiddle each playing its own part. In a backstep (the most famous examples are probably Stanley's *Clinch Mountain Backstep* and Earl Scruggs's *Earl's Breakdown*) whole beats are deleted from a given measure by a particular player, so that mandolin and banjo, for example, are suddenly moving in different time. The temporal disjunction resolves before the end of the piece, but may cyclically return. As Joti Rockwell describes, this is a fundamental disruption of musical expectation, in which a listener projects a given beat forward in time, anticipating the rise and fall of the notes to come, but the projected regularity suddenly fails.[59]

Backsteps generally come to resolution, and enjoyably so, but the pleasures of *Clinch Mountain Backstep* or *Earl's Breakdown* are not merely in the tension a disruption of metrical expectation can produce, because such disruptions themselves can be part of a generic expectation about bluegrass music. Part of the pleasure, then, may come from appreciation of virtuosity in the complex rhythms and their execution, both of which are required to bring everything back into time. But pleasure may also come from engagement with the motion of the beat both imaginatively and physically (at the neural level and at the level of gross motor activity, such as tapping one's fingers or feet). As listeners wait for the errant pulse elided by a backstep to return, it may be the case that they take pleasure not just in the virtuoso abilities of the performer but in their own ability to pursue the beat and catch it on its return—to have their own imagined time and the time of the music finally come to coincide, to have imagined perception and rhythmic sound rejoin. Such tracing of the lost pulse and finding it again would, I argue, be intensely pleasurable insofar as it engages the distributed neural systems of aesthetic experience. I would predict that imagery networks would be actively engaged, as well as the larger default mode network, and that experimental work would bear this out. Indeed, such a finding would comport well with the engagement of the default mode network (along with systems of reward and emotion) in visual aesthetics, where the world outside and the world within meet in new delight. Again, as I argued above, the distributed networks of imagery may be a gateway to the intensity of aesthetic pleasures.

While the virtuosity of bluegrass—in performance or for a listener—offers one view of the varying pleasures that may come from the tensions surrounding musical repetition, the problem of novelty in music has a variety of resolutions. A different and more classical example can be found in Beethoven's late works, where in exploring the relationship between repetition and novelty the composer pushed the boundaries of classical musical structure (for some critics in the years after his death, he pushed them too far).[60] Opus 120, 33 Variations on a Waltz by Anton Diabelli, gives crucial insight into a structure of aesthetic experience that places repetition in tension with novelty. The later compositions have been flashpoints for theorists of music, but also for concepts of aesthetics that engage with music and musical appreciation. The *Diabelli Variations* were composed over four years, late in Beethoven's life. The basis of the piece is a few bars of a waltz by a competent but undistinguished composer, Anton Diabelli, who invited a number of Austrian stars to produce new variations on his theme. Beethoven eventually decided to do so, but, in a staggering achievement, turned a simple, somewhat pedestrian theme into perhaps the single best piano composition of his life.

The very idea of thirty-three revisions of one simple, unremarkable theme is extraordinary (and self-consciously ambitious, modeled, perhaps, on Bach's thirty-two *Goldberg Variations*), and Beethoven relies on tools for variety that are both highly restricted and visionary. The *Diabelli Variations* tend toward one key (C major, occasionally C minor or E-flat major), but now and then they burn up the chromatic scale (C major needs no sharps or flats, but variations 16 and 28 are freely chromatic), pushing the key as far as it can go without changing or falling apart. The variations are also written with a number of different time signatures and speeds, and they transform a waltz into everything from a march to a minuet and fugue. Perhaps most important, Beethoven relied on a level of technical skill in his performer that is itself virtuoso, requiring flourishes, punishing trills and runs, dynamically changing tempos, sudden modulations of sound, syncopations, and demanding rhythms. As much as Beethoven was accused of writing visual and not aural music in his late compositions (thanks to his deafness), these pieces foreground performance skills. A simple waltz like Anton Diabelli's calls only for a pianist's basic technical competence and enough good will (or professional obligation) to play for dancing couples (see figure 8). It is not just ironic that

Beethoven calls the most from his performer in recasting such simplicity. The very motion of the pianist's body thus reconfigures the motion of the dancers, calling forth a kind of technical mastery that might make anyone breathless who watches it (see figure 9, Variation 31).

Beethoven, Solomon proposes, is transforming—revaluing, in my terms—Diabelli in order to enact the transfiguration of the everyday. The waltz was one of the most quotidian of musical forms, familiar to the drawing room of every bourgeois and aristocratic household (it was also the evolution of a folk dance, the *ländler*, and thus reached beyond the privileged classes).[61] The transformations of waltz in the *Diabelli Variations* are in part generic, recasting the theme as march, minuet, or fugue. Generic transformations, however, often lend themselves to burlesque or parody, and Kinderman finds ample evidence for parody (as "re-use and not travesty") in the variations.[62] There are echoes of the kinds of finger exercises pianists use for practice or warmup, upping the ante on Beethoven's own ability to transform nothing into something, but also giving a comedic nod to his performer's own craft. I laugh aloud in Variation 13 at the tiny *piano* responses to the bold shouts of the dominant renditions of the theme.[63] Like Ovid, Beethoven mixes feelings, from languor and anger to laughter, and like Hogarth, he invites listeners at every minute to follow the thread, find the theme, and marvel at its transformation.

Musical structure, though, certainly classical musical structure, means this pursuit is subject to certain rules. Music is in some sense repetition: a chorus, refrain, coda, or theme and variation give a work predictable structure.[64]

Knowledge of a particular musical idiom such as nineteenth-century European classicism allows listeners, especially expert ones, to predict the end of a phrase, a change of key, the next note, the duration of a pause, and even when a piece has come to the appropriate close. Indeed, the reliance of classical composition on tonal conventions means that the expectations of certain kinds of tension and resolution are inescapable: in the triad system (based on three-note chords), there can be no complete circle of rising and falling tones, only a slight mismatch that classical music exploits to provide balance by tonal progression (what is called "equal temperament"). Classical music structures have predictable progressions that alert listeners to order and closure by hitting the notes that close the circuit, from high to low and back again.[65] True novelty here would be stepping outside the tonal scale altogether, toward, say, atonal music and Schoenberg. Beethoven pushes the limits of classicism in his later work, but he does not violate them.

It is the predictability of music that, in part, gives it the potential for pleasure, allowing us to feel the synchronic achievement of what we think will come with what we actually experience, but the reward value of music is still not a priori predictable.[66] Our responses depend on our expectations—of genre, composer, performer, context, mood, or individual work. With the *Diabelli Variations* the game of repetition and prediction becomes the ground against which the unexpected appears: we *know* Diabelli's waltz theme will return, but not when or in what guise. As Charles Rosen observes, in the music of Haydn, Mozart, and Beethoven, humor is the essential form that this classical aesthetic takes: "The incongruous [becomes] seen as exactly right, the out-of-place suddenly turning out to be just where it ought to be" (96). This is a world in which novelty has peculiarly and deliberately limited value. In the case of the *Diabelli Variations,* the theme is known; the methods of closure are known, too. But the music can still delight. Beethoven plays with, satisfies, and even defeats expectations; even the frustrations of the piece can produce pleasure—laughter, tension, and joy. (When the theme returns, for example, in Variation 20, it sounds *piano* and oh-so-slowly, as if it has been beaten into submission by the *sforzata* of Variation 19.) With each transformation, new relations of value emerge. Not only is Diabelli both diminished and exalted, but each juxtaposition of tempo or genre gives new meaning to what has gone before. This is the essence of how parody functions: "the material of cliché becomes an aesthetic object," and the new work revalues what we had known by adding not just new perspectives, but new emotional evaluations (we laugh, are embarrassed, excited, or pleasantly educated).[67]

The way that the *Variations* represent and transform what we have heard is striking, full of echoes and of homage to Beethoven himself, his peers, and his musical world—Haydn in Variation 12, Beethoven's own *Moonlight Sonata* in Variation 8, Mozart's *Don Giovanni* in Variation 22—as well as the sometimes cacophonous sounds of practices and lessons, where ornamentation is (almost) endlessly replayed in search of perfection. It is not hard to see these echoes as acknowledgment of the degree to which Beethoven, in his increasingly profound deafness, is making beauty out of images and memories as much as sounds.[68] The *Diabelli Variations* might be taken as a claim—loud, unmistakable, compelling—that loss of hearing leads to no loss of the beauty of sound for this man, and that the ability of the mind to manipulate its own version of sensation is a perfect crucible for aesthetic delight. The echoes of what had been heard and what can still be perfectly imagined by the composer can themselves be transformed into new beauty.[69]

We should pause here to consider again the fact that Beethoven begins with a waltz, a dance: the Sister Arts, again, are never far behind. The diverse tempos of the *Variations* are explicitly linked to bodily motion: march, fugue (etymologically, "escape"), and minuet. The entire work ultimately returns to the dance form: Beethoven "cannot bring back Diabelli's waltz at the end after his monumental treatment of it, so he transforms it into a minuet, an evocation of a world that has [historically] disappeared."[70] Hogarth would recognize the synergistic drive toward motion, but also toward social and artistic order. In the final years of his life Beethoven was increasingly interested in the model of artistic unity he understood to be that of classical Greece, where the dithyramb combined dance and choral poetry, or the Pindaric ode involved the motion of a chorus (in the strophe, or turn; the antistrophe, or counterturn; and the epode, or stand).[71] Such fabled unity was understood in the wake of Winckelmann and other Hellenists as a kind of spiritual union.[72] Beethoven, however, did not see this unity as purely a matter for the exalted, and indeed, Opus 120 "stands as a sign for the earthly stuff out of which the celestial is spun."[73] If the folk dances, courtship rituals, and common repertoire of sound can explode into the starshine of the *Diabelli Variations*, it is worth noting that for Beethoven, this comes out of a reconfiguration of aesthetic values *and* artistic modes.

Endings and Rebirth: Van Gogh and Erasure

Let us consider one further way in which art can be, unpredictably, revalued: by erasure. This is the haunting possibility that lurks behind Beethoven's late compositions, the works of deafness, where imagination and vibration take over part or all of the work of sound. Keats similarly engages the possibilities of sensory negation in service of aesthetic life. What, though, with vision? As I have shown, there are a number of reasons to think that even seemingly static visual images may achieve effects through promoting our imagination of motion. The dynamic potential of any work of visual art is one thing, however; the ultimate foreclosure of the visible is another. Sight is in fact always discontinuous, whether that discontinuity is manifested in the saccadic movements that take the eye from one component of a scene to another, the blinks that interrupt the focus, or even the embroidery of the visual field that makes the blind spot in the eye's foveal pit unnoticeable. These contingencies and interruptions are inherent to a dynamic sense, but they are part of aesthetic experience, too.

I turn, therefore, to a case in which illusion and visual mystery are at the heart of aesthetic experience. Vincent van Gogh undertook an experiment with beauty's loss. An ink sketch (held in the Van Gogh Museum in Amsterdam) is the only completely visible remnant of a lost painting: "Wild Vegetation" is a haunting drawing (now monochromatic, but perhaps not always so) sent by Van Gogh to his brother and patron.[74] The image—of trees, wild flowers, and weeds—leaves only the barest suggestion of the structure of landscape and foliage (figure 5). Sometime in mid-1889,

Van Gogh ran out of canvas and painted *Ravine* on top of the completed painting of *Wild Vegetation*, a loss confirmed by conservationist Meta Chavannes in 2006.[75] One might be forgiven for feeling the loss irreparable. Elaine Scarry in *On Beauty and Being Just* points out that beauty makes us seek to preserve it: we may want the beautiful object to be forever preserved, replicated into eternity. Painting over something (presumably) precious outrages this sense of care; indeed, the sketch of "Wild Vegetation" suggests that there was something of beauty, and Van Gogh's correspondence leaves us aware that he felt this overpainting to be a necessary sacrifice.

However time or necessity may strike, alter, or destroy the beautiful, in another sense beauty is always necessarily a momentary event, even in the space of painting. Hogarth's *Analysis of Beauty* suggests one reason why this is the case. At the heart of the *Analysis* is Hogarth's theory of what he calls the serpentine line:

> It is a pleasing labour of the mind to solve the most difficult problems; allegories and riddles, trifling as they are, afford the mind amusement: and with what delight does it follow the well-connected thread of a play, or novel, which ever increases as the plot thickens, and ends most pleas'd, when that is most distinctly unravell'd? The eye hath this sort of enjoyment in winding walks, and serpentine rivers, and all sorts of objects, whose forms . . . are composed . . . of the *waving* and *serpentine lines.*[76]

Such figures "*lea[d] the eye a wanton kind of chase,* and from the pleasure that gives the mind, intitles [them] to the name of beautiful" (33, emphasis in original). There is one line that is superlative—not all twists are true. He takes a waving line, a line moving sinuously on two axes, then imagines that line wrapped around a cone so that it curves and winds in all three dimensions. Such a serpentine line invites pursuit, and it does so because it always disappears, passing up and behind and out of sight as it curves away from the eye. This for Hogarth is the foundation on which the experience of beauty is laid, and it is an experience that is based not just on disappearance but on the illusion (or actuality) of motion. The mind engages in a play of pursuit, but such play, at first glance entirely imaginary, is even more exciting when it blends reality with it, as Hogarth illustrates by describing his pleasure in watching a country dance, delighted most "particularly when [his] eye eagerly pursued a favourite dancer, through all the windings of the figure, who then was bewitching to the sight, as the imaginary ray, we were speaking of, [the serpentine line] was dancing with her all the time" (34). The imaginary ray—the serpentine line—implies that beauty is dynamic: as we follow the beautiful, we "give *movement* . . . to the eye itself" (34). The serpentine line itself moves on and disappears behind the cone: it is an abstraction that continues into space even when one cannot see it. The experience of beauty is a process structured by motion and by disappearance (indeed, the bodily contours left in the sand by wrestlers at work in Winckelmann suggest this as well).

Ravine (figure 3) can, I suggest, be approached as Van Gogh's own engagement with this terrain of motion, pursuit, and undulating lines, and as a very conscious attempt to hint at a lost beauty while creating a new one. Unlike other moments when Van Gogh reused a canvas, he did not white out the earlier painting; with *Ravine* he used the texture of the first work as scaffolding on which to erect the second. The thickness of the brush strokes, the mysterious circles beneath the surface, and the contrasting paint that peeks between some of the lines are visible to the naked eye. The image and the texture in this painting do not always, thus, match, and this mismatch gestures toward another structure, another vision of beauty, behind (physically) and before (temporally) the structure of *Ravine*. This striking departure from Van Gogh's earlier practice suggests an aesthetic experiment, one born of necessity. To what end? X-rays of the canvas show that both *Ravine* and *Wild Vegetation* (figure 4) have a vortical structure, swirling from the outer edges of the canvas into the center. At the heart of the sketch and the lost painting are a lush swirl of plant life; at the center of *Ravine* is a winding gorge, where water seems to be drawn, twisting behind the curve of the land, until it disappears beyond the frontiers of sight and the thickness of paint. The magic of perspective produces, in two dimensions, the illusion of depth by conjuring an in fact invisible (vanishing) point; depth is then "visible" only as imagery after all.[77] But the vanishing act here is more intricate. Van Gogh may not have had in mind an explicit reference to Hogarth's disappearing line of beauty as he sacrificed one beautiful object to create a new one, but Van Gogh knew the painter's craft of sight full well, and he pays homage to the techniques of imagery that underpin the experience of perspective in painting. The layered paintings and the swirling structure suggest that in leaving the visible textural and structural remnants of one painting as the basis for another, Van Gogh left a riddle for his viewers—most immediately his own brother—to decode, a riddle about how beauty can transform, and about the way that painting concerns illusions of sight as much as perceptual reality. *Wild Vegetation*'s swirling foliage has new life in the path of water as it goes into the depths of the *Ravine*, even if that life is only hinted on the surface.

Van Gogh was particularly pleased, Chavannes and Van Tilborgh show, with what he had done with the new painting, and it seems that such a potential for transformation was part of Van Gogh's creative process from the first sketch of "Wild Vegetation."[78] The drawing (figure 5) was made using reeds that Van Gogh cut and shaped by hand. Charles Stuckey argues that "this idiosyncratic graphic medium could capture movement more effectively than oils. Such a realization seemingly marked a turning point in Vincent's evolution [in the late 1880s]. When he painted out-of-doors in Provence, he explained that thanks to the mistral winds, 'the canvas is shaking all the time. It does not bother me when I am drawing.' . . . Whatever the case, henceforth, the brushwork in Vincent's paintings would take on the rhythmic logic of his drawings," carrying motion—almost an aesthetic constant—within them in their swooping texture and vortical force.[79] It is thus that the swift passage of beauty was always already part of the aesthetic structure he was creating in the works of this period.

Van Gogh's transformation of one work of art into another, then, might seem in some ways a loss, but in his obsessive revisiting of this particular landscape at Arles, Van Gogh left the clue to its resurrection. Part of that clue lies in the reed-woven work of "Wild Vegetation," a sketch of flora itself made with a sculpted bit of grass. The worlds of art and nature intertwine here most certainly, with the mistral breathing into paper and the artist using part of the natural world to transcribe its own image. On describing the gorge in which he painted *Ravine*, and painted over *Wild Vegetation*, Van Gogh writes that it was "pleasant to work in such a wild place, where you have to bury the easel into the rocks so that the wind doesn't spoil everything with dirt." As Chavannes and Van Tilborgh discover, however, the earth left its mark in *Ravine,* too, in the form of microscopic twigs embedded in the paint.[80]

At one level, Van Gogh is undertaking a sacrifice, a painful transformation, of one object and landscape of beauty for another. Given the loss of *Wild Vegetation*, then, it might be that what we have in *Ravine* is a remembered painting, a structure of beauty-as-echo, but the fact that Van Gogh left the impasto of the original painting and even used it to create the effects of the second makes it more than simply Van Gogh's private memory at stake or an artifact of scholarly history and X-ray technology. In maintaining and manipulating the contours of the first work, Van Gogh leaves us a trace to be followed. We ought to understand the painting as seeking to train viewers to look harder, to look differently, to seek what is vanishing—the raised paint of a twist of foliage transformed into a swirl of foam, the illusion of perspective itself, the water folding in on itself in the gorge, the trace of the artist's departed hand in the texture of the paint, or perhaps even a more fundamental awareness of the momentary experience of beauty. The painting for Van Gogh carried with it the knowledge that beauty could be revalued, and that the layers of perception that structure aesthetic experience exist in dynamic relation with one another.

Chavannes and Van Tilborgh have given viewers access to that knowledge differently, but the painting itself conveys that story of revaluation in multiple ways.

Conclusion: *Carmen Perpetuum*

The painful yet pleasurable revaluation that can come with aesthetic perception or with the struggle to view and re-view the work of art points once more toward the ever-present potential of aesthetic experience to take us out of one set of ideas and into another—and even from one medium to another. In exploring the dynamics of aesthetic experience, we can understand why the Sister Arts are always intertwined, never far behind one another in the imaginative engagements art evokes. I return to Ovid as I close because he blends the arts and draws us into contemplation of aesthetic experiences at the limits of our normal engagement with pleasure. Now, Ovid himself might laugh with joy at Van Gogh's medium and his transformation of one object of beauty into another, even while he recognized the pain and the necessity of the transformation that underwrites it. While a canvas has no memory, it can carry echoes, as one painting echoes the twisting dance of the one the lies beneath its surface and as a painter remembers what his need to create had lost.

In the *Metamorphoses,* Ovid's bizarre figures foreground dynamic changes, and imagination, but also the ways that remembering aesthetic experience may change our thinking. Ovid draws our attention to the Sister Arts, both as a master of ekphrasis (descriptions of visual art) and in the tales he tells, from Pygmalion (sculpture) to Arachne (the pictorial arts) to Orpheus or Syrinx and Pan (music).[81] Ovid freezes beautiful objects and people in moments of transformation, when beauty is changing, passing into something else and away. These transformations are always incomplete—hence both prospective and retrospective—and evoke as much pain and threat as beauty. The case of Syrinx, a young nymph, pursued with threat of rape by Pan, is exemplary:

> the scornful nymph
> Fled through the wilderness and came at last
> To Ladon's peaceful sandy stream, and there,
> Her flight barred by the river, begged her sisters,
> The water-nymphs, to change her; and, when Pan
> Thought he had captured her, he held instead
> Only the tall marsh reeds, and, while he sighed,
> The soft wind stirring in the reeds sent forth
> A thin and plaintive sound; and he, entranced
> By this new music and its witching tones,
> Cried "You and I shall stay in unison!"
> And waxed together the reeds of different lengths
> And made the pipes that keep his darling's name.[82]

In this poem, Pan, patron of music, transforms a threatened nymph's fragile visible beauty and her mournful, plaintive sound into the instrument of his own durable art.[83] But it also layers what one might see and hear now with remembered sight and remembered sound, as one stands at the frontier—the moment when new music is being made. Ultimately, aesthetic experience holds within it the seeds of dynamic transformation, but this means that it is not solely about the future. Ovid himself wrote *Metamorphoses* in the hope that it would enter into memory and become, as he put it, a *carmen perpetuum*, a song never ending in its transformation and evolution in readers' minds (Philip Glass takes up the challenge in his slowly evolving piano composition, *Metamorphosis*).[84]

I have again evoked memory here, as I close, to indicate the deep implications of aesthetic experience for changing our lives, as well as to signal a key future path of research in aesthetics. The default mode network does not just underpin imagery and intense aesthetic experience, it is key to memory, too.[85] Imagery itself involves drawing on remembered experience. More than this, at a neural level, autobiographical memory employs the medial prefrontal cortex and the posterior cingulate cortex, both of which are activated (the anterior medial prefrontal cortex extensively so) in powerful aesthetic responses; in addition, many of the brain areas sensitive to emotion in aesthetic response (see figure 15), especially the hippocampus and the medial prefrontal cortex, perform functions essential to memory as well.[86] Indeed, given the way in which imagery and reward rely on prior experience, I think it impossible to dissociate aesthetic experience from memory circuitry. But this is not just a question of overlapping tissue or analogous functions. Rather, it points toward networked interactions in which large swaths of interconnected neurons work together to perform a number of complex functions. The involvement of the default mode network in intense aesthetic experience is one way in which this is visible, but the other grouped firing patterns that characterize aesthetic response (see figures 11–14) are another. The interconnection of memory and aesthetics suggests to me that memory processes should be greatly affected by strong aesthetic experience, and this has implications for the role of the arts in education. Understanding these interactions is crucial to attaining a more complete understanding of aesthetics and its component processes, and one of the priorities of future empirical research in this area should be to explore these connections.[87] Such work will enable us to speak with more precision about what we learn from the aesthetic, and how we learn it.

I have maintained in this book that something essential to aesthetic experience does persist, even as the events and objects of aesthetic experience pass away. Beauty and its kin create new levels and new measures of the aesthetic power in the representations of value—newly created, unexpected value—which are fundamental to aesthetic experience. Aesthetic experiences—of beauty, awe, fear, sublimity, or even experiences for which there is no easy name—are events; they will and must disappear. But the relations of value they evoke produce new possibilities, and they do so in part because they open up and give access to an extraordinary neural architecture. A sight, a sound, a line of poetry can be a gateway not just to an inner landscape of thoughts and ideas, but can turn on a densely interconnected network of neurons, a network which underpins a broad range of cognitive functions. Aesthetic experience is human experience, and it draws on extraordinary resources within us. Art can change how we think and feel in the now, and in engaging systems for emotion and reward as well as for imagery and even memory in the core network, it can change how we think and feel in the future. The effects of aesthetic experience thus can be both critically minute and ecstatically broad-ranging.

The new possibilities aesthetic experience can bring have physical consequences and neural instantiations, but they also exist out of brain and out of mind; they may be new generic, creative, and even physical configurations that themselves lead to new relations among the arts—Beethoven's revaluation of waltz is only one example that sews dance to music and the motion of fingers and notes. Indeed, as much as all imagery tends toward the multisensory, the arts blend into other aesthetic space by the very nature of perception: beautiful faces become the stuff of painting, or are transformed into eerily graceful trees; dance weaves sound together with sight and motion (even when, as with the work of the Judson collective, the only music is the sound of a body in motion); and landscapes enter paintings and painterly idioms appear in gardens.

It is also the nature of aesthetic experience, with its continual reconfiguration of what we find valuable, to spur us to seek new comparisons, new interpretations, new metaphors, new modes of understanding and perceiving. As aesthetic experience opens up new connections, it also opens up the paths of creativity, and it may do so in part by creating connections between ideas and experiences that on their surface are so distant as to seem unrelated.[88] It is thus that the arts beget both more art, more extra-artistic pleasures, and, simultaneously, more criticism—the drive to repetition Scarry evokes—as well as encouraging us to push the boundaries of what we understand to be *art* toward different forms and different modes.[89]

We might hope beauty is a sign of something eternal (Justice and the Good, as Plato argues? Truth, as Shaftesbury and Keats suggest?), for how could something so perfect, so powerful that it resonates into yet undiscovered countries, be nothing more than the truth of a moment? But aesthetic experience is about overturning and refining initial predictions in my account. As I have argued, the unpredicted, evolving rewards of aesthetic experience are key to aesthetic experience on a neural level, and as they are integrated into the fabric of memory and imagination, they may become part of our future predictions—our hopes and beliefs about the world. This means that the varieties of aesthetic experience are essential to what aesthetics is; it is absolutely necessary that some people don't see things as you do or as I do. Aesthetics is all about newly created and reconfigured value, about something that wasn't there in quite the same way before, something that was in part created in the brain and that leaves traces in how we go forward. This is not all that aesthetic experience is or may be. There is more to be discovered about the role of the default mode network and of memory processes, about the broader somatic context of aesthetic experience, about the varieties of aesthetic emotions, about the differences in artistic modes, about the relations between art and the pleasures outside art, and about the differences between us. This book is only one of many beginnings, and I hope it sparks new research.

Appendix: "The Brain on Art" (Excerpt)

---

fMRI Scanning Procedures

Functional magnetic imaging (fMRI) scans were carried out at New York University's Center for Brain Imaging using a 3T Siemens Allegra scanner and a Nova Medical Head coil (NM011 head transmit coil). Artworks were projected onto a screen in the bore of the magnet and viewed through a mirror mounted on the head coil.

The 109 artworks were divided into four sets (different subsets per observer, depending on order) and shown over the course of four functional scans using a slow event-related design. During these functional scans, the blood-oxygen-level-dependent (BOLD) signal was measured from the entire brain using thirty-six 3 mm sections aligned approximately parallel to the anterior commissure to posterior

Adapted from: Edward A. Vessel, G. Gabrielle Starr, and Nava Rubin, "The Brain on Art: Intense Aesthetic Experience Activates the Default Mode Network," *Frontiers in Human Neuroscience* 6, no. 66 (2012). doi:10.3389/fnhum.2012.00066.

commissure plane (in-plane resolution 3 × 3 mm, repetition time [TR] = 2 s, echo time [TE] = 30 ms, flip angle [FA] = 80 deg.). Each trial began with a 1 second (s) blank period, which was followed by a blinking fixation point for 1 s. An artwork was then displayed for 6 s, followed by a blank screen for 4 s, during which the observer pressed a key corresponding to a recommendation. An additional 0, 2, or 4 s blank interval was inserted pseudorandomly between trials to jitter trial timing. The average trial length was 13.14 s.

The sixteen observers (eleven male, thirteen right-handed; paid, recruited at New York University, with normal or corrected to normal vision) were also run in a localizer scan containing blocks of objects, scrambled objects, faces, and places. This 320 s scan consisted of four 18 s blocks of each stimulus type, during which the observer performed a "one-back" task (the observers monitor for exact repeats of an image). Each block of images in this part of the study consisted of sixteen stimulus images plus two repeats, each presented for 800 ms, with a 200 ms interstimulus interval. The full-color images were placed on top of phase-scrambled versions of the same stimuli filling a 500 × 500 pixel square to control for differences in size across stimulus categories.

A high-resolution (1 mm^3) anatomical volume (MPRage sequence) scan was obtained after the functional scans for registration and spatial normalization purposes.

Behavioral Data Analysis

For the observers' recommendations collected during the scanning session, a measure of agreement across individuals was computed by taking the set of 109 recommendations for every pair of observers and computing the Pearson correlation coefficient. Images with any missing recommendation values were excluded from the correlations in a pairwise manner. One observer gave no "4" recommendations and was therefore excluded from subsequent analyses relying on the contrast of "4" versus "1" responses. Similarly, a measure of across-observer agreement was computed for each item of the nine-item questionnaire collected after the scanning session. For each item, the Pearson correlation coefficient was computed for each pair of observers.

Factor Analysis of Evaluative Questionnaire

The responses on the nine-item questionnaire produced by each observer to each artwork ($16 \times 109 = 1{,}744$ trials total) were then converted to z scores (a measure of the deviation of individual ratings from the mean rating) within observers and concatenated into a single large matrix of scores. Principal components extraction was used to identify factors with eigenvalues greater than one. Two emotional/evaluative factors survived and were rotated using the "direct oblmin" method, which does not require that the factors be orthogonal. Scores on these two factors were computed for each of the 1,744 trials using regression (see figure 15).

fMRI Data Analysis

The scans were preprocessed using the FMRIB Software Library (FSL, Oxford, UK) to correct for slice timing and motion, and were high-pass filtered at 0.0125 Hz. Subsequent analyses were performed using BrainVoyager QX software (Brain Innovation, Maastricht, the Netherlands). After alignment with observer-specific high-resolution anatomical images, the scans were normalized to Talairach space,[1] blurred with an 8 mm Gaussian kernel, and z-scored.

4-vs.-1 Whole-Brain Analysis

To identify regions sensitive to observer recommendation, a whole-brain random effects group-level general linear model (GLM) analysis was computed, with the responses of each observer on each of the four possible recommendation levels coded as separate regressors (as a 6 s "on" period for each image convolved with a standard two-gamma hemodynamic response function, HRF). A contrast of the "4" regressors versus the "1" regressors was computed and the resulting statistical map was corrected for multiple comparisons at a false discovery rate (FDR) of $Q < .05$ and a cluster threshold of five 3 mm^3 voxels.[2] This contrast is referred to hereafter as the 4-vs.-1 whole-brain analysis (see figure 18 and figures 11–13).

ROI Analysis

To compare BOLD activation for all four recommendation levels across these regions, the group-level clusters from the 4-vs.-1 analysis were used to draw regions of interest (ROIs), from which we extracted time series for each observer. Using the average (over voxels in the ROI) of non-blurred, z-scored time series for each scan, we obtained individual observer parameter estimates for each of the four recommendation levels using a GLM with a standard two-gamma HRF convolved with a 6 s "on" period for each image (see figures 11–13). Standard errors were computed across observers.

4-vs.-321 Whole-Brain Analysis

To further isolate processes particular to aesthetic response, we computed a second whole-brain contrast relying on the same whole-brain GLM as above, but with a new contrast of only the "4" recommendations versus the average of all the other recommendation levels, balanced to add to zero (for example, a linear contrast of [1 1 1 3] for the 1, 2, 3, and 4 regressors). The same statistical threshold was used to correct for multiple comparisons—FDR of $Q < 0.05$ and a five 3 mm^3 cluster threshold. This contrast will be referred to as the 4-vs.-321 whole-brain analysis (see figure 14. Note that this analysis may lead to the discovery of new activations not found in the original 4-vs.-1 analysis. Given the widely extended and interconnected nature of the resulting whole-brain map, we do not report the full set of activation coordinates but note only that most of the peak activations were coincident with regions reported for the 4-vs.-1 contrast. Group-level ROIs were isolated for four prominent activations not found in the 4-vs.-1 contrast: the anterior medial prefrontal cortex (aMPFC), the left hippocampus (HC), the left substantia nigra (SN), and the left posterior cingulate cortex (PCC). It was not possible to draw an isolated ROI for the aMPFC from this comparison because of the large swath of activation. We therefore drew a more restricted ROI for the aMPFC based on the 4-vs.-1 whole-brain contrast but with a statistical threshold of $P < .001$.

ROI Analysis of Evaluative Factors

The trial-by-trial scores for the two factors extracted from the principal components factor analysis of the nine-item evaluative questionnaire were used to create BOLD predictors by convolving with a standard two gamma hemodynamic response function with a length of one TR (2 s) and a delay of one TR relative to image onset. This middle TR was chosen as a compromise because of our uncertainty about when, during a 6 s viewing, an observer was able to integrate enough information across successive fixations of an artwork to generate an affective response. The resulting time courses were combined with an "image on" predictor and orthonormalized using the Gram-Schmidt process before being entered into a GLM predicting BOLD activation in each of the ROI's identified in the whole brain analysis (see figure 15).

Individual Differences Analysis of Evaluative Questionnaire

We performed an analysis of individual differences in responses to the nine-item evaluative questionnaire and their relationship to BOLD signal activation. Each observer's recommendations and subsequent responses on the nine items were converted to z scores and then concatenated into a single large matrix (16 observers × 109 images = 1,744 rows). We performed a stepwise regression analysis in SPSS

(IBM, Somers, New York) of observers' recommendations against their responses to the nine items to eliminate redundant terms or terms that had no significant predictive power for recommendations. Individual standardized beta weights were then computed for how well each of the items surviving this procedure predicted recommendations, entered in order from most to least predictive at the group level. The resulting beta weights, which can be conceptualized as reflecting the weight an observer places on a particular emotion/evaluation when making recommendations, were used to predict the size (across observers) of the 4-vs.-1 BOLD effect in the set of ROIs identified in the whole-brain recommendation-based analysis. This yielded an overall R^2 for each ROI and beta weights for each of the items with associated confidence intervals. A significant effect in this analysis would indicate that variability *across* observers in the size of the BOLD effect in an ROI is related to variability in how much individual observers weigh a particular emotion/evaluation when making recommendations (see figure 16).

Notes

Preface

1. For example, the terms beautiful, sublime, sweet, exquisite, interesting, divine, cute, awesome, and so on are historically specific and do not denote the same experiences or classes of objects over time. See, for example, Mary Carruthers, "Sweetness," *Speculum* 81, no. 4 (2006); Carruthers, "Varietas: A Word of Many Colors," *Poetica: Zeitschrift für Sprach- und Literaturwissenschaft* Fall (2009); Ronald Paulson, *The Beautiful, Novel, and Strange: Aesthetics and Heterodoxy* (Baltimore, MD: Johns Hopkins University Press, 1995); Sianne Ngai, "Stuplimity: Shock and Boredom in Twentieth-Century Aesthetics," *Postmodern Culture* 10, no. 2 (2000); and Ngai, "The Cuteness of the Avant Garde," *Critical Inquiry* 31 (Summer 2005).

2. On the evolution of aesthetics, see Paul Guyer, "The Origins of Modern Aesthetics: 1711–35," in *The Blackwell Guide to Aesthetics*, ed. Peter Kivy (London: Blackwell, 2004). David Marshall shows the capacious way in which aesthetic experience was understood in the eighteenth century, even before aesthetics proper began: "intense experiences with and of art [but also including landscapes and tableaux appreciated as art] . . . are far from the disinterested "museum experience" [some describe] . . . as the paradigm and endpoint of eighteenth-century aesthetics," *The Frame of Art: Fictions of Aesthetic Experience, 1750–1815* (Baltimore, MD:

Johns Hopkins University Press, 2005), 6. On the development of the concept of the arts, see Larry Shiner, *The Invention of Art: A Cultural History* (Chicago: University of Chicago Press, 2001).

3. My wording here is meant to straddle a line, carefully. As I describe below, there is still an explanatory gap between "experience" and its neural underpinnings. We are whole beings, and neural activity does not equate with that wholeness, as I emphasize throughout. But components of experience do have neural correlates—patterns of neural activity without which the experience would be impoverished or impossible.

4. Quoted in Guyer, "The Origins of Modern Aesthetics," 15.

5. Anthony Cooper Shaftesbury, *Characteristics of Men, Manners, Opinions, Times*, ed. Lawrence E. Klein (New York: Cambridge University Press, 1999); Francis Hutcheson, *An Inquiry into the Original of Our Ideas of Beauty and Virtue*, ed. Wolfgang Leidhold (Indianapolis: Liberty Fund, 2004); Adam Smith, *The Theory of Moral Sentiments*, ed. D. D. Raphael and A. L. Macfie (Indianapolis: Liberty Fund, 1984); Immanuel Kant, *Critique of Judgment*, trans. Werner S. Pluhar (Indianapolis: Hackett, 1987); Johann Wolfgang von Goethe, *Theory of Colors*, trans. Charles Eastlake (Cambridge, MA: Harvard University Press, 1970); Hermann von Helmholtz, "On the Relation of Optics to Painting," in *Science and Culture*, ed. David Cahan (Chicago: University of Chicago Press, 1995); von Helmholtz, "On the Physiological Causes of Harmony in Music," in *Science and Culture*, ed. David Cahan (Cambridge, MA: Harvard University Press).

6. See, for example: on visual art, Eric R. Kandel, *The Age of Insight: The Quest to Understand the Unconscious in Art, Mind, and Brain, from Vienna 1900 to the Present* (New York: Random House, 2012); Semir Zeki, *Inner Vision: An Exploration of Art and the Brain* (New York: Oxford University Press, 2000); Patrick Cavanagh, "The Artist as Neuroscientist," *Nature* 434 (2005); U. Kirk, M. Skov, S. Christensen, and N. Nygaard, "Brain Correlates of Aesthetic Expertise: a Parametric fMRI Study," *Brain and Cognition* 69 (2009); G. C. Cupchik, O. Vartanian, A. Crawley, and D. J. Mikulis, "Viewing Artworks: Contributions of Cognitive Control and Perceptual Facilitation to Aesthetic Experience," *Brain and Cognition* 70 (2009); C. J. Cela-Conde, G. Marty, F. Maestú, T. Ortiz, E. Munar, A. Fernández, M. Roca, J. Rosselló, and F. Quesney, "Activation of the Prefrontal Cortex in the Human Visual Aesthetic Perception," *Proceedings of the National Academy of Sciences of the United States of America* 101, no.

16 (2004); S. Lacey, H. Hagtvedt, V. M. Patrick, A. Anderson, R. Stilla, G. Deshpande, X. Hu, J. R. Sato, S. Reddy, and K. Sathian, "Art for Reward's Sake: Visual Art Recruits the Ventral Striatum," *NeuroImage* 55 (2011); and Denis Dutton, *The Art Instinct: Beauty, Pleasure, and Human Evolution* (London: Bloomsbury, 2010). On music, see Oliver Sacks, *Musicophilia* (New York: Knopf, 2007); David Huron, *Sweet Anticipation: Music and the Psychology of Expectation* (Cambridge, MA: MIT Press, 2006); Daniel J. Levitin, *This Is Your Brain on Music: The Science of a Human Obsession* (New York: Penguin, 2007); Levitin, *The World in Six Songs: How the Musical Brain Created Human Nature* (New York: Plume, 2009); Mark J. Tramo, Peter A. Carani, Bertrande Delgutte, and Louis D. Braida, "Neurobiological Foundations for the Theory of Harmony in Western Tonal Music," *Annals of the New York Academy of Sciences* 930 (2001); Mark J. Tramo, Peter A. Carani, Christine K. Koh, Nikos Makris, and Louis D. Braida, "Neurophysiology and Neuroanatomy of Pitch Perception: Auditory Cortex," *Annals of the New York Academy of Sciences* 1060 (2005); Isabelle Peretz, "Listen to the Brain: A Biological Perspective on Musical Emotions," in *Music and Emotion: Theory and Research*, ed. Patrik N. Juslin and John A. Sloboda (New York: Oxford University Press, 2001); Anne J. Blood and Robert Zatorre, "Intensely Pleasurable Responses to Music Correlate with Activity in Brain Regions Implicated in Reward and Emotion," *Proceedings of the National Academy of Sciences of the United States of America* 98 (2001); Anne J. Blood, Robert Zatorre, Robert Bermudez, and Alan C. Evans, "Emotional Responses to Pleasant and Unpleasant Music Correlate with Activity in Paralimbic Brain Regions," *Nature Neuroscience* 2, no. 4 (1999); David Temperley, *Music and Probability* (Cambridge, MA: MIT Press, 2007); and Charles O. Nussbaum, *The Musical Representation: Meaning, Ontology, and Emotion* (Cambridge, MA: MIT Press, 2007). On literature, see Elaine Scarry, *Dreaming by the Book* (New York: Farrar, Straus and Giroux, 1999), Brian J. Boyd, *On the Origin of Stories: Evolution, Cognition, and Fiction* (Cambridge, MA: Belknap Press of Harvard University Press, 2010); Patrick Colm Hogan, *The Mind and Its Stories: Narrative Universals and Human Emotion* (Cambridge: Cambridge University Press, 2003); Lisa Zunshine, *Why We Read Fiction: Theory of Mind and the Novel* (Columbus: Ohio State University Press, 2006); Blakey Vermeule, *Why Do We Care about Literary Characters?* (Baltimore, MD: Johns Hopkins University Press, 2009); Alan Richardson, *The Neural Sublime* (Baltimore, MD: Johns Hopkins University Press, 2010); Ellen Spolsky,

"Making 'Quite Anew': Brain Modularity and Creativity," in *Introduction to Cognitive Cultural Studies*, ed. Lisa Zunshine (Baltimore, MD: Johns Hopkins University Press, 2010); Kay Young, *Imagining Minds: The Neuro-Aesthetics of Austen, Eliot and Hardy* (Columbus, Ohio State University Press, 2010); and Mark Turner, *The Literary Mind* (New York: Oxford University Press, 1997). On other arts, see B. Calvo-Merino, D. E. Glaser, J. Grezes, R. E. Passingham, and P. Haggard, "Action Observation and Acquired Motor Skills: An fMRI Study with Expert Dancers," *Cerebral Cortex* 15 (2005); Ivar G. Hagendoorn, "Some Speculative Hypotheses about the Nature and Perception of Dance and Choreography," *Journal of Consciousness Studies* 11, nos. 3–4 (2005); Catherine Stevens and Shirley McKechnie, "Thinking in Action: Thought Made Visible in Contemporary Dance," *Cognitive Processing* 6 (2005); and U. Hasson, O. Landesman, B. Knappmeyer, I. Vallines, N. Rubin, and D. Heeger, "Neurocinematics: The Neuroscience of Films," *Projections: The Journal for Movies and Mind* 2 (2008). On faces, see Nancy Etcoff, *Survival of the Prettiest: The Science of Beauty* (New York: Anchor, 2000); and Itzhak Aharon, Nancy Etcoff, Dan Ariely, Christopher F. Chabris, Ethan O'Connor, and Hans C. Breiter, "Beautiful Faces Have Variable Reward Value: fMRI and Behavioral Evidence," *Neuron* 32, no. 3 (2001). On neuroaesthetics in general, see Paul Bloom, *How Pleasure Works: The New Science of Why We Like What We Like* (New York: Norton, 2010); Anjan Chatterjee, "Neuroaesthetics: A coming of Age Story," *Journal of Cognitive Neuroscience* 23 (2011); Cinzio Di Dio and Vittorio Gallese, "Neuroaesthetics: A Review," *Current Opinion in Neurobiology* 19 (2009).

Introduction

1. Cicero, *Pro Archia Poeta*, trans. N. H. Watts, in *Orations* (Cambridge, MA: Harvard University Press, 1923), 11:8. The translation in the text is my own.

2. There are several very good accounts of the history of the Sister Arts, including Jean H. Hagstrum, *The Sister Arts: The Tradition of Literary Pictorialism and English Poetry from Dryden to Gray* (Chicago: University of Chicago Press, 1975), and Lawrence I. Lipking, *The Ordering of the Arts in Eighteenth-Century England* (Princeton, NJ: Princeton University Press, 1970), among others.

3. Horace, *Ars Poetica*, in *Satires, Epistles, Ars Poetica*, trans. H. Ruston Fairclough (Cambridge, MA: Harvard University Press, 2005), ll. 361ff. Hagstrum, *Sister Arts,* 9.

4. See, for example, Kant: "Only when their need has been satisfied can we tell who in a multitude of people has taste and who does not." Immanuel Kant, *Critique of Judgment,* trans. Werner S. Pluhar (Indianapolis: Hackett, 1987), 52.

5. Horace, *Ars Poetica,* ll. 361–365.

6. On the permanence of beauty, the foundational work is that of Plato, in the *Symposium*, *Phaedrus*, and the *Republic*. On genius, see in particular Edward Young, *Conjectures on Original Composition* (London, 1759). On the development of the system of taste that seeks to guarantee the reception of "truly" beautiful works (rather than what is merely fashionable or idiosyncratic), see Robert W. Jones, *Gender and the Formation of Taste in Eighteenth-Century Britain: The Analysis of Beauty* (Cambridge: Cambridge University Press, 1998). The foundational twentieth-century work is that of Frank Sibley, especially "Aesthetic Concepts," *Philosophical Review* 68 (1959).

7. Plato, *Republic*, trans. Robin Waterfield (New York: Oxford University Press, 1994). On the gods, see especially 377d–383c; on fears, 381e and 386b–d; on laughter, 389a; on rhythm and music, 398d–400c; on the arts and their proper uses, 400–403c; on painting and poetry together, 596b–601a; on the problem of emotional susceptibility in painting and poetry, 602c–607a. On the moral implications of the love of beauty for Plato, see Plato, *Symposium*, trans. Alexander Nehamas and Paul Woodruff (Indianapolis: Hackett, 1989); G. Gabrielle Starr, "Ethics, Meaning and the Work of Beauty," *Eighteenth-Century Studies* 35, no. 3 (2002); and Elaine Scarry, *On Beauty and Being Just* (Princeton, NJ: Princeton University Press, 1999). On the ethics of ancient aesthetics, see also Edward A. Lippman, *Musical Thought in Ancient Greece* (New York: Columbia University Press, 1964).

8. Erasmus, *Collected Works*, trans. R. A. B. Mynors, 33 vols. (Toronto: University of Toronto Press, 1991), 3:284. Among the most influential of the rhetorical texts, see Aristotle, *On Rhetoric*, trans. George A. Kennedy (New York: Oxford University Press, 1991); and Quintilian, *The Orator's Education*, trans. Donald A. Russell, 5 vols. (Cambridge, MA: Harvard University Press, 2001), bk. 6, chaps. 2–3. The nomenclature for affective

responses changes over time, and terms like *emotion* or *passion* may be both technically and functionally distinct in a given system of thought and culture. I use the terms *emotion* and *affect* generally interchangeably, in part because the word *passion* has taken on a more narrow use over time (now largely referring to the vehement passions of lust, anger, and so on, rather than to the broad array of calm and violent passions to which it once referred). For an excellent account of the passions and their triggers in literature, see Philip Fisher, *The Vehement Passions* (Princeton, NJ: Princeton University Press, 2002). On music and catharsis, see book 8 of Aristotle's *Politics*, and on the afterlife of that idea, see James Beattie, *Essays: On Poetry and Music as They Affect the Mind* (London, 1779). On sympathy, see Adam Smith, *The Theory of Moral Sentiments*, ed. D. D. Raphael and A. L. Macfie (Indianapolis: Liberty Fund, 1984), and James Engell, *The Creative Imagination: Enlightenment to Romanticism* (Cambridge, MA: Harvard University Press, 1981).

9. Kendall Walton, *Mimesis and Make-Believe* (Cambridge, MA: Harvard University Press, 1990), 195–204. See also Peter Lamarque, "How Can We Fear and Pity Fictions?," *British Journal of Aesthetics* 21, no. 4 (1981); Bijoy Boruah, *Fiction and Emotion* (Oxford: Clarendon Press, 1988); Tamar Szabó Gendler and Karson Kovakovich, "Genuine Rational Fictional Emotions," in *Contemporary Debates in Aesthetics and the Philosophy of Art*, ed. Matthew Kieran (Malden, MA: Blackwell, 2005); and Eva M. Dadlez, *What's Hecuba to Him? Fictional Events and Actual Emotions* (University Park: Pennsylvania State University Press, 1997). For a good review of this literature, see Jerrold Levinson, "Emotion in Response to Art: A Survey of the Terrain," in *Emotion and the Arts*, ed. Mette Hjort and Sue Laver (New York: Oxford University Press, 1997).

10. Peter Kivy, *Music Alone: Philosophical Reflections on the Purely Musical Experience* (Ithaca, NY: Cornell University Press, 1990), 161. See also Clive Bell, *Art* (London: Chatto and Windus, 1914). Bell argues that art does not induce standard emotions at all but rather feelings in regard to the aesthetic and perceptual shape of the object. Malcolm Budd lays out a variety of objections to the idea that music evokes everyday emotions in *Music and the Emotions: The Philosophical Theories* (New York: Routledge, 1985). For an opposing view, see Aaron Ridley, *Music, Value and the Passions* (Ithaca, NY: Cornell University Press, 1995).

11. See, for example, Mette Hjort and Sue Laver, eds., *Emotion and the Arts* (New York: Oxford University Press, 1997); Gendler and Kovakovich,

"Genuine Rational Fictional Emotions"; Keith Oatley, "A Taxonomy of the Emotions of Literary Responses and a Theory of Identification in Fictional Narrative," *Poetics* 23 (1994); Oatley, "Emotions and the Story Worlds of Fiction," in *Narrative Impact: Social and Cognitive Foundations*, ed. M. C. Green, J. J. Strange, and T. C. Brock (Mahwah, NJ: Erlbaum, 2002); Boruah, *Fiction and Emotion*; and Lamarque, "How Can We Fear and Pity Fictions?"

12. Plato, *Republic*. See especially 605c–d.

13. On the history of critiques of the imagination, see Richard Kearney, *The Wake of Imagination: Toward a Postmodern Culture* (Minneapolis: University of Minnesota Press, 1988). For a very good account of the rise of imagination as essential for artistic endeavor and a sign of aesthetic value, see Engell, *The Creative Imagination*. On the suspicion of imagery, see Ernest Gilman, *Iconoclasm and Poetry in the English Reformation: Down Went Dagon* (Chicago: University of Chicago Press, 1986), and W.J.T. Mitchell, *Iconology: Image, Text, Ideology* (Chicago: University of Chicago Press, 1987).

14. Scarry, *Dreaming by the Book*.

15. Mitchell, *Iconology*.

16. I take the phrase from W. K. Wimsatt and Monroe Beardsley, *The Verbal Icon* (Lexington: University of Kentucky Press, 1954).

17. On visual imagery accompanying music, see Daniel Levitin, *The World in Six Songs: How the Musical Brain Created Human Nature* (New York: Dutton, 2008). Oliver Sacks gives a good account as well in *Musicophilia* (New York: Knopf, 2007). On imagery and musical composition, see Andrea R. Halpern and Robert Zatorre, "Mental Concerts: Musical Imagery and Auditory Cortex," *Neuron* 47 (2005). I discuss motor imagery and auditory imagery, as well as the imagery of imagined pitch and notes in some detail in chapter 2.

18. Epicurus's own writings barely survived classical antiquity (and only in fragments), but his work lived on primarily though the Roman poet Lucretius, who was much admired and imitated through the late eighteenth century. As the seventeenth-century Epicurean Margaret Cavendish describes the problem of materialism, "*Fancy* cannot be without some *Braines*." Cavendish, *Poems and Fancies* (Menton, UK: Scolar Press, 1972), 44. This strain of materialism runs through eighteenth-century aesthetics, especially in Burke and George Berkeley. See G. Gabrielle

Starr, "Cavendish, Aesthetics, and the Anti-Platonic Line," *Eighteenth-Century Studies* 29, no. 3 (2006), and Richard Kroll, *The Material Word: Literate Culture in the Restoration and Early Eighteenth Century* (Baltimore, MD: Johns Hopkins University Press, 1991).

19. See Edmund Burke, *A Philosophical Enquiry into the Origin of our Ideas of the Sublime and Beautiful* (New York: Oxford University Press, 1990), pt. 5, and Mitchell, *Iconology*, 116–142.

20. See, for example, Zenon Pylyshyn, "Return of the Mental Image: Are There Really Pictures in the Brain?," *Trends in Cognitive Sciences* 7, no. 3 (2003), and Gregoire Borst and Stephen Kosslyn, "Visual Mental Imagery and Visual Perception: Structural Equivalence Revealed by Scanning Processes," *Memory and Cognition* 36, no. 4 (2008).

21. Lipking, *The Ordering of the Arts*.

22. I am grateful to Molly Ott Ambler, who took me to see this piece by the City Ballet in New York.

23. John Keats, *The Complete Poems*, ed. Jack Stillinger (Cambridge, MA: Belknap Press of Harvard University Press, 1982).

24. "Ode on a Grecian Urn" offers a concentrating lens on one way the experience of the arts can be puzzling as well as powerful—a lens more compelling to me as a scholar, perhaps, because of the moment in which Keats is writing: that of the emergence of aesthetics as a philosophical discipline, but also of the discipline of literary criticism, the field devoted to understanding how one particular art attains its cultural and intellectual importance. (If aesthetics offers a generalizable view of the arts, specific disciplinary foci emerge to address differences across artistic objects and experiences.)

25. See, for example, Plato, "Laws II," in *Musical Aesthetics: A Historical Reader*, ed. Edward A. Lippman, vol. 1 (New York: Pendragon Press, 1986). For a modern view of how emotion in music might be mimetic not just in terms of "voice" but also of motion and rhythm, see P. N. Johnson-Laird and Keith Oatley, "Emotions, Music, and Literature," in *Handbook of Emotions*, 3rd ed., ed. Michael Lewis, Jeannette M. Haviland-Jones, and Lisa Feldman Barrett (New York: Guilford Press, 2008). See also Lippman, *Musical Thought in Ancient Greece*.

26. Aristotle, *Poetics* 6; 1450b 1–3, 25–28; 1447a 15–25; 1448a 5; 1454b 10–11); 1460b 8–11; Hagstrum, *Sister Arts*, 5–9.

27. Philip Sidney, "The Defence of Poesy," in *Sidney's "The Defence of Poesy" and Selected Renaissance Literary Criticism*, ed. Gavin Alexandar (New York: Penguin, 2004), 34. On the question of assessment, see Jerome Stolnitz, "On the Cognitive Triviality of Art," *British Journal of Aesthetics* 32 (1992).

28. Berys Gaut, "Art and Cognition," in *Contemporary Debates in Aesthetics and the Philosophy of Art*, ed. Matthew Kieran (Malden, MA: Basil Blackwell, 2006); Martha Nussbaum, *Love's Knowledge: Essays on Philosophy and Literature* (New York: Oxford University Press, 1992); Gregory Currie, "Realism of Character and the Value of Fiction," in *Aesthetics and Ethics: Essays at the Intersection*, ed. Jerrold Levinson (Cambridge: Cambridge University Press, 1998). Denise Gigante argues that modern aesthetics fundamentally involves appetitive experience, and that the concept of "taste" acknowledges this: *Taste: A Literary History* (New Haven, CT: Yale University Press, 2005), 2. On learning through emotional response and engagement, see Jenefer Robinson, *Deeper Than Reason: Emotion and Its Role in Literature, Music, and Art* (New York: Oxford University Press, 2005), and David Novitz, *Knowledge, Fiction and Imagination* (Philadelphia: Temple University Press, 1987).

29. Michael Tye, "The Subjective Qualities of Experience," *Mind* 95, no. 377 (1986): 13; Peter Lamarque, "Learning from Literature," *Dalhousie Review* 77 (1997); Susan L. Feagin, "Imagining Emotions and Appreciating Fiction," in *Emotion and the Arts*, ed. Mette Hjort and Sue Laver (New York: Oxford University Press, 1997).

30. Much of the history of this debate relies on questions about fiction and painting. A more robust account of the knowledge of aesthetics ought to be broadly applicable to the Sisters and beyond them.

31. Peter de Bolla, *Art Matters* (Cambridge, MA: Harvard University Press, 2003), 17.

32. Susan Feagin claims that the arts can give us "a restructuring of experience," "Imagining Emotions and Appreciating Fiction," 60. This is a question of emotion for her: "Art educates the emotions not by giving us knowledge by acquaintance of what they are *really* like, but by expanding our knowledge of the myriad ways affective states can be identified and distinguished from one another" (60).

33. Francis Hutcheson, "To the Author of the Dublin Journal," in *Eighteenth-Century British Aesthetics*, ed. Dabney Townsend (Amityville, NY: Baywood, 1999), 142.

34. Hutcheson argues that "laughter . . . is necessarily pleasant to us" (145).

35. Butler begins his analysis of the pleasures of art, and particularly of the pleasures of poetry, by focusing on humor as well: "jokes can help us to see what is involved in the pleasures of understanding a poem, where once more we so often have the pleasure of matching apparently incongruous conceptual frameworks, to make an implicative sense which is satisfying to us." Christopher Butler, *Pleasure and the Arts* (New York: Oxford University Press, 2004), 7.

36. Jenefer Robinson argues thus that the emotions of art, including laughter, can be morally educative: *Deeper Than Reason,* especially 112–113.

37. Nelson Goodman argues that painting thus is valuable because it makes us see differently: "it may bring out neglected likenesses and differences, force unaccustomed associations, and in some measure remake our world. And if the point of the picture is not only successfully made but is also well-taken, if the realignments it directly and indirectly effects are interesting and important, the picture . . . makes a genuine contribution to knowledge." Nelson Goodman, *Languages of Art: An Approach to a Theory of Symbols*, 2nd ed. (Indianapolis: Hackett, 1976), 33.

38. Keats, "Ode to a Nightingale," in *The Complete Poems*. There is more than an aesthetic response implied in these lines, but the "toll," as a sound that is more than merely sound and more than purely semantic force, is certainly aesthetic, too.

39. Sianne Ngai has reminded us that the aesthetic lexicon goes much deeper than this, pervading our culture; she asks us to focus on terms that are minor in philosophy but highly significant in daily life, such as "cute." The list is indeed long of terms with aesthetic valence that are frequently employed in our cultures, including "bad," "chic," "stylish," "fabulous," "neat," "charming," "sweet," "bold," "cool," "fresh," "epic," "wicked," and so on. Sianne Ngai, "Stuplimity: Shock and Boredom in Twentieth-Century Aesthetics," *Postmodern Culture* 10, no. 2 (2000), and Ngai, "The Cuteness of the Avant Garde," *Critical Inquiry* 31 (Summer 2005).

40. Baumgarten's initial definition of aesthetics as the study of how sensations enter into thought paves the way for an empiricist aesthetics throughout the eighteenth century, and both Burke and Hume are interested in perceptions of the external world as well as with the world of

feelings. Hutcheson, though relatively speaking an idealist, is convinced that emotional perception is part of the foundation of aesthetic experience. Kant famously maintained that judgments concerning beauty are not emotional judgments (while judgments concerning the sublime are) and that the pleasure that accompanies aesthetic judgments is in fact produced by the judgment. Kant's argument depends in part on a somewhat idiosyncratic system whereby emotion is one term among many; emotions, affects, and passion have varying strengths and varying relations to the will and to the moral capacity for resistance. See sections 1.9, 1.13–14, and "General Comment on the Exposition of Aesthetic Reflective Judgments" in Kant, *Critique of Judgment*. The history of the philosophical treatments of emotion and aesthetic experience is complex, but key texts include Hutcheson, *An Inquiry into the Original of our Ideas of Beauty and Virtue,* ed. Wolfgang Leidhold (Indianapolis: Liberty Fund, 2004); David Hume, "Of the Standard of Taste," in *Eighteenth-Century British Aesthetics,* ed. Dabney Townsend (Amityville, NY: Baywood, 1999); Burke, *A Philosophical Enquiry into the Origin of our Ideas of the Sublime and Beautiful*; Georg Hegel, *Introductory Lectures on Aesthetics*, trans. Bernard Bonsanquet, ed. Michael Inwood (New York: Penguin, 1993); Theodor Adorno, *Aesthetic Theory*, trans. Robert Hullot-Kentor (Minneapolis: University of Minnesota Press, 1997); and Gerard Genette, *The Aesthetic Relation*, trans. G. M. Goshgarian (Ithaca, NY: Cornell University Press, 1999).

41. Frank Sibley, "Particularity, Art and Evaluation," *Aristotelian Society Supplementary Volume* 48 (1974), and Sibley, "Aesthetic and Nonaesthetic," *Philosophical Review* 74, no. 2 (1965).

42. Equally, Robert Solomon argues that all emotions are evaluative, with similar implications for aesthetics: *The Passions: Emotions and the Meaning of Life* (Indianapolis: Hackett, 1993), 132–134. Hume argues that taste is based on the "finer emotions of the mind": "Of the Standard of Taste," 233. Prinz writes, "An artwork is aesthetically good (bad) for an evaluator if that evaluator upholds aesthetic standards that dispose those who internalize them to experience an emotion of appreciation (depreciation): a. An aesthetic standard is a norm governing emotional responses to features of artworks, including intrinsic features and their mode of production; b. To uphold a standard is to internalize it or to defer to someone who internalizes it": "Can Critics Be Dispassionate? The Role of Emotion in Aesthetic Judgment," paper presented at a meeting of the American Society for Aesthetics, Houston, 2004.

43. See Peter de Bolla: "the great value of art lies in its power to prompt us to share experiences, worlds, beliefs, and differences. And our *affective* experiences of art provide a terrain upon which these singular worlds, beliefs, and differences may be mapped," *Art Matters,* 15. See also Christopher Butler: "literary and visual works of art can provoke a particular type of understanding, which gives us pleasure in new-connection-making structures, which are very often, perhaps primarily, metaphorical," *Pleasure and the Arts,* 10. I argue that these connection-making structures are literal.

44. See Peter de Bolla: "In the philosopher Morris Weitz's term, art is an 'open concept'—it must accommodate the permanent possibility of change, expansion, or novelty," *Art Matters,* 11.

45. There are significant debates about which of these dimensions is the most important and which are in fact constitutive. Jesse Prinz gives a wonderful critical resume of emotion theories broadly understood in *Gut Reactions: A Perceptual Theory of Emotion* (New York: Oxford University Press, 2006). See also the monographs by Edmund T. Rolls, *Emotion Explained* (New York: Oxford University Press, 2005); Joseph LeDoux, *The Emotional Brain: The Mysterious Underpinnings of Emotional Life* (New York: Simon and Schuster, 1998); and Antonio Damasio, *The Feeling of What Happens: Body and Emotion in the Making of Consciousness* (New York: Harcourt, 1999). The amygdala and insula also carry out other functions but are essential parts of fear and disgust circuitry (there are other components of the circuitry of these emotions as well.) On fear and the amygdala, see C. D. Blanchard and R. J. Blanchard, "Innate and Conditioned Reactions to Threat in Rats with Amygdaloid Lesions," *Journal of Comparative and Physiological Psychology* 81 (1972); M. Davis, "The Role of the Amygdala in Emotional Learning," *International Review of Neurobiology* 36 (1994); LeDoux, *The Emotional Brain;* and Elizabeth A. Phelps, "Emotion and Cognition: Insights from Studies of the Human Amygdala," *Annual Review of Psychology* 527 (2006). On the insula and disgust, see D. S. Husted, N. A. Shapira, and W. K. Goodman, "The Neurocircuitry of Obsessive-Compulsive Disorder and Disgust," *Progress in Neuro-Psychopharmacology & Biological Psychiatry* 30 (2006); and M. L. Phillips, A. W. Young, C. Senior, M. Brammer, C. Andrew, S.C.R. Williams, J. A. Gray, and A. S. David, "A Specific Neural Substrate for Perceiving Facial Expressions of Disgust," *Nature* 389 (1997).

46. The phrase is taken from Tor D. Wager, Lisa Feldman Barrett, Eliza Bliss-Moreau, Kristen A. Lindquist, Seth Duncan, Hedy Kober, Josh Joseph, Matthew Davidson, and Jennifer Mize, "The Neuroimaging of Emotion," in *Handbook of Emotions*, 3rd ed., ed. Michael Lewis, Jeannette M. Haviland-Jones, and Lisa Feldman Barrett (New York: Guilford Press, 2008).

47. Neural activity in reward processing is a computational signal that indicates the strength of a reward, as well as registering the difference between "wanting" a reward and "liking" it. It also can compute the difference between our expected reward and what we actually receive. See Tiago V. Maia, "Reinforcement Learning, Conditioning, and the Brain: Successes and Challenges," *Cognitive, Affective, & Behavioral Neuroscience* 9, no. 4 (2009).

48. Anne. J. Blood and Robert Zatorre, "Intensely Pleasurable Responses to Music Correlate with Activity in Brain Regions Implicated in Reward and Emotion," *Proceedings of the National Academy of Sciences of the United States of America* 98 (2001); Thomas Jacobsen, Ricarda I. Schubotz, Lea Höfel, and D. Yves von Cramon, "Brain Correlates of Aesthetic Judgment of Beauty," *NeuroImage* 29 (2006); Hideaki Kawabata and Semir Zeki, "Neural Correlates of Beauty," *Journal of Neurophysiology* 91 (2004); Oshin Vartanian and V. Goel, "Neuroanatomical Correlates of Aesthetic Preference for Paintings," *NeuroReport* 15 (2004).

49. Edward A. Vessel, G. Gabrielle Starr, and Nava Rubin, "The Brain on Art: Intense Aesthetic Experience Activates the Default Mode Network," *Frontiers in Human Neuroscience* 6, no. 66 (2012).

50. On the overlap of the default mode network and imagery networks, see Samuel T. Moulton and Stephen Kosslyn, "Imagining Predictions: Mental Imagery as Mental Emulation," *Philosophical Transactions of the Royal Society of London, Series B, Biological Sciences* 264 (2009), and Dennis Hassabis, Dharshan Kurmara, and Eleanor A. Maguire, "Using Imagination to Understand the Neural Basis of Episodic Memory," *Journal of Neuroscience* 27, no. 52 (2007). I argue in chapter 2 that the distributed nature of imagery processes gives them something of a leg up in giving access to the broader web of aesthetic response.

51. Evaluative conditioning/associative learning is another model for explaining how emotion influences learned behaviors. A conditioned stimulus (one that we have learned to evaluate based on a reinforcement

paradigm) is coupled with a neutral stimulus, and the previously neutral stimulus begins to take on the emotional evaluation associated with the conditioned stimulus. However, this model does not fully describe what happens with aesthetic experience, either, though emotional associations may contribute to aesthetic experience.

52. See Ellen Spolsky, "Making 'Quite Anew': Brain Modularity and Creativity," in *Introduction to Cognitive Cultural Studies,* ed. Lisa Zunshine (Baltimore, MD: Johns Hopkins University Press, 2010). Spolsky argues that "multiple sense modalities" are key to Raphael's representation of the problem of the transfiguration of Christ.

53. For a review of the literature on this subject, see Maia, "Reinforcement Learning." On reward prediction localization, see Brian Knutson and Jeffrey C. Cooper, "Functional Magnetic Resonance Imaging of Reward Prediction," *Current Opinion in Neurology* 18 (2005).

54. An evolutionary psychologist might argue that sometime in the Pleistocene era the architecture of the human brain was essentially established; anything of which we are capable now we were generally capable of then. On average, culture changes faster than does human biology. Discussions of gene-culture coevolution are interesting in this regard, however, and give us examples where this is not the case. For example, the evolution of the gene that enables the digestion of cow's milk evolved closely with the domestication of cattle: Clare Holden and Ruth Mace, "Phylogenetic Analysis of the Evolution of Lactose Digestion in Adults," *Human Biology* 81, nos. 5–6 (2009). For solid critiques of some instances of the influence of evolutionary psychology on literary study, see Patrick Colm Hogan, *Cognitive Science, Literature and the Arts* (New York: Routledge, 2003), chap. 8, and Jonathan Kramnick, "Against Literary Darwinism," *Critical Inquiry* 37, no. 2 (2011).

55. Mara Miller, *The Garden as an Art* (Albany: State University of New York Press, 1993); Denis Dutton, *The Art Instinct: Beauty, Pleasure, and Human Evolution* (London: Bloomsbury, 2010); Steven Pinker, *How the Mind Works* (New York: Norton, 1999). See also a special issue of the *Journal of Aesthetics and Art Criticism* on environmental aesthetics, vol. 56, no. 2 (Spring 1998).

56. Edward A. Vessel and Nava Rubin, "Beauty and the Beholder: Highly Individual Taste for Abstract, but Not Real-World Images," *Journal of Vision* 10, no. 2 (2010).

57. Alan Richardson eloquently critiques these kind of failed explanations in *The Neural Sublime* (Baltimore: Johns Hopkins University Press, 2010): "At their crudest, they may suggest, say, that 'mating programs' evolutionarily designed into the human genome drive the romantic chess games played out in a given Jane Austen novel" (5).

58. Blakey Vermeule shows this with elegance in *Why Do We Care about Literary Characters?* (Baltimore, MD: Johns Hopkins University Press, 2009), in which she argues that what makes the novel unique is the convergence of evolutionary imperatives with the cultural demands of a particular historical moment. Vermeule is a standout in this field, along with Ellen Spolsky and Lisa Zunshine: all three are keenly aware of the way in which the basic evolutionary forces that shape human cognition only become the canvas on which other forces are at work. Vermeule, for example, explains how the social and cultural particulars of eighteenth-century Britain mean concerns about sympathy and imagined characters emerge in a particular shape (eighteenth-century novels). Spolsky is interested in how human creativity is enabled by the evolved brain and mind, and Zunshine has explored the ways in which culture both acts on and through our cognitive architecture and is itself subject to the evolved architecture of cognition. Zunshine's *Why We Read Fiction: Theory of Mind and the Novel* (Columbus: Ohio State University Press, 2006) shows us how the evolved need for a theory of mind underpins our experiences of fiction, while her *Strange Concepts and the Stories They Make Possible* (Baltimore, MD: Johns Hopkins University Press, 2009) explores the ways in which the tensions in our cognitive architecture help produce literary fascinations.

59. An underconstrained problem is one in which the available variables are unable to provide a unique solution. For example, if you draw a circle on a window, that same field could circumscribe a bug on the pane, a robin twenty feet away, or an elephant somewhere in the distance: two dimensional representations cannot adequately represent something that exists in three.

60. Thomas Nagel, "What Is It Like to Be a Bat?," *Philosophical Review* 83, no. 4 (1974). Evolution can indeed give us intriguing clues as to the kinds of stories human beings like or the types of social interaction and theories of mind on which literature must be based, and which novelists and poets creatively exploit and manipulate.

61. For a clear and eloquent statement about some of the advantages of a cognitive approach to literary studies (as opposed to an evolutionary one), see the introduction to a special issue of *Poetics Today*: Alan Richardson and Francis F. Steen, "Literature and the Cognitive Revolution: An Introduction," *Poetics Today* 23, no. 1 (2002).

62. The work my collaborators and I have done combines objective measures (fMRI) with behavioral experiments that involved self-reports of emotion and gave subjects room to describe their own experiences more fully in written form. As Stephen Kosslyn points out, knowledge of neuroanatomy is not particularly useful without a measure of behavior.

63. Geoffrey Hartman, *The Fate of Reading* (Chicago: University of Chicago Press, 1975) 22; Nagel, "What Is It Like to Be a Bat?"; Kevis Goodman, "On Geoffrey Hartman's Psycho-Aesthetics," *Wordsworth Circle* 37, no. 1 (2006).

64. There are several key players espousing different positions in the debate over what literature "does" in this sense. The idea of poems "doing" things most significantly can be traced to the work of I. A. Richards. See I. A. Richards, *Principles of Literary Criticism* (New York: Routledge, 2001); Wimsatt and Beardsley, *The Verbal Icon*; Stanley Fish, "Literature in the Reader: Affective Stylistics," *New Literary History* 2, no. 1 (1970); and Michel Riffaterre, "The Stylistic Approach to Literary History," *New Literary History* 2, no. 1 (1970).

Chapter 1

1. Processing fluency theory argues, perhaps much as does Kant, that ease of neural processing, manifesting the suitability of an object to our neural activity, is the basis for aesthetic pleasure. Kant starts his investigation from the seeming necessity of judgments about the beautiful and posits that the way in which imagination presents images to us in conformity with its own principles produces the pleasure of beauty. See the section "Analytic of the Beautiful" in Immanuel Kant, *Critique of Judgment*, trans. Werner S. Pluhar (Indianapolis: Hackett, 1987). On processing fluency, see Rolf Reber, Norbert Schwarz, and Piotr Winkielman, "Processing Fluency and Aesthetic Pleasure: Is Beauty in the Perceiver's Processing Experience?," *Personality and Social Psychology Review* 8, no. 4 (2004). For a contrary view, see Ingo Rentschler, Martin Jüttner, Alexander Unzicker, and Theodor Landis, "Innate and Learned Components of Human Visual Preference," *Current Biology* 9 (1999).

2. Eric Kandel does a masterful job of exploring these subjective contours (as well as universal features of perception) for a single subgenre in a single period, Viennese portraiture, in *The Age of Insight: The Quest to Understand the Unconscious in Art, Mind, and Brain, from Vienna 1900 to the Present* (New York: Random House, 2012). He gives a slightly different account of emotion, in that by focusing on portraiture he generally assumes a congruity between the emotion represented and the emotion elicited by a work of art. With other forms of visual art such a conformity does not exist, as I discuss below.

3. Robert L. Solso, *Cognition and the Visual Arts* (Cambridge, MA: MIT Press, 1996); Semir Zeki, *Inner Vision: An Exploration of Art and the Brain* (New York: Oxford University Press, 2000); Irving Biederman and Edward A. Vessel, "Perceptual Pleasure and the Brain," *American Scientist* 94 (2006).

4. Following Shaftesbury and Kant, a number of philosophers have argued that pure aesthetic judgments ought to be free from "interest"—from desire, merely personal considerations (warm memories, and so forth), conceptions of utility, and even any concern about the existence of the object itself. Arthur Schopenhauer gives one of the most influential statements of an aesthetic attitude in *The World as Will and Representation* (New York: Dover Publications, 1966), 1:178ff. See also E. Bullough, "'Psychical Distance' as a Factor in Art and as an Aesthetic Principle," *British Journal of Psychology* 5 (1912), and Jerome Stolnitz, "On the Origins of 'Aesthetic Disinterestedness,'" *Journal of Aesthetics and Art Criticism* 20 (1961). For a critique, see George Dickie, "The Myth of the Aesthetic Attitude," *American Philosophical Quarterly* 1 (1964).

5. The rise of behaviorism after William James largely relegated the discussion of the subjective and bodily dimensions of emotion to philosophy. Perhaps most important in this history is the tradition of phenomenology. See Maurice Merleau-Ponty, *Phenomenology of Perception*, trans. Colin Smith (New York: Routledge, 2002).

6. Eva M. Dadlez gives a good résumé of these arguments in *What's Hecuba to Him? Fictional Events and Actual Emotions* (University Park: Pennsylvania State University Press, 1997). She focuses on the question of belief, arguing that valid beliefs about moral life motivate emotional responses to art. Jesse Prinz, however, in *Gut Reactions: A Perceptual Theory of Emotion* (New York: Oxford University Press, 2006) convincingly argues that belief is not necessary to emotions in daily life. He also

contends that maintaining a belief requirement for emotions relies on outmoded psychological concepts. In his view, emotions are also an indispensable part of all aesthetic evaluations (see his two conference papers, "Can Critics Be Dispassionate? The Role of Emotion in Aesthetic Judgment," presented at a meeting of the American Society for Aesthetics, Houston, 2004, and "Emotion and Aesthetic Value," presented at a meeting of the American Philosophical Association, Pacific Division, San Francisco, 2007). Jenefer Robinson has given a strong and convincing defense of emotional responses to art in the absence of belief in *Deeper Than Reason: Emotion and Its Role in Literature, Music, and Art* (New York: Oxford University Press, 2005).

7. Research has shown that patients with impaired emotional responses have altered beliefs about outcomes on gambling tasks: Antoine Bechara, Hannah Damasio, Daniel Tranel, and Antonio Damasio, "Deciding Advantageously before Knowing the Advantageous Strategy," *Science* 275 (1997); Antonio Damasio, *Descartes' Error: Emotion, Reason, and the Human Brain* (New York: HarperCollins, 1995). The field of neuroeconomics has in part been built on studying the influence of emotion on decision making. See also, for example, the body of work on racial bias, where it is now clear that fear processing is independent of stated and defended beliefs: Elizabeth A. Phelps, C. J. Cannaistraci, and W.A. Cunningham, "Intact Performance on an Indirect Measure of Race Bias Following Amygdala Damage," *Neuropsychologia* 41 (2003); Allen J. Hart, Paul J. Whalen, Lisa M. Shin, Sean C. McInerney, Hakan Fischer, and Scott L. Rauch, "Differential Response in the Human Amygdala to Racial Outgroup vs. Ingroup Face Stimuli," *NeuroReport* 11, no. 11 (2000). It is also arguable that insofar as emotions emerge from perceptual input (what we see, hear, or otherwise sense can be the stimulus that drives an emotion), perception can be constrained not so much by belief as by the heuristics that govern the processing of perceptual systems. Contemporary philosophers enamored of the belief condition tend to turn to appraisal theories of emotion for support. Such theories contend that emotions are elicited and differentiable based on subjective evaluations of events; these evaluations would generally require beliefs about these events, but these beliefs need not be veridical. In addition, appraisal theories do not contend that appraisals are necessary and sufficient conditions for emotional response. The use of games for the elicitation of emotion in experimental conditions testifies to the ways in which the appraisal of events can be directed at fictional circumstances (and when the payoff of

the imaginary is in fact real). For a good summary of appraisal theory, see Gerald L. Clore and Andrew Ortony, "Appraisal Theories: How Cognition Shapes Affect into Emotion," in *Handbook of Emotions*, 3rd ed., ed. Michael Lewis, Jeannette M. Haviland-Jones, and Lisa Feldman Barrett (New York: Guilford Press, 2008), and Klaus R. Scherer, "Appraisal Theory," in *Handbook of Cognition and Emotion*, ed. Tim Dalgleish and Mick Power (New York: Wiley, 1999). For a more detailed view of the stages of appraisal as neural processing, see Didier Grandjean and Klaus R. Scherer, "Unpacking the Cognitive Architecture of Emotion Processes," *Emotion* 8, no. 3 (2008). Robert Gordon gives an interesting solution to the belief problem in part by distinguishing classes of emotions and focusing on the question of knowledge in *The Structure of Emotions: Investigations in Cognitive Philosophy* (Cambridge: Cambridge University Press, 1990).

8. Nico H. Frijda, "The Psychologists' Point of View," in *Handbook of Emotions*, 3rd ed., ed. Michael Lewis, Jeannette M. Haviland-Jones, and Lisa Feldman Barrett (New York: Guilford Press, 2008), 72. Some theorists argue that the concept of the action tendency was developed primarily in the study of negative emotions and that in general, it is harder to link an action tendency to positive emotions such as joy, which if anything have very generalized action tendencies to a variety of behaviors (why pick out skipping or singing, for example?): Barbara L. Fredrickson and Michael A. Cohn, "Positive Emotions," in *Handbook of Emotions*, 3rd ed., ed. Michael Lewis, Jeannette M. Haviland-Jones, and Lisa Feldman Barrett (New York: Guilford Press, 2008). On the phenomenon of "depressive realism," see, in summary, Prinz, *Gut Reactions,* 8, as well as Tiffany Fu, Wilma Koutstaal, Cynthia H. Y. Fu, Lucia Poon, and Anthony J. Cleare, "Depression, Confidence, and Decision: Evidence against Depressive Realism," *Journal of Psychopathology and Behavioral Assessment* 27, no. 4 (2005), and Lauren B. Alloy and Lyn Y. Abramson, "Judgment of Contingency in Depressed and Nondepressed Students: Sadder But Wiser?," *Journal of Experimental Psychology: General* 108, no. 4 (1979).

9. See Tamar Szabó Gendler and Karson Kovakovich, "Genuine Rational Fictional Emotions," in *Contemporary Debates in Aesthetics and the Philosophy of Art*, ed. Matthew Kieran (Malden, MA: Blackwell, 2005); Prinz, *Gut Reactions;* and Frijda, "The Psychologists' Point of View."

10. See Keith Oatley and P. N. Johnson-Laird, "The Communicative Theory of Emotions: Empirical Tests, Mental Models, and Implications for Social Interaction," in *Striving and Feeling: Interactions among Goals, Affect, and Self-Regulation*, ed. Leonard L. Martin and Abraham Tesser (Hillsdale, NJ: Erlbaum, 1996).

11. Jaak Panksepp, "The Affective Brain and Core Consciousness: How Does Neural Activity Generate Emotional Feelings?," in *Handbook of Emotions*, 3rd ed., ed. Michael Lewis, Jeannette M. Haviland-Jones, and Lisa Feldman Barrett (New York: Guilford Press, 2008).

12. Klaus R. Scherer, "Toward a Concept of 'Modal Emotions,'" in *The Nature of Emotion*, ed. P. Ekman and R. J. Davidson (New York: Oxford University Press, 1994), 27, emphasis in original. See also Lisa Feldman Barrett, "Are Emotions Natural Kinds?," *Perspectives on Psychological Science* 1, no. 1 (2006).

13. For a dissenting view, which claims that the basic emotions are the *only* product of art, see P. N. Johnson-Laird and Keith Oatley, "Emotions, Music, and Literature," in *Handbook of Emotions*, 3rd ed., ed. Michael Lewis, Jeannette M. Haviland-Jones, and Lisa Feldman Barrett (New York: Guilford Press, 2008). The basic emotions are objects of representation in painting, poetry, and music (Stravinsky portrays the fear surrounding the sacrifice of the dancer in the *Rite of Spring*, for example) but we do not always feel these emotions in response to art, and it is quite probable that the frequency with which we might feel particular emotional responses to artworks differs from the frequency with which we feel those emotions in everyday life. Just because, for example, we are shown a representation of an angry man, we do not necessarily feel anger or fear in response, though we might be likely to do so in real life. It is also clear that people are able to identify the emotions represented by works of art with consistency (Johnson-Laird and Oatley, "Emotions, Music, and Literature"; M. De Vega, I. Leon, and J. M. Diaz, "The Representations of Changing Emotions in Reading Comprehension," *Cognition and Emotion* 10, no. 3 [1996]; Isabelle Peretz and Lisa Gagnon, "Dissociation between Recognition and Emotional Judgements for Melodies," *Neurocase* 5 [1999]). The distinction between experience and representation has had a significant history in debates surrounding aesthetic thought and emotion theory and research.

14. David Hume, "Of the Standard of Taste," in *Eighteenth-Century British Aesthetics*, ed. Dabney Townsend (Amityville, NY: Baywood,

1999), 233; Edmund Burke, *A Philosophical Enquiry into the Origin of our Ideas of the Sublime and Beautiful* (New York: Oxford University Press, 1990).

15. Peter Kivy, *Music Alone: Philosophical Reflections on the Purely Musical Experience* (Ithaca, NY: Cornell University Press, 1990), 161.

16. Marcel Zentner, Didier Grandjean, and Klaus R. Scherer, "Emotions Evoked by the Sound of Music: Characterization, Classification, and Measurement," *Emotion* 8, no. 4 (2008).

17. See Peter de Bolla, *Art Matters* (Cambridge, MA: Harvard University Press, 2001), 16–17. It is worth noting the significance of cultural differences here as well; the subjects of Zentner and colleagues were francophone, and we have these terms only in translation: Marcel Zentner, Didier Grandjean, and Klaus R. Scherer, "Emotions Evoked by the Sound of Music: Characterization, Classification, and Measurement," *Emotion* 8, no. 4 (2008). But experiments with Noh masks provide further evidence of the way emotion structures may be conserved even when emotional interpretations vary: see Michael J. Lyons Ruth Campbell, Andre Plante, Mike Coleman, Miyuki Kamachi, and Shigeru Agamatsu, "The Noh Mask Effect: Vertical Viewpoint Dependence of Facial Expression Perception," *Proceedings: Biological Sciences* 267, no. 1459 (2000).

18. Zentner et al., "Emotions Evoked by the Sound of Music," 495; Nico H. Frijda and Louise Sundararajan, "Emotion Refinement: A Theory Inspired by Chinese Poetics," *Perspectives on Psychological Science* 2 (2007).

19. There also may be differences in the emotional palette of aesthetic experience as compared to everyday life. For example, representations of and responses to emotion vary by artistic genre. Anger matters in some genres—tragedy or the social novel—as does fear—again, in tragedy, but also in thrillers and horror. One might seek out artworks that elicit emotions one feels absent in daily life, from romance novels to horror movies; moreover, one might preferentially seek out these kinds of works based on one's own emotional predispositions, or one might seek genres given high value in one's culture. These might skew the emotions of aesthetic life in a variety of directions in comparison with those of an individual's baseline emotional world.

20. Tor D. Wager, Lisa Feldman Barrett, Eliza Bliss-Moreau, Kristen A. Lindquist, Seth Duncan, Hedy Kober, Josh Joseph, Matthew Davidson, and Jennifer Mize, "The Neuroimaging of Emotion," in *Handbook of*

Emotions, 3rd ed., ed. Michael Lewis, Jeannette M. Haviland-Jones, and Lisa Feldman Barrett (New York: Guilford Press, 2008), 251; K. Luan Phan, Tor D. Wager, S. F. Taylor, and I. Liberzon, "Functional Neuroimaging Studies of Human Emotions," *CNS Spectrums* 9, no. 4 (2004).

21. Fredrickson and Cohn, "Positive Emotions"; Wager et al., "The Neuroimaging of Emotion," 258–260. See also John D. Teasdale, Robert J. Howard, Sally G. Cox, Yvonne Ha, M. Brammer, S.C.R. Williams, and Stuart A. Checkley, "Functional MRI Study of the Cognitive Generation of Affect," *American Journal of Psychiatry* 156, no. 2 (1999).

22. Anne J. Blood and Robert Zatorre, "Intensely Pleasurable Responses to Music Correlate with Activity in Brain Regions Implicated in Reward and Emotion," *Proceedings of the National Academy of Sciences of the United States of America* 98 (2001); Robert Zatorre, "Music, the Food of Neuroscience?," *Nature* 434, no. 7031 (2005). See also Istvan Molnar-Szakacs and Katie Overy, "Music and Mirror Neurons: From Motion to 'E'motion," *SCAN* 1 (2006); Stefan Koelsch, Thomas Fritz, D. Yves Von Cramon, Karsten Müller, and Angela Friederici, "Investigating Emotion with Music: An fMRI Study," *Human Brain Mapping* 27 (2006); Alf Gabrielsson, "Emotions in Strong Experiences with Music," *Music and Emotion: Theory and Research*, ed. Patrik N. Juslin and John A. Sloboda (New York: Oxford University Press, 2001); V. Menon and Daniel J. Levitin, "The Rewards of Music Listening: Response and Physiological Connectivity of the Mesolimbic System," *NeuroImage* 28 (2005); Isabelle Peretz and Robert J. Zatorre, "Brain Organization for Music Processing," *Annual Review of Psychology* 56 (2005); and Edward A. Vessel, G. Gabrielle Starr, and Nava Rubin, "The Brain on Art: Intense Aesthetic Experience Activates the Default Mode Network," *Frontiers in Human Neuroscience* 6 (2012).

23. Laurel J. Trainor and L. A. Schmidt, "Processing Emotions Induced by Music," in *The Cognitive Neuroscience of Music*, ed. Isabelle Peretz and Robert Zatorre (New York: Oxford University Press, 2004), 316; Wager et al., "The Neuroimaging of Emotion," 259–260; H. L. Urry, J. B. Nitschke, I. Dolksi, D. C. Jackson, K. M. Dalton, C. J. Mueller, M. A. Rosenkranc, C. D. Ryff, B. H. Singer, and R. J. Davidson, "Making a Life Worth Living: Neural Correlates of Well-Being," *Psychological Science* 15, no. 6 (2004); Isabelle Peretz, "Listen to the Brain: A Biological Perspective on Musical Emotions," in *Music and Emotion: Theory and Research*, ed. Patrik N. Juslin and John A. Sloboda (New York: Oxford

University Press, 2001); Anne J. Blood, Robert Zatorre, Patrick Bermudez, and Alan C. Evans, "Emotional Responses to Pleasant and Unpleasant Music Correlate with Activity in Paralimbic Brain Region," *Nature Neuroscience* 2, no. 4 (1999).

24. Trainor and Schmidt, "Processing Emotions Induced by Music," 316–317. Citing Blood and Zatorre, "Intensely Pleasurable Responses to Music," Bromberger and colleagues found that evaluative processes are unaffected by right hemisphere lesions, suggesting again the importance of left hemispheric activity for responses to visual art: Bianca Bromberger, Rebecca Sternschein, Page Widick, William Smith, and Anjan Chatterjee, "The Right Hemisphere in Aesthetic Perception," *Frontiers in Human Neuroscience* 5 (2011).

25. Valorie N. Salimpoor, Mitchel Benovoy, Gregory Longo, Jeremy R. Cooperstock, and Robert J. Zatorre, "The Rewarding Aspects of Music Listening Are Related to Degree of Emotional Arousal," *PLoS ONE* 4, no. 10 (2009); Oliver Grewe, Frederik Nagel, Reinhard Kopiez, and Eckart Altenmuller, "Emotions over Time: Synchronicity and Development of Subjective, Physiological, and Facial Affective Reactions to Music," *Emotion* 7, no .4 (2007); Nikki S. Rickard, "Intense Emotional Responses to Music: A Test of the Physiological Arousal Hypothesis," *Psychology of Music* 32 (2004); I. Nyklicek, J. F. Thayer, and L. J. P. Van Doornen, "Cardiorespiratory Differentiation of Musically Induced Emotions," *Journal of Psychophysiology* 11 (1997).

26. We used a factor analysis to determine which of the nine emotional and evaluative terms were significantly correlated with the evaluation of the strength of the overall aesthetic response to individual paintings. Factor analyses help determine the least number of categories necessary to describe the patterns of the data (to capture the greatest variance). Factors thus do not entirely map to the categories of the original analysis but are composites, and individual categories "load" into the composite so that each factor is composed of categories assigned a weighted value adding up to 1. We identified two factors, one largely positive (composed primarily of beauty, pleasure, and joy) and one largely negative (fear, disgust, sadness, and confusion), with awe appearing in both factors, though contributing more strongly to the positive factor than to the negative.

27. Wager et al.,, "The Neuroimaging of Emotion." On the ventral striatum, see 259; on the inferior frontal gyrus, see 259; see also plates 15.1, 15.2, and 15.3 for the anterior medial prefrontal cortex, substantia nigra,

superior frontal gyrus, inferior frontal gyrus, and striatum. The medial prefrontal cortex was activated in around 50 percent of the studies reviewed by Phan and colleagues, who suggest that it offers "a plausible interaction zone between affective and cognitive processing": Phan et al., "Functional Neuroimaging Studies of Human Emotions," 262. See also Richard D. Lane, Eric. M. Reiman, Margaret M. Bradley, Peter J. Lang, Geoffrey L. Ahern, R. J. Davidson, and Gary E. Schwartz, "Neuroanatomical Correlates of Pleasant and Unpleasant Emotion," *Neuropsychologia* 35, no. 11 (1997).

28. Electroencephalography is a technique that measures changes in electrical impulses from the scalp; fMRI measures changes in oxygen metabolism, and positron emission tomography uses a radioactive glucose analog to measure metabolism as well. New techniques in fMRI, including multivoxel pattern analysis, promise to give improved resolution, as well as enabling the confident attribution of fMRI signal to small amounts of brain tissue: Kenneth A. Norman, Sean M. Polyn, Greg J. Detre, and James V. Haxby, "Beyond Mind-Reading: Multi-Voxel Pattern Analysis of fMRI Data," *Trends in Cognitive Sciences* 10, no. 9 (2006).

29. Antonio Damasio, *The Feeling of What Happens: Body and Emotion in the Making of Consciousness* (New York: Harcourt, 1999), 50. Cited in Trainor and Schmidt, "Processing Emotions Induced by Music," 314.

30. For a good review of hemispheric bias and emotion, see Nelson Torro Alves, Sérgio S. Fukusima, and J. Antonio Aznar-Casanova, "Models of Brain Asymmetry in Emotional Processing," *Psychology and Neuroscience* 1, no. 1 (2008).

31. Augustine, *Confessions*, trans. Henry Chadwick (New York: Oxford University Press, 1991), 15.

32. John Keats, "On Seeing the Elgin Marbles," in *The Complete Poems*, ed. Jack Stillinger (Cambridge, MA: Belknap Press of Harvard University Press, 1982).

33. Salimpoor et al., "The Rewarding Aspects of Music Listening"; Grewe et al., "Emotions over Time"; Jaak Panksepp, "The Emotional Sources of 'Chills' Induced by Music," *Music Perception* 13, no. 2 (1995).

34. Trainor and Schmidt, "Processing Emotions Induced by Music," 312; Koelsch et al., "Investigating Emotion with Music"; Wolfgang Tschacher, Steven Greenwood, Volker Kirchberg, Stéphanie Wintzerith, Karen van Den Berg, and Martin Tröndle, "Physiological Correlates of Aesthetic

Perception of Artworks in a Museum," *Psychology of Aesthetics, Creativity, and the Arts* 6, no. 1 (2012).

35. Research was carried out at NYU in conformity with the procedures of the University Committee on Activities Involving Human Subjects. The Catalogue of Museum Images Online may be found at: http://camio.oclc.org. We set a maximum size for images of no more than 20° of visual angle in their greatest dimension and a maximum area no more than 75 percent of a 20° box. Stimuli were presented and responses were collected using a Macintosh G4 running Matlab 6.5 and the Psychophysics Toolbox: D. H. Brainard, "The Psychophysics Toolbox," *Spatial Vision* 10 (1997).

36. We sought to minimize recognition by selecting images not commonly reproduced. Most of our subjects recognized no images, and no observer recognized more than five. Subjects ranged from novices to several who had completed some undergraduate study in art history. The 1–4 scale meant that subjects could not give a "neutral" response but had to discriminate in either the positive or negative direction. We administered the Positive and Negative Affect Schedule (PANAS), as it offers a stable, internally consistent way of measuring mood: D. Watson, L. A. Clark, and A. Tellegen, "Development and Validation of Brief Measures of Positive and Negative Affect: The PANAS Scales," *Journal of Personality and Social Psychology* 54 (1988).

37. I adapt this definition from Edmund T. Rolls, *Emotion Explained* (New York: Oxford University Press, 2005), 2 passim.

38. On reward and emotion, see, for example, Rolls, *Emotion Explained*, and Joseph E. LeDoux and Elizabeth A Phelps, "Emotional Networks in the Brain," in *Handbook of Emotions*, 3rd ed., ed. Michael Lewis, Jeannette M. Haviland-Jones, and Lisa Feldman Barrett (New York: Guilford, 2008).

39. Frijda, "The Psychologists' Point of View," 72.

40. See, for example, A. Verdejo-Garcia, M. Pérez-Garcia, andAntoine Bechara, "Emotion, Decision-Making and Substance Dependence: A Somatic-Marker Model of Addiction," *Current Neuropharmacology* 4, no. 1 (2006): 17–31; Rita Goldstein and Nora D. Volkow, "Drug Addiction and Its Underlying Neurobiological Basis: Neuroimaging Evidence for the Involvement of the Frontal Cortex," *American Journal of Psychiatry* 159, no. 10 (2002); and Ann E. Kelley, "Memory and Addiction: Shared Neural Circuitry and Molecular Mechanisms," *Neuron* 44 (2004).

41. See Rolls, *Emotion Explained*, and LeDoux and Phelps, "Emotional Networks in the Brain."

42. See, for example, Bechara et al., "Deciding Advantageously"; Jess Benhabib and A. Bisin, "Modeling Internal Commitment Mechanisms and Self-Control: A Neuroeconomics Approach to Consumption-Saving Decisions," *Games and Economic Behavior* 52, no. 2 (2005); and Ming Hsu, Cedric Anen, and Steven R. Quartz, "The Right and the Good: Distributive Justice and Neural Encoding of Equity and Efficiency," *Science* 320, no. 5879 (2008). For a good review, see Steven R. Quartz, "Reason, Emotion and Decision-Making: Risk and Reward Computation with Feeling," *Trends in Cognitive Sciences* 13, no. 5 (2009).

43. Blood and Zatorre, "Intensely Pleasurable Responses to Music"; Salimpoor et al., "The Rewarding Aspects of Music Listening"; Hideaki Kawabata and Semir Zeki, "Neural Correlates of Beauty," *Journal of Neurophysiology* 91 (2004); Menon and Levitin, "The Rewards of Music Listening"; Valorie N. Salimpoor, Mitchel Benovoy, Kevin Larcher, Alain Dagher, and Robert J. Zatorre, "Anatomically Distinct Dopamine Release during Anticipation and Experience of Peak Emotion to Music," *Nature Neuroscience* 14, no. 2 (2011).

44. Tomohiro Ishizu and Semir Zeki, "Toward a Brain-Based Theory of Beauty," *PLoS ONE* 6, no. 7 (2011). This study evaluates aesthetic experience along what the authors posit to be a single, bipolar axis: beautiful–ugly. A more multidimensional approach might reveal broader activations. In addition, while a group-level analysis produced a region of overlap common to music and visual art, it is unclear whether and to what degree responses overlap in any individual participant. Still, this is a promising and important first effort to describe aesthetic response across artistic modes.

45. Oshin Vartanian, "Conscious Experience of Pleasure in Art," in *Neuroaesthetics*, ed. Martin Skov and Oshin Vartanian (Amityville, NY: Baywood, 2009), 264.

46. As John Guillory notes, "the problem of 'aesthetic value' is not in fact a perennial problem, but can be posed as such only after the divergence of aesthetics and political economy, and as a consequence of the repression of their convergent origin," *Cultural Capital* (Chicago: University of Chicago Press, 1993).

47. Adorno, *Aesthetic Theory*; Nussbaum, *Love's Knowledge*.

48. Biederman and Vessel, "Perceptual Pleasure and the Brain."

49. See, for example, G. H. Orians, "An Evolutionary Perspective on Aesthetics," *Bulletin of Psychology and the Arts* 2 (2001), or Nancy Etcoff, *Survival of the Prettiest: The Science of Beauty* (New York: Doubleday, 1999).

50. See T. V. Maia, "Reinforcement Learning, Conditioning, and the Brain: Successes and Challenges," *Cognitive, Affective & Behavioral Neuroscience* 9, no. 4 (2009), on the wanting versus liking distinction. See a discussion of wanting versus liking in painting in Vessel et al., "The Brain on Art."

51. On the ways that mood can change our experience, see, for example, work that shows the so-called Mozart effect (increased performance on a spatial task following musical experience) is probably due to mood and arousal effects: William Forde Thompson, E. Glenn Schellenberg, and Gabriela Husain, "Arousal, Mood, and the Mozart Effect," *Psychological Science* 12, no. 3 (2001). Daniel Levitin describes the new perspective given by aesthetic experience nicely with regard to the Beatles' "She Loves You" and the revelation of a new way to close a musical sequence in *The World in Six Songs: How the Musical Brain Created Human Nature* (New York: Plume, 2009), 107ff.

52. See, for example, Paul Glimcher, *Foundations of Neuroeconomic Analysis* (New York: Oxford, 2010); Scott A. Huettel, C. Jill Stowe, Evan M. Gordon, Brent T. Warner, and Michael L. Platt, "Neural Signatures of Economic Preferences for Risk and Ambiguity," *Neuron* 49 (2006); Michael L. Platt and Scott A. Huettel, "Risky Business: The Neuroeconomics of Decision Making under Uncertainty," *Nature Neuroscience* 11, no. 4 (2008); Camelia M. Kuhnen and Brian Knutson, "The Neural Basis of Financial Risk Taking," *Neuron* 47 (2005); and Benhabib and Bisin, "Modeling Internal Commitment Mechanisms and Self-Control."

53. Malcolm Heath, *Unity in Greek Poetics* (Oxford: Clarendon Press, 1989). See also Larry Shiner, *The Invention of Art: A Cultural History* (Chicago: University of Chicago Press, 2001).

54. V. S. Ramachandran makes an argument for the importance of the peak-shift effect, whereby desire for exaggerations of preferred, rewarding, features of the world around us and the objects and people in it emerge naturally from neural processes. He uses this to describe the emergence of tools of caricature and changes in fashion, but it has limited applications

for aesthetics more broadly: see *The Tell-Tale Brain: A Neuroscientist's Quest for What Makes Us Human* (New York: Norton, 2011), 206–214.

55. Vessel and Rubin, "Beauty and the Beholder: Highly Individual Taste for Abstract, but Not Real-World Images," *Journal of Vision* 10, no. 2 (2010), and Vessel et al., "The Brain on Art."

56. See, for example, Salimpoor et al., "The Rewarding Aspects of Music Listening."

57. See Mark Meerum Terwogt and Flora Van Grinsven, "Musical Expression of Moodstates," *Psychology of Music* 19 (1991); Laurel J. Trainor and Sandra E. Trehub, "The Development of Referential Meaning in Music," *Music Perception* 9 (1992); and Patrik N. Juslin and Petri Lauuka, "Expression, Perception, and Induction of Musical Emotions: A Review and a Questionnaire Study of Everyday Listening," *Journal of New Music Research* 33 (2004), cited in Trainor and Schmidt, "Processing Emotions Induced by Music."

58. The average across-observer correlations were as follows: pleasure 0.13, fear 0.49, disgust 0.29, sadness 0.38, confusion 0.32, awe 0.30, joy 0.16, sublime 0.17, and beautiful 0.17, respectively (standard deviations ranging from 0.10 to 0.20). Fear had the highest correlation, and was the only one of statistical significance ($P = .054$, $\alpha = .05$). The peculiar position of fear makes sense in that fear tends to have a comparatively highly conserved architecture across people and animals, as a response to perceived threat. See LeDoux and Phelps, "Emotional Networks in the Brain."

59. Zentner et al., "Emotions Evoked by the Sound of Music." For other factors, including age, class, and gender, surrounding individual differences with music, see David J. Hargreaves and Adrian C. North, "Experimental Aesthetics and Liking for Music," in *Handbook of Music and Emotion: Theory, Research, Applications*, ed. Patrik N. Juslin and John A. Sloboda (New York: Oxford University Press, 2010).

60. For a wonderful account of the aesthetics of surprise, see Christopher R. Miller, *Surprise: The Poetics of the Unexpected from Milton to Austen* (forthcoming, Cornell University Press).

61. Eric Kandel puts the emotional interpretability of faces to great use in his discussion of responses to portraiture in *The Age of Insight.*

62. Vessel et al., "The Brain on Art."

63. Marcus E. Raichle and Abraham Z. Snyder, "A Default Mode of Brain Function: A Brief History of an Evolving Idea," *NeuroImage* 37 (2007); Samuel T Moulton and Stephen Kosslyn, "Imagining Predictions: Mental Imagery as Mental Emulation," *Philosophical Transactions of the Royal Society of London, Series B, Biological Sciences* 264 (2009).

64. Debra A. Gusnard and Marcus E. Raichle, "Searching for a Baseline: Functional Imaging and the Resting Human Brain," *Nature Reviews: Neuroscience* 2 (2001); Stephen M. Smith, Peter T. Fox, Karla L. Miller, David C. Glahn, P. Mickle Fox, Clare E. Mackay, Nicola Filippini, Kate E. Watkins, Roberto Toro, Angela R. Laird, and Christian F. Beckmann, "Correspondence of the Brain's Functional Architecture during Activation and Rest," *Proceedings of the National Academy of Sciences of the United States of America* 106, no. 31 (2009); H. Laufs, K. Krakow, P. Sterzer, E. Eger, A. Beyerle, A. Salek-Haddadi, and A. Kleinschmidt, "Electroencephalographic Signatures of Attentional and Cognitive Default Modes in Spontaneous Brain Activity Fluctuations at Rest," *Proceedings of the National Academy of Sciences of the United States of America* 100, no. 19 (2003); R. Nathan Spreng, Raymond A. Mar, and Alice S. N. Kim, "The Common Neural Basis of Autobiographical Memory, Prospection, Navigation, Theory of Mind and the Default Mode: A Quantitative Meta-Analysis," *Journal of Cognitive Neuroscience* 21, no. 3 (2008).

65. Locher, Smith, and Smith have shown experimentally and quantitatively what most of us suspect experientially and qualitatively—the aesthetic experience associated with viewing reproductions of art on slides or computer screens is less powerful than in museum settings. However, they have also shown that training mitigates these differences for some works of art, and that some works maintain their power despite reproduction. It is probable not just that works of art in varying forms of presentation may have different effects but that experimentation itself changes the experience. Altering paintings certainly does change the experience (and that is one reason my work with Vessel and Rubin used real museum images, altered only to limit maximum size). I make no claim that some works of art in my work with Rubin and Vessel might have been more powerful in their original form than in the MRI, or that all of the responses might have been more powerful thus. But I believe that the categorical difference we found showed that people did have powerful aesthetic experiences. Locher and colleagues note that in some circumstances their participants

"accommodated to the screen image" and "were able to adjust to the fact that they were looking at reproductions and 'look past' the limitations of the medium": Paul J. Locher, Jeffrey K. Smith, and Lisa F. Smith, "The Influence of Presentation Format and Viewer Training in the Visual Arts on the Perception of Pictorial and Aesthetic Qualities of Paintings," *Perception* 30 (2001): 450.

66. J. R. Simpson, A. Z. Snyder, D. A. Gusnard, and M. E. Raichle, "Emotion-Induced Changes in Human Medial Prefrontal Cortex: I. During Cognitive Task Performance," *Proceedings of the National Academy of Sciences of the United States of America* 93 (2001); J. R. Simpson, A. Z. Snyder, D. A. Gusnard, and M. E. Raichle, "Emotion-Induced Changes in Human Medial Prefrontal Cortex: II. During Anticipatory Anxiety," *Proceedings of the National Academy of Sciences of the United States of America* 93 (2001); J. Geday and A. Gjedde, "Attention, Emotion, and Deactivation of Default Activity in Inferior Medial Prefrontal Cortex," *Brain and Cognition* 69, no. 2 (2009); Jessica R. Andrews-Hanna, Jay S. Reidler, Jorge Sepulcre, Renee Poulin, and Randy L. Buckner, "Functional-Anatomic Fractionation of the Brain's Default Network," *Neuron* 65, no. 4 (2010).

67. Rebecca Saxe and Nancy Kanwisher, "People Thinking about Thinking People: The Role of the Temporo-parietal Junction in 'Theory of Mind,'" *NeuroImage* 19 (2003). The default mode connection is made in Randy L. Buckner and Daniel C. Carroll, "Self-Projection and the Brain," *Trends in Cognitive Sciences* 11, no. 2 (2007). For a summary of the medial prefrontal cortex and theory of mind, see C. N. Macrae, T. F. Heatherton, and W. M. Kelley, "A Self Less Ordinary: The Medial Prefrontal Cortex and You," in *The Cognitive Neurosciences*, 3rd ed., ed. Michael S. Gazzaniga (Cambridge, MA: MIT Press, 2004).

68. Arnaud D'Argembeau, Fabienne Collette, Martial Van der Linden, Steven Laureys, Guy Del Fiore, Christian Degueldre, Andre Luxen, and Eric Salmon, "Self-Referential Reflective Activity and Its Relationship with Rest: A PET Study," *NeuroImage* 25 (2005); Arnaud D'Argembeau, David Stawarczyk, Steve Majerus, Fabienne Collette, Martial Van der Linden, Dorothée Feyers, Pierre Maquet, and Eric Salmon, "The Neural Basis of Personal Goal Processing When Envisioning Future Events," *Journal of Cognitive Neuroscience* 22, no. 8 (2009); W. M. Kelley, C. N. Macrae, C.L. Wyland, S. Caglar, Souheil Inati, and T. F. Heatherton, "Finding the Self? An Event-Related fMRI Study," *Journal of Cognitive*

Neuroscience 14, no. 5 (2002); S. Gallagher, "Philosophical Conceptions of the Self: Implications for Cognitive Science," *Trends in Cognitive Sciences* 4, no. 1 (2000); J. M. Moran, C. N. Macrae, T. F. Heatherton, C. L. Wyland, and W. M. Kelley, "Neuroanatomical Evidence for Distinct Cognitive and Affective Components of Self," *Journal of Cognitive Neuroscience* 18, no. 9 (2006).

69. For general considerations on trait storage and the specificity of personal knowledge, see Stanley B. Klein, "The Cognitive Neuroscience of Knowing One's Self," in *The Cognitive Neurosciences*, 3rd ed., ed. Michael S. Gazzaniga (Cambridge, MA: MIT Press, 2004). Klein and colleagues argue, based on studies of patients with amnesia but who maintain consistent trait self-knowledge, that there is a separate subsystem for identifying the self that is distinct from memory or from social knowledge, but their argument relies heavily on episodic memories of others and does not explore the social implications of trait knowledge itself.

70. For an overview of much recent work on cultural difference, with some attention to the default mode network, see Shinobu Kitayama and Jiyoung Park, "Cultural Neuroscience of the Self: Understanding the Social Grounding of the Brain," *SCAN* 5 (2010). Cultural differences in self-concept are instantiated within the same neural framework; differences in how the relation of self and other are understood can shift activations within particular neural regions.

71. See Maia, "Reinforcement Learning," and Rolls, *Emotion Explained*, chap. 8, for summary accounts.

72. Michael D. Greicius, Ben Krasnow, Allan L. Reiss, and Vinod Menon, "Functional Connectivity in the Resting Brain: A Network Analysis of the Default Mode Hypothesis," *Proceedings of the National Academy of Sciences of the United States of America* 100, no. 1 (2003).

73. Peter Fransson and Guillaume Marrelec, "The Precuneus/Posterior Cingulate Cortex Plays a Pivotal Role in the Default Mode Network: Evidence from a Partial Correlation Network Analysis," *NeuroImage* 42 (2008): 1183.

74. Fransson and Marrelec, "The Precuneus/Posterior Cingulate Cortex."

75. Buckner and Carroll, "Self-Projection and the Brain," 54.

76. The key area here is the temporoparietal junction. On theory of mind and literature, see especially Lisa Zunshine, *Why We Read Fiction:*

Theory of Mind and the Novel (Columbus: Ohio State University Press, 2006); Blakey Vermeule, *Why Do We Care about Literary Characters?* (Baltimore, MD: Johns Hopkins University Press, 2009); and Kay Young, *Imagining Minds: The Neuro-Aesthetics of Austen, Eliot, and Hardy* (Columbus, Ohio State University Press, 2010).

77. On the connection between the default mode network and memory, see Moulton and Kosslyn, "Imagining Predictions," and Demis Hassabis, Dharshan Kumaran, Seralynn D. Vann, and Eleanor A. Maguire, "Patients with Hippocampal Amnesia Cannot Imagine New Experiences," *Proceedings of the National Academy of Sciences of the United States of America* 105, no. 5 (2007). Son Preminger suggests that, if aesthetic engagement involves the default mode network (and we know now that it does), this may be one way we can have transformative aesthetic experiences: "Transformative Art: Art as a Means for Long-Term Neurocognitive Change," *Frontiers in Human Neuroscience* 6 (2012).

78. I am indebted to Jesse Prinz for this formulation.

79. The tendency toward left hemisphere lateralization found by Vessel and colleagues, as I suggested above, might indicate the degree to which putatively negative emotions are reclaimed in an aesthetic context as not to be avoided but embraced. More work can be done on this peculiarity of emotional response. It is also necessary to do more work to differentiate between powerful negative and positive aesthetic experiences—not just beauty versus ugliness but beauty versus, say, the grotesque, where what is experienced and understood as aversion becomes savored or desired (even while aversive). In addition, there is some similarity here to what Maslow called "peak experiences," in which he includes "aesthetic perception" as one class of experiences that, in their extreme, can be transformative and transcendent: Abraham Maslow, *Toward a Psychology of Being*, 3rd ed. (New York: Wiley, 1999), 85. Alf Gabrielsson describes studies of musical peak experiences on Maslow's model, with the revision that musical peak experiences can involve negative emotions. While peak experiences may share some characteristics with strong aesthetic experiences, in Maslow's view they include responses that are not necessarily aesthetic (religious ecstasy, parental love, and so on), and emotional responses (including loss of control, and inexpressibility) not found in our study. In other words, an aesthetic experience, even a powerful aesthetic experience, need not be a peak experience, and vice versa. Gabrielsson, "Emotions in Strong Experiences with Music," 431–432.

80. Determining the sequence of these events awaits further experimentation. But the presence of connections in both directions between the medial prefrontal cortex and thalamus is well established. See G. E. Alexander and M. D. Crutcher, "Functional Architecture of Basal Ganglia Circuits: Neural Substrates of Parallel Processing," *Trends in Neurosciences* 13 (1990); G. E. Alexander, M. R. DeLong, and P. L. Strick, "Parallel Organization of Functionally Segregated Circuits Linking Basal Ganglia and Cortex," *Annual Review of Neuroscience* 9 (1986); F. A. Middleton and P. L. Strick, "Basal-Ganglia 'Projections' to the Prefrontal Cortex of the Primate," *Cerebral Cortex* 12 (2002); and M. Steriade and R. R. Llinás, "The Functional States of the Thalamus and the Associated Neuronal Interplay," *Physiological Reviews*, 68 (1988).

81. Kant, "Analytic of the Beautiful," especially 61–62. The free play of imagination and understanding sets the stage for the universality of the experience of beauty. Francis F. Steen echoes the Kantian argument in a cognitive frame, arguing that aesthetic experience arrives at a kind of "truth" that identifies "a significant and systematic relation between certain orders that are externally manifest and the internal manifest order of certain aspects of our being," Steen, "A Cognitive Account of Aesthetics," in *The Artful Mind*, ed. Mark Turner (New York: Oxford University Press, 2006), 69.

82. See Kant, *Critique of Judgment*, especially 115, 116, 235, and 120–121. On the mathematically sublime (that which is impossible to imagine because of its magnitude), see 103–118, and on the dynamically sublime (that which overpowers with its might), see 119–126.

83. Blaise Pascal, *Pensées*, trans. Honor Levi (New York: Oxford University Press, 2008), 72–73: "A human being is only a reed, the weakest in nature, but he is a thinking reed. To crush him, the whole universe does not have to arm itself. A mist, a drop of water is enough to kill him. But if the universe were to crush the reed, the dying man would be nobler than his killer, since he knows that he is dying, and that the universe has the advantage over him. The universe knows nothing about this."

84. Baruch Spinoza, *Ethics, Treatise on the Emendation of the Intellect, and Selected Letters*, trans. Samuel Shirley, ed. Seymour Feldman (Indianapolis: Hackett, 1991), 110, 11; Propositions 11 and 12.

85. Kant, *Critique of Judgment*, 44. This comparison "forms the basis of a very special power of discriminating and judging. This power . . . merely

compares the given presentation in the subject with the entire presentational power, of which the mind becomes conscious when it feels its own state. The presentations given in a judgment may be empirical (and hence aesthetic), but if we refer them to the object, the judgment we make by means of them is logical. On the other hand, even if the given presentations were rational, they would still be aesthetic if, and to the extent that, the subject referred them, in his judgment, solely to himself (to his feeling)" (44–45).

86. Elaine Scarry in *On Beauty and Being Just* (Princeton, NJ: Princeton University Press, 1999) argues that beauty speaks to the sense of care that is part of the Heideggerian being-in-the-world.

87. De Bolla, *Art Matters*, 12.

Chapter 2

1. W.J.T. Mitchell gives an excellent account of the history of imagery and imagination in this regard. See also Elaine Scarry, *Dreaming by the Book* (New York: Farrar, Straus and Giroux, 1999); Richard Kearney, *The Wake of Imagination: Toward a Postmodern Culture* (Minneapolis: University of Minnesota Press, 1988); James Engell, *The Creative Imagination: Enlightenment to Romanticism* (Cambridge, MA: Harvard University Press, 1981); and Ellen Esrock, *The Reader's Eye: Visual Imaging as Reader Response* (Baltimore, MD: Johns Hopkins University Press, 1994).

2. Michelle Leona Goodin describes the implications of the Molyneux problem for British literary criticism and aesthetics in "The Spectator & the Blind Man: Seeing & Not-Seeing in the Wake of Empiricism" (PhD diss., New York University, 2009).

3. Joseph Addison, *The Spectator*, ed. Donald F. Bond, 5 vols. (Oxford: Clarendon Press, 1965), 3:536–537.

4. William Hogarth, *The Analysis of Beauty*, ed. Ronald Paulson (New Haven, CT: Yale University Press, 1997), 21.

5. Hogarth, *The Analysis of Beauty*, 21.

6. I first began to think about the implications of this after a conversation with Dorothy Hale in 2000, in which she reminded me of William Empson's declaration that "literary critics have stubbornly refused to pay any attention" to individual differences in imagery ("Rhythm and Imagery in English Poetry," *British Journal of Aesthetics* 2 [1962], 47). Several tests for vividity and controllability, primarily visual, exist: The Vividness of

Visual Imagery Questionnaire, the Betts Questionnaire Upon Mental Imagery, the Gordon Test of Visual Imagery Control, the Verbalizer-Visualizer Questionnaire, and the Vividness of Movement Imagery Questionnaire: respectively, D. F. Marks, "Visual Imagery Differences in the Recall of Pictures," *British Journal of Psychology* 64 (1973); P. W. Sheehan, "A Shortened Form of Betts' Questionnaire Upon Mental Imagery," *Journal of Clinical Psychology* 23 (1967); A. Richardson, *Mental Imagery* (New York: Springer, 1969); A. Isaac, D. F. Marks, and D. G. Russell, "An Instrument for Assessing Imagery for Movement: The Vividness of Movement Imagery Questionnaire," *Journal of Mental Imagery* 10 (1986); idem. In *The Neural Sublime* (Baltimore, MD: Johns Hopkins University Press, 2010), Alan Richardson takes up this debate to point out that it may be true that contemporary readers are becoming less likely to visualize.

7. Hitoshi Okada, Kazuo Matsuoka, and Takeo Hatakeyama, "Individual Differences in the Range of Sensory Modalities Experienced in Dreams," *Dreaming* 15, no. 2 (2005). Okada and colleagues show that imagery of taste, smell, and cutaneous sensation are the least common forms of mental imagery during dreaming. About one quarter of subjects experience taste and smell in dreams, while around 60 percent experience cutaneous sensation always or occasionally (109).

8. Stephen Kosslyn, "Aspects of a Cognitive Neuroscience of Mental Imagery," in *Essential Sources in the Scientific Study of Consciousness*, ed. Bernard J. Baars, William P. Banks, and James B. Newman (Cambridge, MA: MIT Press, 2003); Zenon Pylyshyn, "Is the Imagery Debate Over? If So, What Was It About?," in *Language, Brain, and Cognitive Development: Essays in Honor of Jacques Mehler*, ed. Emmanuel Dupoux (Cambridge, MA: MIT Press, 2001); Stephen Kosslyn, "Mental Imagery," in *Conversations in the Cognitive Neurosciences*, ed. Michael S. Gazzaniga (Cambridge, MA: MIT Press, 1997); Martha J. Farah, "The Neural Basis of Mental Imagery," in *Essential Sources in the Scientific Study of Consciousness*, ed. Bernard J. Baars, William P. Banks, and James B. Newman (Cambridge, MA: MIT Press, 2003); Stephen Kosslyn, *Image and Mind* (Cambridge, MA: Harvard University Press, 1980); Stephen Kosslyn, W. L. Thompson, and G. Ganis, *The Case for Mental Imagery* (New York: Oxford University Press, 2006). See also Horace Barlow, Colin Blakemore, and Miranda Weston-Smith, eds., *Images and Understanding* (New York: Cambridge University Press, 1990), and Ned Block, ed., *Imagery* (Cambridge, MA: MIT Press, 1981).

9. I first encountered these terms for describing the debate in Stephen E. Palmer, *Vision Science: From Photons to Phenomenology* (Cambridge, MA: MIT Press, 1991).

10. Pylyshyn, "Return of the Mental Image."

11. I take the idea of the round green ball from Burke's discussion of beauty in the *Enquiry*. It is worth noting that Burke believes that the power of poetry does not rely on imagery at all.

12. Zenon Pylyshyn, "Return of the Mental Image: Are There Really Pictures in the Brain?," *Trends in Cognitive Sciences* 7, no. 3 (2003): 115.

13. Certain smells, like that of strawberry, make it easier for us to taste sugar. Djordjevic and colleagues show that the imagined smell of strawberry does the same: Jelena Djordjevic, Robert J. Zatorre, and M. Jones-Gotman, "Effects of Perceived and Imagined Odors on Taste Detection," *Chemical Senses* 29 (2004). Visual imagery, however, has no such effect: Jelena Djordjevic, Robert J. Zatorre, and M. Jones-Gotman, "The Mind's Nose: Effects of Odor and Visual Imagery on Odor Detection," *Psychological Science* 15, no. 3 (2004).

14. Richard J. Stevenson and Trevor I. Case, "Olfactory Imagery: A Review," *Psychonomic Bulletin & Review* 12, no. 2 (2005): 252. Stevenson and Case caution that more work needs to be done to differentiate phenomenal imagery and performance on experimental tasks that might stem from other causes. One important problem with some work on taste imagery is that the behavior used to verify the effects of such imagery is salivation. It is unclear in these circumstances whether we are dealing with an image or simply a conditioned stimulus.

15. Maria Olkkonen, Thorsten Hansen, and Karl R. Gegenfurtner, "Color Appearance of Familiar Objects: Effects of Object Shape, Texture, and Illumination Changes," *Journal of Vision* 8, no. 5 (2008). My thanks to Ned Block for this citation.

16. Even if there are similar or even identical brain regions involved in both imagery and perception, that does not make either one of them involve an image—this is Pylyshn's point in the classic debate. (Cf. W.J.T. Mitchell, *Iconology: Image, Text, Ideology* [Chicago: University of Chicago Press, 1987].) Ultimately, there is no need to make a strong claim that either imagery or perception depends on a *pictorial* model, for it is clear that the processes of imagery stretch across multiple sensory modes and engage a variety of kinds of data.

17. See Floris P. de Lange, Peter Hagoort, and Ivan Toni, "Neural Topography and Content of Movement Representations," *Journal of Cognitive Neuroscience* 17, no. 1 (2005). For a critical analysis of this data, see G. Gabrielle Starr, "Multi-Sensory Imagery," in *Introduction to Cognitive Cultural Studies*, ed. Lisa Zunshine (Baltimore, MD: Johns Hopkins University Press, 2010).

18. L. Fadiga, G. Buccino, Laila Craighero, L. Fogassi, Vittorio Gallese, and G. Pavesi, "Corticospinal Excitability Is Specifically Modulated by Motor Imagery: A Magnetic Stimulation Study," *Neuropsychologica* 37 (1999); R. Hashimoto and J. C. Rothwell, "Dynamic Changes in Corticospinal Excitability during Motor Imagery," *Experimental Brain Research* 125 (1999); Young H. Sohn, Nguyet Dang, and Mark Hallett, "Suppression of Corticospinal Excitability during Negative Motor Imagery," *Journal of Neurophysiology* 90 (2003); Paolo M. Rossini, Simone Rossi, Patrizio Pasqualetti, and Franca Tecchio, "Corticospinal Excitability Modulation to Hand Muscles during Movement Imagery," *Cerebral Cortex* 9 (1999); Carlo A. Porro, Maria Pia Francescato, Valentina Cettolo, Mathew E. Diamond, Patrizia Baraldi, Chiava Zuiani, Massimo Bazzocchi, and Pietro E. di Prampero, "Primary Motor and Sensory Cortex Activation during Motor Performance and Motor Imagery: A Functional Magnetic Resonance Imaging Study," *Journal of Neuroscience* 16, no. 23 (1996). Transcranial magnetic stimulation is a noninvasive technique that allows stimulation of brain cells to determine functional specificity.

19. Andrea R. Halpern, "Mental Scanning in Auditory Imagery for Songs," *Journal of Experimental Psychology: Learning, Memory, and Cognition* 14, no. 3 (1988).

20. Samuel T. Moulton and Stephen Kosslyn, "Imagining Predictions: Mental Imagery as Mental Emulation," *Philosophical Transactions of the Royal Society, Series B, Biological Sciences* 264 (2009): 1275, 1274.

21. George Sandys, *Ovid's Metamorphoses Englished by G.S.* (London, 1628), 19, slightly orthographically modernized.

22. John Keats, "The Eve of St. Agnes," in *Complete Poems*, ed. Jack Stillinger (Cambridge, MA: Belknap Press of Harvard University Press, 1982), ll. 56–57, 66–67.

23. I am indebted to John C. Harpole for this reminder.

24. Stevenson and Case, "Olfactory Imagery"; J. A. Stevens, "Olfactory Dreams: Phenomenology, Relationship to Volitional Imagery and Odor Identification," *Imagination, Cognition and Personality* 24, no. 1 (2005).

25. For a fuller review of the variety of multisensory imagery, see Starr, "Multi-Sensory Imagery."

26. The processes involved in these categories of auditory imagery differ phenomenologically and physiologically. For example, music seems to use some areas of the brain that other sounds do not, perhaps because of the way that musical pitch works.

27. Ken W. Grant, Virginie van Wassenhove, and David Poeppel, "Detection of Auditory (Cross-Spectral) and Auditory-Visual (Cross-Modal) Synchrony," *Speech Communication* 44 (2004).

28. For literary scholars, synesthesia refers to imagery that blends senses together in the mode of Keats in "Ode to a Nightingale": "I cannot see what flowers are at my feet, / Nor what soft incense hangs upon the boughs." For neuroscientists, however, synesthesia involves the involuntary and persistent coupling of different sensory modalities: an individual with synesthesia will *always* see the number seven as yellow, or hear high C as green. The experience is automatic. The most prominent explanations for these phenomena involve neural development. Sensory data are aggregate early in the development of the human brain and in perception itself; dissociation and differentiation (color from sound, say) are the result of developmental processes. This differentiation occurs abnormally, or fails to occur, in individuals with synesthesia. Synesthetes can experience this blending in imaginative conditions as well: a woman who, on seeing the number seven always sees the color yellow, for example, also sees yellow when thinking "5 + 2" or "3 + 4." V. S. Ramachandran and E. M. Hubbard, "Synaesthesia: A Window into Perception, Thought and Language," *Journal of Consciousness Studies* 8, no. 12 (2001). Their discussion of language is speculative, and of it I am skeptical. For follow-on discussion, see Karl Pribram, "Commentary on 'Synaesthesia' by Ramachandran and Hubbard," *Journal of Consciousness Studies* 10, no. 3 (2003), and E. M. Hubbard and V. S. Ramachandran, "Refining the Experimental Lever: A Reply to Shanon and Pribram," *Journal of Consciousness Studies* 10, no. 3 (2003); see also, relatedly, Mike J. Dixon, Daniel Smilek, Cera Cudahy, and Philip M. Merikle, "Five Plus Two Equals Yellow," *Nature* 406 (2000). For an unusual case, see Michaela Esslen Beeli and Lutz Jancke, "Synaesthesia: When Coloured Sounds

Taste Sweet," *Nature* 434 (2005). Synesthetes include Vladimir Nabokov, David Hockney, and Jimi Hendrix, and around one in 25,000 of the general population. In lived synesthesia, some couplings predominate, such as auditory-visual and typographic-color, while others are exceedingly rare, such as synesthesia involving taste or smell, as Richard E. Cytowic shows: "Synesthesia: Phenomenology and Neuropsychology. A Review of Current Knowledge," *Psyche* 2, no. 10 (1995). Sean Day, in suggestive research, proposes that the most common form of synesthetic imagery in the English-language literature—blends of touch and sound—are not those most common in lived synesthesia, in which blends of sound and sight predominate: "Synaesthesia and Synaesthetic Metaphors," *Psyche* 2, no. 32 (1996). There is clearly a mismatch: neurological concepts of synesthesia and what individuals with synesthesia experience differ greatly from the blending of sensory imagery in metaphor and art. The more fruitful cognitive approach to blended forms of imagery may thus be through exploring multisensory images. Cytowic lays out the basics. It is inherited, more women than men are synesthetes, and fewer right-handed individuals than left-handed are synesthetes ("Synesthesia," secs. 2 and 3). Cytowic should be taken with some skepticism in his discussion of the emotional components of synesthesia because of his reliance on somewhat outdated models of emotional processing.

29. Barbara Cerf-Ducastel, Pierre-Francois Van de Moortele, Patrick MacLeod, Denis Le Bihan, and Annick Faurion, "Interaction of Gustatory and Lingual Somatosensory Perceptions at the Cortical Level in the Human: A Functional Magnetic Resonance Imaging Study," *Chemical Senses* 26 (2001); Stevenson and Case, "Olfactory Imagery."

30. On the relation of grasping to visual "what" and "where" pathways, see S. C. Prather, John R. Votaw, and K. Sathian, "Task-Specific Recruitment of Dorsal and Ventral Visual Areas During Tactile Perception," *Neuropsychologia* 42 (2004). On motor imagery, vision, and grasping, see Laurel J. Buxbaum, Scott H. Johnson-Frey and Megan Bartlett-Williams, "Deficient Internal Models for Planning Hand-Object Interactions in Apraxia," *Neuropsychologia* 43 (2005).

31. See Minming Zhang, Valerie D. Weisser, Randall Stilla, S. C. Prather and K. Sathian, "Multisensory Cortical Processing of Object Shape and Its Relation to Mental Imagery," *Cognitive, Affective, & Behavioral Neuroscience* 4, no. 2 (2004); K. Sathian, "Visual Cortical Activity

during Tactile Perception in the Sighted and the Visually Deprived," *Developmental Psychobiology* 46 (2005).

32. Rainer Goebel, Darius Khorram-Sefat, Lars Muckli, Hans Hacker and Wolf Singer, "The Constructive Nature of Vision: Direct Evidence from Functional Magnetic Resonance Imaging Studies of Apparent Motion and Motion Imagery," *European Journal of Neuroscience* 10, no. 5 (1998).

33. James J. Gibson, "The Theory of Affordances," in *Perceiving, Acting, Knowing*, ed. Robert Shaw and John Bransford (New York: Wiley, 1977).

34. J. Kevin O'Regan and Alva Noë, "A Sensorimotor Account of Vision and Visual Consciousness," *Behavioral and Brain Sciences* 24 (2001).

35. J. A. Stevens, "Interference Effects Demonstrate Distinct Roles for Visual and Motor Imagery during the Mental Representation of Human Action," *Cognition* 95 (2005). Much research into imagery uses interference to determine functional exclusivity. So, for example, experience that relies on visual imagery or vision can be altered or inhibited by other visual activity. It is hard, thus, to concentrate both on the details of a picture in front of you and on the imagined details of an imagined image at the same time. However, we can concentrate on the detail of a piece of music while also looking intently at a painting, or imagining one. We cannot do both as easily together as we can separately, but we can do them together. We can measure the degree of difficulty or challenge involved in such potentially interfering activities by measuring the amount of time it takes to do them together as opposed to separately. Stevens shows that imagining someone else moving can be inhibited more by visual interference than by motor interference. Imagining ourselves moving, however, shows more effects of interference from motor activity than from visual imagery. In general "visual and motor imagery [are] cooperative processes," but not always. Similar results to Stevens's, concerning the difference between imagining yourself moving something and imagining someone else doing so, may be found in Stephen Kosslyn, William L. Thompson, Mary J. Wraga, and Nathaniel M. Alpert, "Imagining Rotation by Endogenous versus Exogenous Forces: Distinct Neural Mechanisms," *NeuroReport* 12 (2001). See also B. Calvo-Merino, D. E. Glaser, J. Grezes, R.E. Passingham, and P. Haggard, "Action Observation and Acquired Motor Skills: An fMRI Study with Expert Dancers," *Cerebral Cortex* 15 (2005).

36. Stevens, "Interference Effects," 345.

37. For an overview, see Giacomo Rizzolatti and Laila Craighero, "The Mirror-Neuron System," *Annual Review of Neuroscience* 27 (2004). On learning and mirror neurons, see also Katja Stefan, Leonard G. Cohen, Julie Duque, Riccardo Mazzochio, Pablo Celnik, Lumi Sawaki, Leslie Ungerleider, and Joseph Classen, "Formation of a Motor Memory by Action Observation," *Journal of Neuroscience* 25, no. 41 (2005); James M. Kilner, Karl J. Friston, and Chris D. Frith, "The Mirror-Neuron System: A Bayesian Perspective," *NeuroReport* 18, no. 6 (2007); Laurie Carr, Marco Iacoboni, Marie-Charlotte Dubeau, John C. Mazziotta, and Gian Luigi Lenzi, "Neural Mechanisms of Empathy in Humans: A Relay from Neural Systems for Imitation to Limbic Areas," *Proceedings of the National Academy of Sciences of the United States of America* 100, no. 9 (2003); R. Hari, N. Forss, S. Avikainen, E. Kirveskari, S. Salenius, and Giacomo Rizzolatti, "Activation of Human Primary Motor Cortex During Action Observation: A Neuromagnetic Study," *Proceedings of the National Academy of Sciences of the United States of America* 95 (1998); Marco Iacoboni, Istvan Molnar-Szakacs, Vittorio Gallese, G. Buccino, John C. Mazziotta, and Giacomo Rizzolatti, "Grasping the Intentions of Others with One's Own Mirror Neuron System," *PLoS Biology* 3 (2005); Ilan Dinstein, Uri Hasson, Nava Rubin, and David Heeger, "Brain Areas Selective for Both Observed and Executed Movements," *Journal of Neurophysiology* 98 (2007); Marco Iacoboni, R. P. Woods, M. Brass, H. Bekkering, and John C. Mazziotta, "Cortical Mechanisms of Human Imitation," *Science* 286 (1999); S. H Johnson-Frey, F. R. Maloof, R. Newman-Norlund, C. Farrer, Souheil Inati, and S. T. Grafton, "Actions or Hand-Object Interactions? Human Inferior Frontal Cortex and Action Observation," *Neuron* 39 (2003); and L. Aziz-Zadeh, L. Koski, E. Zaidel, John C. Mazziotta, and Marco Iacoboni, "Lateralization of the Human Mirror Neuron System," *Journal of Neuroscience* 26 (2006). Evidence for mirror neurons remains stronger for other primates than for humans.

38. For a critique of mirror neurons, see Gregory Hickok, "Eight Problems for the Mirror Neuron Theory of Action Understanding in Monkeys and Humans," *Journal of Cognitive Neuroscience* 21, no. 7 (2009). Hickok argues that the activity attributed to mirror neurons is generalizable across motor systems. For the broader context of empathy in the brain beyond mirror neurons, see Jean Decety and Philip L. Jackson, "The Functional Architecture of Human Empathy," *Behavioral and Cognitive Neuroscience Reviews* 3, no. 2 (2004). On the motor networks involved in the perception of others' actions and intentions, see: S.-J.

Blakemore and J. Decety, "From the Perception of Action to the Understanding of Intention," *Nature Reviews: Neuroscience* 2 (2001).

39. On the empathy connection, see Joe Cambray, "Towards the Feeling of Emergence," *Journal of Analytical Psychology* 51 (2006), and Decety and Jackson, "The Functional Architecture of Human Empathy." For a good account of the mirror system, empathy, and its implications for portraiture, see Eric R. Kandel, *The Age of Insight: The Quest to Understand the Unconscious in Art, Mind, and Brain, from Vienna 1900 to the Present* (New York: Random House, 2012), 415–418.

40. Adam Smith, *The Theory of Moral Sentiments*, ed. D. D. Raphael and A. L. Macfie (Indianapolis: Liberty Fund, 1984), 10.

41. For example, Smith, *The Theory of Moral Sentiments,* 143ff.

42. Swift writes,

> Corinna, . . .
> . . .
> Seated on a three-leg'd chair,
> Takes off her artificial hair:
> Now, picking out a crystal eye,
> She wipes it clean, and lays it by.
> Her eyebrows from a mouse's hide,
> Stuck on with art on either side,
> Pulls off with care, . . .
> Now dexterously her plumpers draws,
> That serve to fill her hollow jaws.
> Untwists a wire; and from her gums
> A set of teeth completely comes.
> . . .
> With gentlest touch, she next explores
> Her shankers, issues, running sores;
> Effects of many a sad disaster.
> . . .
> She takes a bolus e'er she sleeps;
> And then between two blankets creeps.
> With pains of love tormented lies;
> Or if she chance to close her eyes,
> Of Bridewell and the compter dreams,
> And feels the lash, and faintly screams.
> . . .

> But how shall I describe her arts
> To recollect the scattered parts?
> Or show the anguish, toil, and pain,
> Of gathering up herself again? (ll. 9–15, 17–20, 37–41, 67–70)

Jonathan Swift, "A Beautiful Young Nymph Going to Bed," in *The Complete Poems*, ed. Pat Rogers (New York: Penguin, 1989); John Sitter, "Touching Satire" paper presented at a meeting of the American Society for Eighteenth-Century Studies, Montreal, 2006.

43. Hogarth, *The Analysis of Beauty*, 21.

44. F. Attneave and P. Farrar, "The Visual World behind the Head," *American Journal of Psychology* 90 (1977).

45. David Freedberg and Vittorio Gallese, "Motion, Emotion and Empathy in Esthetic Experience," *Trends in Cognitive Sciences* 11, no. 5 (2007). Elsewhere Freedberg argues that the strongest evidence for the aesthetic importance of mirror effects is that they are automatic (see his "Memory in Art: History and the Neuroscience of Response," in *The Memory Process,* ed. Suzanne Nalbantian, Paul M. Matthews, and James L. McClelland [Cambridge, MA: MIT Press, 2011]), and that such automatic, unconscious activations of mirror neurons have emotional effects. The most significant issue here is in the second part of the equation. Not everyone has the empathetic responses such an analysis would propose, nor do individuals always have these responses to a given image. I do not wish to suggest that unconscious, fast emotional responses based on mirror neurons do not necessarily exist (and I believe they might), but rather that this can't be all of the picture.

46. Cinzia di Dio, Emiliano Macaluso, and Giacomo Rizzolatti, "The Golden Beauty: Brain Response to Classical and Renaissance Sculptures," *PLoS ONE* 11 (2007).

47. Stefan Koelsch, Thomas Fritz, D. Yves Von Cramon, Karsten Müller, and Angela Friederici, "Investigating Emotion with Music: An fMRI Study," *Human Brain Mapping* 27 (2006).

48. On the rise of the silent audience in Europe, see James H. Johnson, *Listening in Paris: A Cultural History* (Berkeley: University of California Press, 1996), and Richard Leppert, "The Social Discipline of Listening," in *Aural Cultures,* ed. Jim Drobnik (Toronto: YYZ Books, 2004): 19–36. For an excellent review of the scholarship, see William Weber, "Did People Listen in the 18th Century?" *Early Music* 25 (1997).

49. Daniel J. Levitin, *The World in Six Songs: How the Musical Brain Created Human Nature* (New York: Dutton, 2009), 101. See also Robert Zatorre, "Music, the Food of Neuroscience?," *Nature* 434, no. 7031 (2005), and Daniel J. Levitin, "The Neural Correlates of Temporal Structure in Music," *Music and Medicine* 1, no. 1 (2009).

50. Isabelle Peretz and Robert J. Zatorre summarize the evidence showing links between music and motion developed through musical training: "Brain Organization for Music Processing," *Annual Review of Psychology* 56 (2005), 102ff.

51. See Aaron Ridley, *Music, Value and the Passions* (Ithaca, NY: Cornell University Press, 1995), 81ff.; Carroll Pratt, *The Meaning of Music* (New York: McGraw-Hill, 1931); Eduard Hanslick, *The Beautiful in Music*, trans. Gustav Cohen (New York: Da Capo Press, 1974), 37ff.; Koelsch et al., "Investigating Emotion with Music"; and Charles O. Nussbaum, *The Musical Representation: Meaning, Ontology, and Emotion* (Cambridge, MA: MIT Press, 2007).

52. Malcolm Budd, *Music and the Emotions: The Philosophical Theories* (New York: Routledge, 1985).

53. Nussbaum, *The Musical Representation,* 61.

54. See A. Lomax, "The Cross-Cultural Variation of Rhythmic Style," in *Interaction Rhythms: Periodicity in Human Behavior*, ed. M. Davis (New York: Human Sciences Press, 1982), and Martin Clayton, Rebecca Sager, and Udo Will, "In Time with the Music: The Concept of Entrainment and Its Significance for Ethnomusicology," *ESEM CounterPoint* 1 (2004).

55. Patrik N. Juslin, Simon Liljeström, Daniel Västfjäll, and Lars-Olov Lundqvist, "How Does Music Evoke Emotions? Exploring the Underlying Mechanisms," in *Handbook of Music and Emotions: Theory, Research and Applications*, ed. Patrik N. Juslin and John A. Sloboda (New York: Oxford University Press, 2010).

56. Deborah L. Harrington, Kathleen Y. Haaland, and Neal Hermanowicz, "Temporal Processing in the Basal Ganglia," *Neuropsychology* 12, no. 1 (1998).

57. Andrea R. Halpern and Robert Zatorre, "When That Tune Runs through Your Head: A PET Investigation of Auditory Imagery for Familiar Melodies," *Cerebral Cortex* 9, no. 7 (1999): 703. Halpern and colleagues argue that much more work needs to be done to ascertain whether

we really are doing something like humming along, or whether parts of our brains usually used for motor activity "may be involved in some more general aspect of auditory imagery, such as image generation of preparation, regardless of any potential subvocal contribution to the image": Andrea R. Halpern, Robert J. Zatorre, Marc Bouffard, and Jennifer A. Johnson, "Behavioral and Neural Correlates of Perceived and Imagined Musical Timbre," *Neuropsychologia* 42 (2004): 1291. This work is very good, but the interpretation of the subthreshold SMA (supplementary motor area) activation they find with imagined timbre is tricky. They argue that because timbre is not vocalizable, any motor activity in imagined timbre should not come from imagined vocalization. Therefore the subthreshold SMA activation should come from something else. However, they note that "although subvocalizing the timbre of an instrument is difficult, the timbre was accompanied by pitch, with itself is easily vocalizable" (1291).

58. Scarry suggests a special place for poetry in this regard, as well: "Yet because of the sound of the poem, the palpable touch of the interior parts of the mouth glancing across one another even in silent reading, and because of the visual scanning of the lines, the material surface of the poem is closer to" painting: *Dreaming by the Book,* 8. Recent investigations show that the perception of metrical stress involves motor imagery: Andre Aleman and Mascha Van't Wout, "Subvocalization in Auditory-Verbal Imagery: Just a Form of Motor Imagery?," *Cognitive Processing* 5 (2004). Hermann Ackermann, Klaus Mathiak, and Richard B. Ivry, "Temporal Organization of 'Internal Speech' as a Basis for Cerebellar Modulation of Cognitive Functions," *Behavioral and Cognitive Neuroscience Reviews* 3, no. 1 (2004).

59. Empson, "Rhythm and Imagery in English Poetry," 46.

60. Gerard Manley Hopkins, "The Woodlark," in Seamus Heaney and Ted Hughes, eds., *The Rattle Bag* (Boston: Faber and Faber, 1982).

61. Horace, *Ars Poetica,* in *Satires, Epistles, Ars Poetica,* trans. H. Ruston Fairclough (Cambridge, MA: Harvard University Press, 2005), l. 274, p. 473.

62. J. Decety, M. Jeannerod, D. Durozard and G. Baverel, "Central Activation of Autonomic Effectors during Mental Simulation of Motor Actions in Man," *Journal of Physiology* 462 (1993), cited in Grant et al., "Detection of Auditory (Cross-Spectral) and Auditory-Visual (Cross-Modal) Synchrony."

63. Gerard Manley Hopkins, "Pied Beauty," in *The Major Works*, ed. Catherine Phillips (New York: Oxford University Press, 2002), 132.

64. Ellen J. Esrock makes a different argument for a multimodal representation as a component of reading in "Embodying Literature," *Journal of Consciousness Studies* 11, nos. 5–6 (2004).

65. Frances Ferguson also places imagery at the heart of aesthetics: "my view is that the advent of aesthetics as a more or less distinct area of philosophical speculation marks an intensification of interest in the mental image and in the difficulties of assimilating it to the problems of ontology and epistemology, on the one hand, and to those of ethics, on the other" because "the imagination suggests the interconnections between consciousness and matter," *Solitude and the Sublime: Romanticism and the Aesthetics of Individuation* (New York: Routledge, 1992), 1, 6.

66. Colin Martindale, "The Pleasures of Thought: A Theory of Cognitive Hedonics," *Journal of Mind and Behavior* 5, no. 1 (1984).

67. Emily A. Holmes, Anna E. Coughtrey, and Abigail Connor, "Looking at or through Rose-Tinted Glasses? Imagery Perspective and Positive Mood," *Emotion* 8, no. 6 (2008); Emily A. Holmes, Andrew Mathews, Bundy Mackintosh, and Tim Dalgleish, "The Causal Effect of Mental Imagery on Emotion Assessed Using Picture-Word Cues," *Emotion* 8, no. 3 (2008).

68. Kosslyn and colleagues suggest that motor imagery produces associative knowledge: "imagining making movements might not only exercise the relevant brain areas, but also build associations among processes implemented in different areas, which in turn facilitate complex performance."

69. Vincent D. Costa, Peter J. Lang, Dean Sabatinelli, Francesco Versace, and Margaret M. Bradley, "Emotional Imagery: Assessing Pleasure and Arousal in the Brain's Reward Circuitry," *Human Brain Mapping* 31 (2010); Dean Sabatinelli, Peter J. Lang, Margaret M. Bradley, and Tobias Flaisch, "The Neural Basis of Narrative Imagery: Emotion and Action," *Progress in Brain Research* 156 (2006). Their findings implicate the nucleus accumbens, the medial prefrontal cortex (also found in our research on aesthetics), and the amygdala.

70. Mark R. Dadds, Dana Bovbjerg, William H. Redd, and Tim R. H. Cutmore, "Imagery in Human Classical Conditioning," *Psychological Bulletin* 122, no. 1 (1997).

71. Eduardo Paulo Morawski Vianna, Nasir Naqvi, Antoine Bechara and Daniel Tranel, "Does Vivid Emotional Imagery Depend on Body Signals?," *International Journal of Psychophysiology* 72 (2009). See the somatic marker hypothesis about emotion in Antonio Damasio, *The Feeling of What Happens: Body and Emotion in the Making of Consciousness* (New York: Harcourt, 1999). In his view, emotional experience involves feedback between activity in the central nervous system (especially the brain) and in the peripheral nervous system.

72. I call this work suggestive because the study focused only on three paintings, but the initial results suggest that further research is warranted: Fortunato Battaglia, Sarah H. Lisanby, and David Freedberg, "Corticomotor Excitability During Observation and Imagination of a Work of Art," *Frontiers in Human Neuroscience* 5 (2011).

73. Elizabeth Bishop, "At the Fishhouses," in *The Complete Poems, 1929–1979* (New York: Noonday, 1983).

74. Moulton and Kosslyn, "Imagining Predictions." Demis Hassabis, Dharshan Kumaran, and Eleanor A. Maguire investigate detailed participants' imaginings of navigating scenes in "Using Imagination to Understand the Neural Basis of Episodic Memory," *Journal of Neuroscience* 27, no. 52 (2007).

75. On the overlapping of memory and forward planning in the default mode network, see Peter Fransson and Guillaume Marrelec, "The Precuneus/Posterior Cingulate Cortex Plays a Pivotal Role in the Default Mode Network: Evidence from a Partial Correlation Network Analysis," *NeuroImage* 42 (2008).

76. See Hassabis et al., "Using Imagination to Understand the Neural Basis of Episodic Memory." For examples of the kinds of imaginative tasks found to recruit areas of the default mode network, see Demis Hassabis, Dharshan Kumaran, Seralynne D. Vann, and Eleanor A. Maguire, "Patients with Hippocampal Amnesia Cannot Imagine New Experiences," *Proceedings of the National Academy of Sciences of the United States of America* 105, no. 5 (2007).

77. See Nathan R. Spreng, Raymond A. Mar, and Alice S. N. Kim, "The Common Neural Basis of Memory, Prospection, Navigation, Theory of Mind, and the Default Mode: A Quantitative Meta-Analysis," *Journal of Cognitive Neuroscience* 21, no. 3 (2008). Vessel and colleagues in "The Brain on Art" show the classic rebound to baseline in default mode

regions. Connectivity of the default mode network is established in Michael D. Greicius, Ben Krasnow, Allan L. Reiss, and Vinod Menon, "Functional Connectivity in the Resting Brain: A Network Analysis of the Default Mode Hypothesis," *Proceedings of the National Academy of Sciences of the United States of America* 100, no. 1 (2003). On default mode connectivity and imagination, see Y. Østby, K. B. Walhovd, C. K. Tamnes, H. Grydeland, L. T. Westlye, A. M. Fjell, "Mental Time Travel and Default-Mode Network Functional Connectivity in the Developing Brain," *Proceedings of the National Academy of Sciences* 109, no. 42 (2012): 16800–16804.

78. John A. Sloboda, "Music in Everyday Life: The Role of Emotions," in *Handbook of Music and Emotion: Theory, Research, Applications*, ed. Patrik N. Juslin and John A. Sloboda (New York: Oxford University Press, 2010). Sloboda gives an excellent summary of the research on ways in which emotion is not always evoked by music in everyday experience, rather than in special situations (concerts and other intense listening experiences). Important here is that everyday listening tends to lead to relatively mild emotional responses; it also involves a number of negative emotions, and is often highly personal. People also, it seems, generally have to want to respond to music emotionally in order for it to have a powerful effect (see especially 509ff.).

79. Son Preminger in "Transformative Art" has recently speculated that this might occur, as we have in part demonstrated, through the default mode network.

80. Catherine Stevens and Shirley McKechnie, "Thinking in Action: Thought Made Visible in Contemporary Dance," *Cognitive Processing* 6 (2005), Calvo-Merino et al., "Action Observation and Acquired Motor Skills"; Ivar G. Hagendoorn, "Some Speculative Hypotheses about the Nature and Perception of Dance and Choreography," *Journal of Consciousness Studies* 11, nos. 3–4 (2005).

81. E. H. Gombrich, *Art and Illusion: A Study in the Psychology of Pictorial Representation* (Princeton, NJ: Princeton University Press, 2000), pt. 3; Wolfgang Iser, *The Act of Reading* (Baltimore, MD: Johns Hopkins University Press, 1980). Kandel takes up the beholder's share in his *Age of Insight*.

Chapter 3

1. For this reason, my close reading of "Ode on a Grecian Urn" does not play the same kind of evidentiary role that close readings often do in literary criticism, where they may be made to carry the kind of "benevolent normativity" that Geoffrey Hartmann warned us to beware. I offer an extreme form of vivid reading that is intended to show how Keats forecloses vivid imagining, even in the strongest case. For influential engagements with "Ode on a Grecian Urn" and the question of beauty and poetic form, see especially John Middleton Murry, *Keats* (New York: Noonday, 1955); Cleanth Brooks, *The Well Wrought Urn: Studies in the Structure of Poetry* (New York: Harcourt Brace, 1947); Earl Wasserman, *The Finer Tone* (Baltimore, MD: Johns Hopkins University Press, 1967); Helen H. Vendler, *The Odes of John Keats* (Cambridge, MA: Belknap Press of Harvard University Press, 1983); and Barbara Herrnstein Smith, *Poetic Closure: A Study of How Poems End* (Chicago: University of Chicago Press, 1968).

2. For an excellent account of Keats's exploitation of imagery, see Alan Richardson, *The Neural Sublime* (Baltimore, MD: Johns Hopkins University Press, 2010).

3. Keats's terms are an echo of Shaftesbury's early eighteenth-century essay on beauty: "Sensus Communis, an Essay on the Freedom of Wit and Humour," in Anthony Cooper Shaftesbury, *Characteristics of Men, Manners, Opinions, Times*, ed. Lawrence E. Klein (New York: Cambridge University Press, 1999), 65.

4. Before the eighteenth century there was, as we have seen, a rich variety of discussions of questions about the arts, as well as about beauty, the sublime, and other terms of evaluative response (including the ethics of such responses); but there was no coherent cultural or philosophical domain that sought to adjudicate these questions. The culture of taste, the concept of aesthetic value, and a dedicated philosophical and cultural discourse emerge slowly, so that it is not really until the mid- to late nineteenth century that one might say that aesthetics as a discipline properly exists. See, among others, Paul Guyer, "The Origins of Modern Aesthetics: 1711–35," in *The Blackwell Guide to Aesthetics*, ed. Peter Kivy (London: Blackwell, 2004).

5. For detail on the persistence of Aristotelian thought, see Ross Hamilton, *Accident: A Philosophical and Literary History* (Chicago: University of

Chicago Press, 2008). On the blendings, contests, and revisions of ancient and modern forms of knowledge in the neoclassical period, see especially Richard Kroll, *The Material Word: Literate Culture in the Restoration and Early Eighteenth Century* (Baltimore, MD: Johns Hopkins University Press, 1991).

6. On aesthetics and empiricism, see Frances Ferguson, *Solitude and the Sublime: Romanticism and the Aesthetics of Individuation* (New York: Routledge, 1992), and G. Gabrielle Starr, "Cavendish, Aesthetics, and the Anti-Platonic Line," *Eighteenth-Century Studies* 29, no. 3 (2006). On part of the debates around neoclassicism and aesthetics, especially with Shaftesbury, see Ronald Paulson, *The Beautiful, Novel, and Strange: Aesthetics and Heterodoxy* (Baltimore, MD: Johns Hopkins University Press, 1995).

7. Fuseli's 1765 translation of Winckelmann brought his work to the attention of English-speaking readers; Keats's acquaintance with the Fuseli translation is well accepted. See, for example, James L. O'Rourke, *Keats's Odes and Contemporary Criticism* (Gainesville: University Press of Florida, 1998). A number of studies pursue the connection between Winckelmann and Keats, from Pater's *Renaissance* to, more recently, A. W. Phinney, "Keats in the Museum: Between Aesthetics and History," *Journal of English and Germanic Philology* 90, no. 2 (1991); David Ferris, *Silent Urns: Romanticism, Hellenism, Modernity (Cultural Memory in the Present)* (Stanford: Stanford University Press, 2000); and Martin Aske, *Keats and Hellenism: An Essay* (New York: Cambridge University Press, 2005).

8. Johann Winckelmann, "On the Imitation of the Painting and Sculpture of the Greeks," in *German Essays on Art History*, trans. Henry Fuseli, ed. Gert Schiff (New York: Continuum, 1988) 2.

9. Winckelmann, "On the Imitation of the Painting and Sculpture of the Greeks," 4.

10. Barbara Maria Stafford, "Beauty of the Invisible: Winckelmann and the Aesthetics of Imperceptibility," *Zeitschrift für Kunstgeschichte* 43, no. 1 (1980): 65. Stafford gives a cogent account of the idea of invisible beauty in Winckelmann and in neoclassical and romantic aesthetics. Michael Fried notes, "Surrounded by the most physically perfect human beings in all history, in circumstances that made possible intimate familiarity with their perfection, the Greek wasn't satisfied simply to represent the latter in his art. Instead the great, exemplary, originary achievement of the ancient

Greeks turns out to have been grounded in a recognition of the need to go beyond natural beauty in the direction of the ideal," "Antiquity Now: Reading Winckelmann on Imitation," *October* 37, Summer (1986): 88.

11. As Jonah Siegel writes, "At best, the works of great originary genius to which Winckelmann had paid homage were Hellenistic copies of irretrievably lost Greek bronzes," *Desire and Excess: The Nineteenth-Century Culture of Art* (Princeton, NJ: Princeton University Press, 2000), 58.

12. For the classic account of the implications of optics for eighteenth-century aesthetics, see Marjorie Hope Nicholson, *Newton Demands the Muse: Newton's "Opticks" and the Eighteenth Century Poets* (Princeton, NJ: Princeton University Press, 1946).

13. For a good account of the history of the marbles, see William St. Clair, *Lord Elgin and the Marbles: The Controversial History of the Parthenon Sculptures* (New York: Oxford University Press, 1998). Jonah Siegel offers a cogent analysis of the effects of the marbles and other classical recoveries on ideas of art in *Desire and Excess*.

14. Keats himself evokes the problem of visibility and of the erasure of beauty when he writes about the marbles and the incongruity of image and perception:

> Such dim-conceived glories of the brain
> > Bring round the heart an undescribable feud;
> So do these wonders a most dizzy pain,
> > That mingles Grecian grandeur with the rude
> Wasting of old time. . . .

"On Seeing the Elgin Marbles," in *Complete Poems*, ed. Jack Stillinger (Cambridge, MA: Belknap Press of Harvard University Press, 1982).

15. Vinzenz Brinkmann and Oliver Primavesi, *Die Polychromie der Archaischen und Frühklassischen Skulptur* (München: Biering & Brinkmann, 2004). On the twentieth-century damage, see St. Clair, *Lord Elgin and the Marbles*.

16. Siegel, *Desire and Excess,* 59, 61. The phrase "mutilated fragments" belongs to George Beaumont, quoted in Siegel, *Desire and Excess*, 298 n. 30. As Siegel puts it, "The close attention of neoclassicism is inverted into distant gazing toward objects that can never be recovered, that are beloved but forever lost. As such, the beauties of antiquity can *only* be mourned as they are spied or 'fancied' in distant images" (55).

17. Percy Bysshe Shelley, "Hymn to Intellectual Beauty" (1816), in *The Complete Poetry of Percy Bysshe Shelley*, ed. Donald H. Reiman, Neil Fraistat, and Nora Crook (Baltimore: Johns Hopkins University Press, 2012).

18. What we perceive here on earth is beauty's image, which "we grasp . . . sparkling through the clearest of our senses." This earthly beauty serves (though still only a reflective brightness) to lead us to the greater brightness and power of Truth, Justice, and the other ideals, which occupy a higher plane of existence. Plato, *Phaedrus*, trans. Alexander Nehamas and Paul Woodruff (Indianapolis: Hackett, 1995), 39. See also Plato, *Symposium*, trans. Alexander Nehamas and Paul Woodruff (Indianapolis: Hackett, 1989).

19. On the importance of history (in part) as material effect in the period, see Alan Liu, *Wordsworth: The Sense of History* (Stanford: Stanford University Press, 1989), and Clifford Siskin, *The Historicity of Romantic Discourse* (New York: Oxford University Press, 1988), among other major critiques.

20. On the relations of the Sister Arts to ideas of aesthetics, see Lawrence I. Lipking, *The Ordering of the Arts in Eighteenth-Century England* (Princeton, NJ: Princeton University Press, 1970); Jean H. Hagstrum, *The Sister Arts: The Tradition of Literary Pictorialism and English Poetry from Dryden to Gray* (Chicago: University of Chicago Press, 1975); and James Engell, *The Creative Imagination: Enlightenment to Romanticism* (Cambridge, MA: Harvard University Press, 1981). On the artistic perception in the Romantic period, see, most famously, M. H. Abrams, *The Mirror and the Lamp: Romantic Theory and the Critical Tradition* (New York: Oxford University Press, 1971).

21. Marshall Brown puts this poem back in context of its Sisters in "Unheard Melodies: The Force of Form," *PMLA* 107, no. 3 (1992).

22. Derrida might argue that the parergon is the figure that signals the completion of the form as well as the problem of formal completion and the perception of that completion: "The *parergon* stands out . . . both from the *ergon* (the work) and from the milieu, it stands out first of all like a figure on a ground. But it does not stand out in the same way as the work. The latter also stand out against a ground. But the parergonal frame stands out against two grounds." Jacques Derrida, *The Truth in Painting*, trans. Geoff Bennington and Ian McLeod (Chicago: University of Chicago Press, 1987), 61.

23. Barbara Herrnstein Smith in *Poetic Closure* notes, "this ode . . . is offered as the poetic report of a train of associations evoked by the poet's response to a specific object, and develops in accord with Keats's notion of the sequence of psychological events in a 'bardic trance'" (230). James Ralston Caldwell, *John Keats's Fancy: The Effect on Keats of the Psychology of His Day* (New York: Octagon, 1965).

24. Murray Krieger, *The Play and Place of Criticism* (Baltimore, MD: Johns Hopkins University Press, 1959), chap. 8.

25. Stephen Palmer, "Gestalt Perception," in *The MIT Encyclopedia of the Cognitive Sciences*, ed. Robert Wilson and Frank Keil (Cambridge, MA: MIT Press, 1999). Reuven Tsur blends insights of Gestalt psychology with those of cognitive science, arguing that poetic meter is most successful when it capitalizes both on our limited cognitive capacity and the demands of Gestalt: "Verse lines can be perceived as perceptual wholes if they can be contained in short-term memory, . . . and the number of units it can hold is limited, according to George Miller (1970), at 'the magical number seven, plus or minus two.' . . . The 'better' or 'simpler' the gestalt of a stimulus pattern, the less mental processing space it occupies, and the metric pattern is therefore more likely to be contained within the scope of short-term memory and perceived as rhythmical. At the same time, according to gestalt theory, greater simplicity of, for example, the metric feet must be modified to make them dependent on and integrated with, for example, the hemistich that is the perceptual whole." Tsur,"Some Cognitive Foundations of 'Cultural Programs,'" *Poetics Today* 23, no. 1 (2002): 73.

26. Smith, *Poetic Closure,* 229–234.

27. I am grateful to an anonymous reviewer for helping with this formulation.

28. This reemergence of sound contributes to the debate, intense for much of the middle of the twentieth century, as to who "says" the final lines of the poem.

29. On masking, see, among others, Charles S. Watson, "Uncertainty, Informational Masking, and the Capacity of Immediate Auditory Memory," in *Auditory Processing of Complex Sounds*, ed. William A. Yost and Charles S. Watson (Hillsdale, NJ: Erlbaum, 1987). On language and the competition between semantically close words, see Wilem J. M. Levelt, "The Architecture of Normal Spoken Language Use," in *Linguistics*

Disorders and Pathologies: An International Handbook, ed. Gerhard Blanken, Juergen Dittman, Hannelore Grimm, John C. Marshall, and Claus W. Wallesch (Berlin: de Gruyter, 1993).

30. Colin Martindale, "The Pleasures of Thought: A Theory of Cognitive Hedonics," *Journal of Mind and Behavior* 5, no. 1 (1984): 76. Martindale is interested in "a variety of seemingly diverse pleasures, e.g., those of solitary thinking, calm contemplation of aesthetic objects, and perception of neutral stimuli in psychological laboratories" (76). His key philosophical and critical influences include Burke, Hegel, George Dickie, and Empson.

31. Edmund Burke argues, "It is certain that . . . the removal or moderation of pain . . . has something in it far from distressing. . . . This feeling, in many cases so agreeable," he calls "delight," and he sees this "delight" as the foundation of the sublime. See Edmund Burke, *A Philosophical Enquiry into the Origin of our Ideas of the Sublime and Beautiful* (New York: Oxford University Press, 1990) 33.

32. For a view of how uniformity in variety produces cognitive pleasure, see Martindale, "The Pleasures of Thought," 67–68.

33. Martindale, "The Pleasures of Thought," 76. Try the experiment yourself: stare at a red object on a white back-ground, or better, a red light, for a minute or so, then look away at something white. You should see a green image in the shape of the red object. Then look at something green. It is important to note that inhibitory pairs are not always intuitively linked, as we see here. The similarity that is needed to produce inhibition has to do with the way that red light and green light are coded by the brain. As Martindale points out, pleasures associated with such processes, which appear in more complex kinds of experience—such reading poetry—have to do with a range of associations that excite and inhibit one another: "It is important to keep in mind that preference for an object is determined not only by the cognitive units directly coding the object but also by cognitive units positively associated with them. To the extent that there are more of such associations, pleasure will be greater so long as the associations do not laterally inhibit one another. Thus, many and diverse associations will produce maximal pleasure" (69).

34. The concept governing this is cognitive load. "Cognitive load" and "limited capacity" are terms used to discuss constraints on the amount and kind of information our brains can process at a given time. In everyday

experience, this might be encountered as the maximum number of items on a grocery list that you can keep in your head at once. We generally experience such limits as flexible, up to a point, and humans are very good at manipulating them—mnemonic devices and medieval memory systems, for example, may make our limitations seem less, but the limits are still there (See Mary Carruthers, *The Book of Memory: A Study of Memory in Medieval Culture* [New York: Cambridge University Press, 1990], and Frances Yates, *The Art of Memory* [Chicago: University of Chicago Press, 1966].) René Descartes made some significant discoveries about cognitive capacity that work well as thought experiments (indeed, many of the fundamental insights that enabled modern cognitive science were made in the seventeenth and eighteenth centuries). Imagine a five-sided figure; easy for most of us. Now, with Descartes, try eleven sides; then a thousand (a chiliagon). Eventually, no one can keep in mind a visual image that displays, distinctly, all of the edges and angles. The problem does not apply only to geometric figures: try to envision five objects—apples, barrels of beer, books. As you increase the number of objects, you cannot "see" each distinctly, even with relatively small numbers, like thirteen. Réne Descartes, *Discourse on Method and Meditations on First Philosophy*, trans. Donald A. Cress (Indianapolis: Hackett, 1988), 92–93. The simplest explanation for these phenomena is that we only have so much ability to process information at once. On the limits with visual imagery, see Stephen Kosslyn, "Aspects of a Cognitive Neuroscience of Mental Imagery," in *Essential Sources in the Scientific Study of Consciousness*, ed. Bernard J. Baars, William P. Banks, and James B. Newman (Cambridge, MA: MIT Press, 2003). On auditory limits, see Andre Aleman, Mark R. Nieuwenstein, Koen B. E. Böcker, and Edward H. F. de Haan, "Music Training and Mental Imagery Ability," *Neuropsychologia* 38 (2000).

35. Martha J. Farah and A. F. Smith, "Perceptional Interference and Facilitation with Auditory Imagery," *Perception & Psychophysics* 33 (1983). See also above, chapter 2.

36. I am indebted to Chris Collins for helping me fine-tune this argument.

37. Helen Vendler argues that "Ode on a Grecian Urn" offers models of aesthetic experience in the varying ways in which we "encounter" the urn. I have argued that the poem also offers models of aesthetic pleasures in the ways sensation itself is either manipulated or foreclosed. Vendler, *The Odes of John Keats,* 116–152.

38. This is Siegel's argument in *Desire and Excess*.

39. On the dissolution of the sublime, see Mark Algee-Hewitt, "The Afterlife of the Sublime: Toward a New History of Aesthetics in the Long Eighteenth Century." PhD diss., New York University, 2008.

40. Peter de Bolla, *The Discourse of the Sublime: Readings in History, Aesthetics, and the Subject* (New York: Oxford University Press, 1989); Ferguson, *Solitude and the Sublime;* Paulson, *The Beautiful, Novel, and Strange;* Samuel Holt Monk, *The Sublime: A Study of Critical Theories in XVIII-Century England* (Ann Arbor: University of Michigan Press, 1960).

41. Ovid, *Ovid's Metamorphoses in Fifteen Books, Translated by the Most Eminent Hands*, ed. Samuel Garth (London: 1717), 25. The original reads:

> "fer, pater," inquit "opem! si flumina numen habetis,
> qua nimium placui, mutando perde figuram!"
> vix prece finitā torpor gravis occupat artūs,
> mollia cinguntur tenui praecordia libro,
> in frondem crinēs, in ramos bracchia crescunt,
> pes modo tam velox pigris radicibus haeret,
> ora cacumen habet: remanet nitor unus in illa.
> > Hanc quoque Phoebus amat positāque in stipite dextrā
> > sentit adhuc trepidare novo sub cortice pectus
> > conplexusque suis ramos ut membra lacertis
> > oscula dat ligno; refugit tamen oscula lignum.

42. On Ovid as a standard for the aesthetics of novelty, see Paulson, *The Beautiful, Novel, and Strange*. On the humorous status of the *Metamorphoses*, see G. Gabrielle Starr, "Burney, Ovid, and the Value of the Beautiful," *Eighteenth-Century Fiction* 24, no. 1 (2012), and Jean-Marc Frécaut, *L'esprit et l'humor chez Ovide* (Grenoble: Presses Universitaires de Grenoble, 1972). Chaucer and Dryden are the two English poets most often credited with getting the joke.

43. The foundational paper is Robert B. Zajonc, "Attitudinal Effects of Mere Exposure," *Journal of Personality and Social Psychology* 9, no. 2 (1968).

44. D. E. Berlyne, "Novelty, Complexity, and Hedonic Value," *Attention, Perception, & Psychophysics* 8, no. 5 (1970): 279–86. See also Berlyne, "Novelty and Curiosity as Determinants of Exploratory Behaviour," *British Journal of Psychology, General Section* 41, nos. 1–2 (1950). For a

review and meta-analysis of the studies of novelty and exposure, see Robert F. Bornstein, "Exposure and Affect: Overview and Meta-Analysis of Research, 1968–1987," *Psychological Bulletin* 106, no. 2 (1989). There is significant evidence that children prefer novel stimuli.

45. Hackjin Kim and colleagues have shown differences in early and late reward responses in the nucleus accumbens that feed forward to the orbitofrontal cortex, and that the earlier response in the nucleus accumbens is selectively enacted for novel stimuli. Hackjin Kim, Ralph Adolphs, John P. O'Doherty, and Shinsuke Shimojo, "Temporal Isolation of Neural Processes Underlying Face Preference Decisions," Proceedings of the National Academy of Sciences of the United States of America 104, no. 46 (2007).

46. Walter Benjamin, *Illuminations*, trans. Harry Zohn (New York: Schocken, 1968), 256.

47. On novelty and the early/late function of the nucleus accumbens and orbitofrontal cortex, see Kim et al., "Temporal Isolation of Neural Processes Underlying Face Preference Decisions."

48. Bernini was becoming increasingly well known in the late seventeenth century in England, and Dryden's friend, the painter Geoffrey Kneller, had reputedly studied with Bernini. Christopher Wren and Sir William Temple were particular admirers, and William Wotton made Bernini one of the modern stars in his *Reflections upon Ancient and Modern Learning*. See Joseph M. Levine, *Between the Ancients and Moderns: Baroque Culture in Restoration England* (New Haven, CT: Yale University Press, 1999), 61–102 passim. The sculpture *Apollo and Daphne* at the Villa Borghese became a famous part of the Grand Tour. The statue appeared in many of the earliest guidebooks for Rome (see, for example, Giacomo Manilli's *Villa Borghese: Fuori di Porta Pincians* [Rome, 1650]). George Berkeley's account of the tour (though after Dryden's poem) gives a sense of the growing appeal of the sculptures; the tour, of course, was increasingly popular for aristocratic men after the Restoration. See Edward Chaney, *The Evolution of the Grand Tour* (London: Frank Cass, 1998). See also Jean Hagstrum, who notes that reproductions of Bernini are mentioned in an idealized country house in *Country Conversations* (Henry Wright, 1694): Hagstrum, *Sister Arts,* 112. Hagstrum gives a good account of Dryden's pictorial practice.

49. On the role of the statue in Bernini's reputation, see Rudolf Wittkower, *Bernini* (New York: Phaidon, 1997). It was a breathtaking triumph for the sculptor, who was only twenty-three when he began work on it.

50. Andrea Bolland, "*Desiderio* and *Diletto*: Vision, Touch, and the Poetics of Bernini's *Apollo and Daphne,*" *Art Bulletin* 82, no. 2 (2000).

51. Lipking, *The Ordering of the Arts in Eighteenth-Century England;* Hagstrum, *Sister Arts.*

52. On Dryden's translations of Ovid, see Lee T. Pearcy, *The Mediated Muse: English Translations of Ovid 1560–1700* (Hamden, CT: Archon, 1984), chaps. 5–6. On the importance of translation and imitation, especially of Ovid, see Margaret Doody, *The Daring Muse: Augustan Poetry Reconsidered* (New York: Cambridge University Press, 1985), and on the broader picture of imitation, see Howard Weinbrot, *The Formal Strain: Studies in Augustan Imitation and Satire* (Chicago: University of Chicago Press, 1969).

53. Alice Fulton, "Give: Daphne and Apollo," in *After Ovid: New Metamorphoses*, ed. Michael Hofmann and James Lasdun (New York: Farrar, Straus and Giroux, 1994).

54. We might fruitfully compare Huron's contrastive valence to Edmund Burke's idea of delight. Delight, for him, comes from the release of pain, and is not the same as pleasure.

55. On the aesthetics of surprise, see Christopher R. Miller, "Jane Austen's Aesthetics and Ethics of Surprise," *Narrative* 13, no. 3 (2005), and Miller, "Wordsworth's Anatomies of Surprise," *Studies in Romanticism* 46, Winter (2007).

56. On the twentieth-century history of bluegrass, see Neil Rosenberg, *Bluegrass: A History* (Champaign: University of Illinois Press, 2005). Rosenberg argues that bluegrass was a folk revival style linked to the emergence of the "Nashville sound" of commercial country music.

57. In such an instance, following Huron's model we might say that the probability of failure in performance increases with difficulty, and we respond pleasurably to the unlikely success, which seems to delight, if not surprise us, every time we hear it.

58. Joti Rockwell has given an intriguing description of the motion of the hands in banjo playing as an essential way of representing bluegrass

music mathematically in "Banjo Transformations and Bluegrass Rhythm," *Journal of Music Theory* 53, no. 1 (2009).

59. See Joti Rockwell, "Time on the Crooked Road: Isochrony, Meter, and Disruption in Old-Time Country and Bluegrass Music," *Ethnomusicology* 55, no. 1 (Winter 2011).

60. K. M. Knittel, "Wagner, Deafness, and the Reception of Beethoven's Late Style," *Journal of the American Musicological Society* 51, no. 1 (1998). On the importance of the late style for aesthetics, see Theodor Adorno, *Beethoven: The Philosophy of Music*, trans. Edmund Jephcott, ed. Rolf Tiedemann (Stanford: Stanford University Press, 1998), and Michael Spitzer, *Music as Philosophy: Adorno and Beethoven's Late Style* (Bloomington: Indiana University Press, 2006).

61. Peter Gammond and Andrew Lamb, "Waltz," in *The Oxford Companion to Music*, ed. Alison Latham (New York: Oxford University Press, 2002).

62. William Kinderman, *Beethoven's Diabelli Variations* (New York: Oxford University Press, 1999), 69.

63. Rosen finds it "grotesquely funny": Charles Rosen, *The Classical Style: Haydn, Mozart, Beethoven*, expanded ed. (New York: Norton, 1997), 95.

64. For an excellent description of musical predictability, see David Temperley, *Music and Probability* (Cambridge, MA: MIT Press, 2007).

65. Rosen, *The Classical Style,* 23–29; see also Temperley, *Music and Probability.*

66. David Huron in *Sweet Anticipation* (Cambridge, MA: MIT Press, 2006) calls musical events "innocent bystanders" of emotional responses, and argues against any inherent value. On predictive reward, in addition to Huron, see also Valorie N. Salimpoor, Mitchel Benovoy, Kevin Larcher, Alain Dagher, and Robert J. Zatorre, "Anatomically Distinct Dopamine Release during Anticipation and Experience of Peak Emotion to Music," *Nature Neuroscience* 14, no. 2 (2011).

67. Spitzer, *Music as Philosophy,* 167.

68. Oliver Sacks gives a wonderful account of how composers in general rely on musical imagery rather than instruments in *Musicophilia* (New York: Knopf, 2007).

69. For a good account of the ways that Beethoven's deafness was first understood as a way of accounting for perceived grotesque features of the final compositions, see Knittel, "Wagner, Deafness, and the Reception of Beethoven's Late Style."

70. Rosen, *The Classical Style*, 510.

71. See Maynard Solomon, *Late Beethoven: Music, Thought, Imagination* (Berkeley: University of California Press, 2003), 102ff.

72. Solomon, *Late Beethoven*, 129.

73. Solomon, *Late Beethoven*, 179.

74. Charles Stuckey engages the question of color and fading of Van Gogh's inks in "Rhythmic Lines: Van Gogh's Drawings," *Art in America* 94, no. 3 (2006).

75. Meta Chavannes and Louis Van Tilborgh, "A Missing Van Gogh Unveiled," *Burlington Magazine* 149, August 2007.

76. William Hogarth, *The Analysis of Beauty*, ed. Ronald Paulson (New Haven, CT: Yale University Press, 1997), 33. Emphasis in original.

77. E. H. Gombrich, *Art and Illusion: A Study in the Psychology of Pictorial Representation* (Princeton, NJ: Princeton University Press, 2000), chap. 8.

78. Chavannes and Van Tilborgh argue that Van Gogh was pleased with the result of his reuse of the canvas, but that it was as if he was "almost taken by surprise" when he found himself without materials when he felt the need to paint the ravine in Saint-Rémy (550).

79. Stuckey, "Rhythmic Lines," 183.

80. Letter to Emile Bernard, quoted in Chavannes and Van Tilborgh, "A Missing Van Gogh Unveiled," 548: "cela est amusant de travailler dans des sites bien sauvages où il faut enterrer le chevalet pour que le vent ne vous fiche pas tout par terre."

81. Ovid's description of Europa, for example, may be an ekphrasis relying in part on ancient frescoes of the girl riding a bull. One of these is well preserved in the Museo Archeologico Nazionale in Naples.

82. Ovid, *Metamorphoses*, trans. A. D. Melville (New York: Oxford University Press, 2009), 22.

83. On the ways in which Renaissance writers found a model for the pains of artistic endeavor in Ovid, see Leonard Barkan, *The Gods Made Flesh: Metamorphosis and the Pursuit of Paganism* (New Haven, CT: Yale University Press, 1990).

84. Ovid, *Metamorphoses,* bk. 1, l.4.

85. In "Transformative Art," Son Preminger speculates that this may be one way that art can be provide a "long-term transformative experience": Preminger, "Transformative Art: Art as Means for Long-term Neurocognitive Change," *Frontiers in Human Neuroscience* 6 (2012), doi:10.3389/fnhum.2012.00096.

86. Spreng and colleagues synthesize the evidence for overlap between memory and the default mode network. See R. Nathan Spreng, Raymond A. Marr, and Alice S. N. Kim, "The Common Neural Basis of Autobiographical Memory, Prospection, Navigation, Theory of Mind and the Default Mode: A Quantitative Meta-analysis," *Journal of Cognitive Neuroscience* 21, no. 3 (2008).

87. Work has begun on memory; see the essays in Suzanne Nalbantian, Paul M. Matthews, and James L. McClelland, eds., *Memory Process: Neuroscientific and Humanistic Perspectives* (Cambridge, MA: MIT Press, 2010).

88. Eric Kandel makes a wonderful argument for what he calls the link between the "cognitive unconscious and the creative brain" in chapter 29 of *The Age of Insight.*.

89. Elaine Scarry, *On Beauty and Being Just* (Princeton, NJ: Princeton University Press, 1999), chap. 1.

Appendix

1. J. Talairach and P. Tournoux, *Co-planar Sterotaxic Atlas of the Human Brain: 3-Dimensional Proportional System—An Approach to Cerebral Imaging* (New York: Thieme Medical Publishers, 1988).

2. On computing the false discovery rate, see Y. Benjamini and Y. Hochberg, "Controlling the False Discovery Rate: A Practical and Powerful Approach to Multiple Testing," *Journal of the Royal Statistical Society, Series B, Methodological* 57 (1995): 289–300, and C. R. Genovese, N. A. Lazar, and T. Nichols, "Thresholding of Statistical Maps in Functional Neuroimaging Using the False Discovery Rate," *NeuroImage* 15 (1998): 870–878.

Bibliography

Abrams, M. H. *The Mirror and the Lamp: Romantic Theory and the Critical Tradition.* New York: Oxford University Press, 1971.

Ackermann, Hermann, Klaus Mathiak, and Richard B. Ivry. "Temporal Organization of 'Internal Speech' as a Basis for Cerebellar Modulation of Cognitive Functions." *Behavioral and Cognitive Neuroscience Reviews* 3, no. 1 (2004): 14–22.

Addison, Joseph. *The Spectator.* Ed. Donald F. Bond. Oxford: Clarendon Press, 1965.

Adorno, Theodor. *Aesthetic Theory.* Trans. Robert Hullot-Kentor. Minneapolis: University of Minnesota Press, 1997.

Adorno, Theodor. *Beethoven: The Philosophy of Music.* Trans. Edmund Jephcott, ed. Rolf Tiedemann. Stanford: Stanford University Press, 1998.

Aharon, Itzhak, Nancy Etcoff, Dan Ariely, Christopher F. Chabris, Ethan O'Connor, and Hans C. Breiter. "Beautiful Faces Have Variable Reward Value: fMRI and Behavioral Evidence." *Neuron* 32, no. 3 (2001): 537–551.

Aleman, Andre, Mark R. Nieuwenstein, Koen B. E. Böcker, and Edward H. F. de Haan. "Music Training and Mental Imagery Ability." *Neuropsychologia* 38 (2000): 1664–1668.

Aleman, Andre, and Mascha Van't Wout. "Subvocalization in Auditory-Verbal Imagery: Just a Form of Motor Imagery?" *Cognitive Processing* 5 (2004): 228–231.

Alexander, G. E., and M. D. Crutcher. "Functional Architecture of Basal Ganglia Circuits: Neural Substrates of Parallel Processing." *Trends in Neurosciences* 13 (1990): 266–271.

Alexander, G. E., M. R. DeLong, and P. L. Strick. "Parallel Organization of Functionally Segregated Circuits Linking Basal Ganglia and Cortex." *Annual Review of Neuroscience* 9 (1986): 357–381,

Algee-Hewitt, Mark. "The Afterlife of the Sublime: Toward a New History of Aesthetics in the Long Eighteenth Century." PhD diss., New York University, 2008.

Alloy, Lauren B., and Lyn Y. Abramson. "Judgment of Contingency in Depressed and Nondepressed Students: Sadder But Wiser?" *Journal of Experimental Psychology: General* 108, no. 4 (1979): 441–485.

Alves, Nelson Torro, Sérgio S. Fukusima, and J. Antonio Aznar-Casanova. "Models of Brain Asymmetry in Emotional Processing." *Psychology and Neuroscience* 1, no. 1 (2008): 63–66.

Amodio, D. M., and C. D. Frith. "Meeting of Minds: The Medial Frontal Cortex and Social Cognition." *Nature Reviews: Neuroscience* 7 (2006): 268–277.

Andrews-Hanna, Jessica R., Jay S. Reidler, Jorge Sepulcre, Renee Poulin, and Randy L. Buckner. "Functional-Anatomic Fractionation of the Brain's Default Network." *Neuron* 65, no. 4 (2010): 550–562.

Aristotle. *On Rhetoric*. Trans. George A. Kennedy. New York: Oxford University Press, 1991.

Aristotle. *Politics*. Trans. C.D.C. Reeve. Indianapolis: Hackett, 1998.

Aske, Martin. *Keats and Hellenism: An Essay*. New York: Cambridge University Press, 2005.

Attneave, F., and P. Farrar. "The Visual World behind the Head." *American Journal of Psychology* 90 (1977): 549–563.

Augustine. *Confessions*. Trans. Henry Chadwick. New York: Oxford University Press, 1991.

Aziz-Zadeh, L., L. Koski, E. Zaidel, John C. Mazziotta, and Marco Iacoboni. "Lateralization of the Human Mirror Neuron System." *Journal of Neuroscience* 26 (2006): 2964–2970.

Barkan, Leonard. *The Gods Made Flesh: Metamorphosis and the Pursuit of Paganism*. New Haven, CT: Yale University Press, 1990.

Barlow, Horace, Colin Blakemore, and Miranda Weston-Smith, eds. *Images and Understanding*. New York: Cambridge University Press, 1990.

Barrett, Lisa Feldman. "Are Emotions Natural Kinds?" *Perspectives on Psychological Science* 1, no. 1 (2006): 28–58.

Battaglia, Fortunato, Sarah H. Lisanby, and David Freedberg. "Corticomotor Excitability during Observation and Imagination of a Work of Art." *Frontiers in Human Neuroscience* 5 (2011).

Beattie, James. *Essays: On Poetry and Music as They Affect the Mind*. London, 1779.

Bechara, Antoine, Hannah Damasio, Daniel Tranel, and Antonio Damasio. "Deciding Advantageously before Knowing the Advantageous Strategy." *Science* 275 (1997): 1293–1295.

Beeli, Michaela Esslen, and Lutz Jancke. "Synaesthesia: When Coloured Sounds Taste Sweet." *Nature* 434 (2005): 38.

Bell, Clive. *Art*. London: Chatto and Windus, 1914.

Benhabib, Jess, and A. Bisin. "Modeling Internal Commitment Mechanisms and Self-Control: A Neuroeconomics Approach to Consumption-Saving Decisions." *Games and Economic Behavior* 52, no. 2 (2005): 460–492.

Benjamin, Walter. *Illuminations*. Trans. Harry Zohn. New York: Schocken, 1968.

Benjamini, Y., and Y. Hochberg. "Controlling the False Discovery Rate: A Practical and Powerful Approach to Multiple Testing." *Journal of the Royal Statistical Society, Series B, Methodological* 57 (1995): 289–300.

Berlyne, D. E. "Novelty, Complexity, and Hedonic Value." *Attention, Perception, & Psychophysics* 8, no. 5 (1970): 279–286.

Berlyne, D. E. "Novelty and Curiosity as Determinants of Exploratory Behaviour." *British Journal of Psychology, General Section* 41, nos. 1–2 (1950): 68–80.

Biederman, Irving, and Edward A. Vessel. "Perceptual Pleasure and the Brain." *American Scientist* 94 (2006): 249–255.

Bishop, Elizabeth. *The Complete Poems, 1929–1979.* New York: Noonday, 1983.

Blakemore, S.-J., and J. Decety. "From the Perception of Action to the Understanding of Intention." *Nature Reviews: Neuroscience* 2 (2001): 561–567.

Blanchard, C. D., and R. J. Blanchard. "Innate and Conditioned Reactions to Threat in Rats with Amygdaloid Lesions." *Journal of Comparative and Physiological Psychology* 81 (1972): 281–290.

Block, Ned, ed. *Imagery.* Cambridge, MA: MIT Press, 1981.

Blood, Anne J., and Robert Zatorre. "Intensely Pleasurable Responses to Music Correlate with Activity in Brain Regions Implicated in Reward and Emotion." *Proceedings of the National Academy of Sciences of the United States of America* 98 (2001): 11818–11823.

Blood, Anne J., Robert Zatorre, Patrick Bermudez, and Alan C. Evans. "Emotional Responses to Pleasant and Unpleasant Music Correlate with Activity in Paralimbic Brain Regions." *Nature Neuroscience* 2, no. 4 (1999): 382–387.

Bloom, Paul. *How Pleasure Works: The New Science of Why We Like What We Like.* New York: Norton, 2010.

Bolland, Andrea. "*Desiderio* and *Diletto*: Vision, Touch, and the Poetics of Bernini's *Apollo and Daphne.*" *Art Bulletin* 82, no. 2 (2000): 309–330.

Bornstein, Robert F. "Exposure and Affect: Overview and Meta-Analysis of Research, 1968–1987." *Psychological Bulletin* 106, no. 2 (1989): 265–289.

Borst, Gregoire, and Stephen Kosslyn. "Visual Mental Imagery and Visual Perception: Structural Equivalence Revealed by Scanning Processes." *Memory and Cognition* 36, no. 4 (2008): 849–862.

Boruah, Bijoy. *Fiction and Emotion.* Oxford: Clarendon Press, 1988.

Boyd, Brian J. *On the Origin of Stories: Evolution, Cognition, and Fiction.* Cambridge, MA: Belknap Press of Harvard University Press, 2010.

Brainard, D. H. "The Psychophysics Toolbox." *Spatial Vision* 10 (1997): 443–446.

Brinkmann, Vinzenz, and Oliver Primavesi. *Die Polychromie der Archaischen und Frühklassischen Skulptur*. München: Biering & Brinkmann, 2004.

Brooks, Cleanth. *The Well Wrought Urn: Studies in the Structure of Poetry*. New York: Harcourt Brace, 1947.

Bromberger, Bianca, Rebecca Sternschein, Page Widick, William Smith, and Anjan Chatterjee. "The Right Hemisphere in Aesthetic Perception." *Frontiers in Human Neuroscience* 5 (2011).

Brown, Marshall. "Unheard Melodies: The Force of Form." *PMLA* 107, no. 3 (1992): 465–481.

Buckner, Randy L., and Daniel C. Carroll. "Self-Projection and the Brain." *Trends in Cognitive Sciences* 11, no. 2 (2007): 49–57.

Budd, Malcolm. *Music and the Emotions: The Philosophical Theories*. New York: Routledge, 1985.

Bullough, E. "'Psychical Distance' as a Factor in Art and as an Aesthetic Principle." *British Journal of Psychology* 5 (1912): 87–98.

Burke, Edmund. *A Philosophical Enquiry into the Origin of Our Ideas of the Sublmime and Beautiful*. New York: Oxford University Press, 1990.

Butler, Christopher. *Pleasure and the Arts*. New York: Oxford University Press, 2004.

Buxbaum, Laurel J., Scott H. Johnson-Frey, and Megan Bartlett-Williams. "Deficient Internal Models for Planning Hand-Object Interactions in Apraxia." *Neuropsychologia* 43 (2005): 917–929.

Caldwell, James Ralston. *John Keats's Fancy: The Effect on Keats of the Psychology of His Day*. New York: Octagon, 1965.

Calvo-Merino, B., D. E. Glaser, J. Grezes, R. E. Passingham, and P. Haggard. "Action Observation and Acquired Motor Skills: An fMRI Study with Expert Dancers." *Cerebral Cortex* 15 (2005): 1243–1249.

Cambray, Joe. "Towards the Feeling of Emergence." *Journal of Analytical Psychology* 51 (2006): 1–20.

Carr, Laurie, Marco Iacoboni, Marie-Charlotte Dubeau, John C. Mazziotta, and Gian Luigi Lenzi. "Neural Mechanisms of Empathy in Humans: A Relay from Neural Systems for Imitation to Limbic Areas." *Proceedings of the National Academy of Sciences of the United States of America* 100, no. 9 (2003): 5497–5502.

Carruthers, Mary. *The Book of Memory: A Study of Memory in Medieval Culture*. New York: Cambridge University Press, 1990.

Carruthers, Mary. "Sweetness." *Speculum* 81, no. 4 (2006): 999–1013.

Carruthers, Mary. "Varietas: A Word of Many Colors." *Poetica: Zeitschrift für Sprach- und Literaturwissenschaft* Fall (2009): 33–54.

Cavanagh, Patrick. "The Artist as Neuroscientist." *Nature* 434 (2005): 301–307.

Cavendish, Margaret. *Poems and Fancies*. Menton, UK: Scolar Press, 1972.

Cela-Conde, C. J., G. Marty, F. Maestú, T. Ortiz, E. Munar, A. Fernández, M. Roca, J. Rosselló, and F. Quesney. "Activation of the Prefrontal Cortex in the Human Visual Aesthetic Perception." *Proceedings of the National Academy of Sciences of the United States of America* 101, no. 16 (2004): 6321–6325.

Cerf-Ducastel, Barbara, Pierre-Francois Van de Moortele, Patrick MacLeod, Denis Le Bihan, and Annick Faurion. "Interaction of Gustatory and Lingual Somatosensory Perceptions at the Cortical Level in the Human: A Functional Magnetic Resonance Imaging Study." *Chemical Senses* 26 (2001): 371–383.

Chaney, Edward. *The Evolution of the Grand Tour*. London: Frank Cass, 1998.

Chatterjee, A. "Neuroaesthetics: A Coming of Age Story." *Journal of Cognitive Neuroscience* 23 (2011): 53–62.

Chavannes, Meta, and Louis Van Tilborgh. "A Missing Van Gogh Unveiled." *Burlington Magazine* 149 (August 2007): 546–550.

Cicero. *Pro Archia Poeta*. In *Orations*, vol. 11. Trans. N. H. Watts, 6–41. Cambridge, MA: Harvard University Press, 1923.

Clayton, Martin, Rebecca Sager, and Udo Will. "In Time with the Music: The Concept of Entrainment and Its Significance for Ethnomusicology." *ESEM CounterPoint* 1 (2004): 1–45.

Clore, Gerald L., and Andrew Ortony. Appraisal Theories: How Cognition Shapes Affect into Emotion. In *Handbook of Emotions*. 3rd ed., ed. Michael Lewis, Jeannette M. Haviland-Jones, and Lisa Feldman Barrett, 628–642. New York: Guilford Press, 2008.

Costa, Vincent D., Peter J. Lang, Dean Sabatinelli, Francesco Versace, and Margaret M. Bradley. "Emotional Imagery: Assessing Pleasure and Arousal in the Brain's Reward Circuitry." *Human Brain Mapping* 31 (2010): 1446–1457.

Cupchik, G. C., O. Vartanian, A. Crawley, and D. J. Mikulis. "Viewing Artworks: Contributions of Cognitive Control and Perceptual Facilitation to Aesthetic Experience." *Brain and Cognition* 70 (2009): 84–91.

Currie, Gregory. "Realism of Character and the Value of Fiction." In *Aesthetics and Ethics: Essays at the Intersection*, ed. Jerrold Levinson, 161–181. Cambridge: Cambridge University Press, 1998.

Cytowic, Richard E. "Synesthesia: Phenomenology and Neuropsychology. A Review of Current Knowledge." *Psyche* 2, no. 10 (1995): np.

Dadds, Mark R., Dana Bovbjerg, William H. Redd, and Tim R. H. Cutmore. "Imagery in Human Classical Conditioning." *Psychological Bulletin* 122, no. 1 (1997): 89–103.

Dadlez, Eva M. *What's Hecuba to Him? Fictional Events and Actual Emotions*. University Park: Pennsylvania State University Press, 1997.

Damasio, Antonio. *Descartes' Error: Emotion, Reason, and the Human Brain*. New York: HarperCollins, 1995.

Damasio, Antonio. *The Feeling of What Happens: Body and Emotion in the Making of Consciousness*. New York: Harcourt, 1999.

D'Argembeau, Arnaud, Fabienne Collette, Martial Van der Linden, Steven Laureys, Guy Del Fiore, Christian Degueldre, Andre Luxen, and Eric Salmon. "Self-Referential Reflective Activity and Its Relationship with Rest: A PET Study." *NeuroImage* 25 (2005): 616–624.

D'Argembeau, Arnaud, David Stawarczyk, Steve Majerus, Fabienne Collette, Martial Van der Linden, Dorothée Feyers, Pierre Maquet, and Eric Salmon. "The Neural Basis of Personal Goal Processing When Envisioning Future Events." *Journal of Cognitive Neuroscience* 22, no. 8 (2009): 1701–1713.

Davis, M. "The Role of the Amygdala in Emotional Learning." *International Review of Neurobiology* 36 (1994): 225–266.

Day, Sean. "Synaesthesia and Synaesthetic Metaphors." *Psyche* 2, no. 32 (1996): np.

de Bolla, Peter. *Art Matters*. Cambridge, MA: Harvard University Press, 2001.

de Bolla, Peter. *The Discourse of the Sublime: Readings in History, Aesthetics, and the Subject.* New York: Oxford University Press, 1989.

Decety, Jean, M. Jeannerod, D. Durozard, and G. Baverel. "Central Activation of Autonomic Effectors during Mental Simulation of Motor Actions in Man." *Journal of Physiology* 462 (1993): 549–563.

Decety, Jean, and Philip L. Jackson. "The Functional Architecture of Human Empathy." *Behavioral and Cognitive Neuroscience Reviews* 3, no. 2 (2004): 71–100.

de Lange, Floris P., Peter Hagoort, and Ivan Toni. "Neural Topography and Content of Movement Representations." *Journal of Cognitive Neuroscience* 17, no. 1 (2005): 97–112.

Derrida, Jacques. *The Truth in Painting.* Trans. Ian McLeod and Geoff Bennington. Chicago: University of Chicago Press, 1987.

Descartes, Réne. *Discourse on Method and Meditations on First Philosophy.* Trans. Donald A. Cress. Indianapolis: Hackett, 1988.

De Vega, M., I. Leon, and J. M. Diaz. "The Representations of Changing Emotions in Reading Comprehension." *Cognition and Emotion* 10, no. 3 (1996): 303–321.

Dickie, George. "The Myth of the Aesthetic Attitude." *American Philosophical Quarterly* 1 (1964): 56–66.

di Dio, Cinzia, and Vittorio Gallese. "Neuroaesthetics: A Review." *Current Opinion in Neurobiology* 19 (2009): 682–687. doi:10.1016/j.conb.2009.09.001.

di Dio, Cinzia, Emiliano Macaluso, and Giacomo Rizzolatti. "The Golden Beauty: Brain Response to Classical and Renaissance Sculptures." *PLoS ONE* 11 (2007): e1201.

Dinstein, Ilan, Uri Hasson, Nava Rubin, and David Heeger. "Brain Areas Selective for Both Observed and Executed Movements." *Journal of Neurophysiology* 98 (2007): 1415–1427.

Dixon, Mike J., Daniel Smilek, Cera Cudahy, and Philip M. Merikle. "Five Plus Two Equals Yellow." *Nature* 406 (2000): 365.

Djordjevic, Jelena, Robert J. Zatorre, and M. Jones-Gotman. "Effects of Perceived and Imagined Odors on Taste Detection." *Chemical Senses* 29 (2004): 199–208.

Djordjevic, Jelena, Robert J. Zatorre, and M. Jones-Gotman. "The Mind's Nose: Effects of Odor and Visual Imagery on Odor Detection." *Psychological Science* 15, no. 3 (2004): 143–148.

Doody, Margaret. *The Daring Muse: Augustan Poetry Reconsidered*. New York: Cambridge University Press, 1985.

Dutton, Denis. *The Art Instinct: Beauty, Pleasure, and Human Evolution*. London: Bloomsbury, 2010.

Empson, William. "Rhythm and Imagery in English Poetry." *British Journal of Aesthetics* 2 (1962): 36–54.

Engell, James. *The Creative Imagination: Enlightenment to Romanticism*. Cambridge, MA: Harvard University Press, 1981.

Erasmus. *Collected Works*. 33 vols. Vol. 3, trans. R. A. B. Mynors. Toronto: University of Toronto Press, 1991.

Esrock, Ellen J. "Embodying Literature." *Journal of Consciousness Studies* 11, nos. 5–6 (2004): 79–89.

Esrock, Ellen J. *The Reader's Eye: Visual Imaging as Reader Response*. Baltimore, MD: Johns Hopkins University Press, 1994.

Etcoff, Nancy. *Survival of the Prettiest: The Science of Beauty*. New York: Anchor, 2000.

Fadiga, L., G. Buccino, Laila Craighero, L. Fogassi, Vittorio Gallese, and G. Pavesi. "Corticospinal Excitability Is Specifically Modulated by Motor Imagery: A Magnetic Stimulation Study." *Neuropsychologica* 37 (1999): 147–158.

Farah, Martha J. "The Neural Basis of Mental Imagery." In *Essential Sources in the Scientific Study of Consciousness*, ed. Bernard J. Baars, William P. Banks, and James B. Newman, 469–477. Cambridge, MA: MIT Press, 2003.

Farah, Martha J., and A. F. Smith. "Perceptional Interference and Facilitation with Auditory Imagery." *Perception & Psychophysics* 33 (1983): 475–478.

Feagin, Susan L. "Imagining Emotions and Appreciating Fiction." In *Emotion and the Arts*, ed. Mette Hjort and Sue Laver, 50–62. New York: Oxford University Press, 1997.

Ferguson, Frances. *Solitude and the Sublime: Romanticism and the Aesthetics of Individuation*. New York: Routledge, 1992.

Ferris, David. *Silent Urns: Romanticism, Hellenism, Modernity (Cultural Memory in the Present)*. Stanford: Stanford University Press, 2000.

Fish, Stanley. "Literature in the Reader: Affective Stylistics." *New Literary History* 2, no. 1 (1970): 123–162.

Fisher, Philip. *The Vehement Passions*. Princeton, NJ: Princeton University Press, 2002.

Fransson, Peter, and Guillaume Marrelec. "The Precuneus/Posterior Cingulate Cortex Plays a Pivotal Role in the Default Mode Network: Evidence from a Partial Correlation Network Analysis." *NeuroImage* 42 (2008): 1178–1184.

Frécaut, Jean-Marc. *L'esprit et l'humour chez Ovide*. Grenoble: Presses Universitaires de Grenoble, 1972.

Fredrickson, Barbara L., and Michael A. Cohn. "Positive Emotions." In *Handbook of Emotions*. 3rd ed., ed. Michael Lewis, Jeannette M. Haviland-Jones, and Lisa Feldman Barrett, 777–796. New York: Guilford Press, 2008.

Freedberg, David. "Memory in Art: History and the Neuroscience of Response." In *The Memory Process*, ed. Suzanne Nalbantian, Paul M. Matthews, and James L. McClelland, 337–358. Cambridge, MA: MIT Press, 2011.

Freedberg, David, and Vittorio Gallese. "Motion, Emotion and Empathy in Esthetic Experience." *Trends in Cognitive Sciences* 11, no. 5 (2007): 197–203.

Fried, Michael. "Antiquity Now: Reading Winckelmann on Imitation." *October* 37 (Summer) (1986): 87–97.

Frijda, Nico H. "The Psychologists' Point of View." In *Handbook of Emotions*. 3rd ed., ed. Michael Lewis, Jeannette M. Haviland-Jones, and Lisa Feldman Barrett, 68–87. New York: Guilford Press, 2008.

Frijda, Nico H., and Louise Sundararajan. "Emotion Refinement: A Theory Inspired by Chinese Poetics." *Perspectives on Psychological Science* 2 (2007): 227–241.

Fu, Tiffany, W. Koutstaal, C.H.Y. Fu, L. Poon, and A. J. Cleare. "Depression, Confidence, and Decision: Evidence against Depressive Realism." *Journal of Psychopathology and Behavioral Assessment* 27, no. 4 (2005): 243–252.

Fulton, Alice. "Give: Daphne and Apollo." In *After Ovid: New Metamorphoses*, ed. Michael Hofmann and James Lasdun, 34–35. New York: Farrar, Straus, and Giroux, 1994.

Gabrielsson, Alf. "Emotions in Strong Experiences with Music." In *Music and Emotion: Theory and Research*, ed. Patrik N. Juslin and John A. Sloboda, 431–449. New York: Oxford University Press, 2001.

Gallagher, S. "Philosophical Conceptions of the Self: Implications for Cognitive Science." *Trends in Cognitive Sciences* 4, no. 1 (2000): 14–21.

Gammond, Peter, and Andrew Lamb. "Waltz." In *The Oxford Companion to Music*, ed. Alison Latham, 1366–1367. New York: Oxford University Press, 2002.

Gaut, Berys. "Art and Cognition." In *Contemporary Debates in Aesthetics and the Philosophy of Art*, ed. Matthew Kieran, 115–126. Malden, MA: Basil Blackwell, 2006.

Geday, J., and A. Gjedde. "Attention, Emotion, and Deactivation of Default Activity in Inferior Medial Prefrontal Cortex." *Brain and Cognition* 69, no. 2 (2009): 344–352.

Gendler, Tamar Szabó, and Karson Kovakovich. "Genuine Rational Fictional Emotions." In *Contemporary Debates in Aesthetics and the Philosophy of Art*, ed. Matthew Kieran, 241–253. Malden, MA: Blackwell, 2005.

Genette, Gerard. *The Aesthetic Relation*. Trans. G. M. Goshgarian. Ithaca, NY: Cornell University Press, 1999.

Genovese, C. R., N. A. Lazar, and T. Nichols. "Thresholding of Statistical Maps in Functional Neuroimaging Using the False Discovery Rate." *NeuroImage* 15 (1998): 870–878.

Gigante, Denise. *Taste: A Literary History*. New Haven, CT: Yale University Press, 2005.

Gibson, James J. "The Theory of Affordances." In *Perceiving, Acting, Knowing*, ed. Robert Shaw and John Bransford. New York: Wiley, 1977.

Gilman, Ernest B. *Iconoclasm and Poetry in the English Reformation: Down Went Dagon*. Chicago: University of Chicago Press, 1986.

Glimcher, Paul. *Foundations of Neuroeconomic Analysis*. New York: Oxford, 2010.

Goebel, Rainer, Darius Khorram-Sefat, Lars Muckli, Hans Hacker, and Wolf Singer. "The Constructive Nature of Vision: Direct Evidence from Functional Magnetic Resonance Imaging Studies of Apparent Motion and Motion Imagery." *European Journal of Neuroscience* 10, no. 5 (1998): 1563–1573.

Goethe, Johann Wolfgang von. *Theory of Colors*. Trans. Charles Eastlake. Cambridge, MA: Havard University Press, 1970.

Goldstein, Rita, and Nora D. Volkow. "Drug Addiction and Its Underlying Neurobiological Basis: Neuroimaging Evidence for the Involvement of the Frontal Cortex." *American Journal of Psychiatry* 159, no. 10 (2002): 1642–1652.

Gombrich, E. H. *Art and Illusion: A Study in the Psychology of Pictorial Representation*. Princeton, NJ: Princeton University Press, 2000.

Goodin, Michelle Leona. "The Spectator & the Blind Man: Seeing & Not-Seeing in the Wake of Empiricism." PhD diss., New York University, 2009.

Goodman, Kevis. "On Geoffrey Hartman's Psycho-Aesthetics." *Wordsworth Circle* 37, no. 1 (2006): 17–19.

Goodman, Nelson. *Languages of Art: An Approach to a Theory of Symbols*. 2nd ed. Indianapolis: Hackett, 1976.

Gordon, Robert. *The Structure of Emotions: Investigations in Cognitive Philosophy*. Cambridge: Cambridge University Press, 1990.

Grandjean, Didier, and Klaus R. Scherer. "Unpacking the Cognitive Architecture of Emotion Processes." *Emotion* 8, no. 3 (2008): 341–351.

Grant, Ken W., Virginie van Wassenhove, and David Poeppel. "Detection of Auditory (Cross-Spectral) and Auditory-Visual (Cross-Modal) Synchrony." *Speech Communication* 44 (2004): 43–53.

Greicius, Michael D., Ben Krasnow, Allan L. Reiss, and Vinod Menon,. "Functional Connectivity in the Resting Brain: A Network Analysis of the Default Mode Hypothesis." *Proceedings of the National Academy of Sciences of the United States of America* 100, no. 1 (2003): 253–258.

Grewe, Oliver, F. Nagel, R. Kopiez, and E. Altenmüller. "Emotions over Time: Synchronicity and Development of Subjective, Physiological, and Facial Affective Reactions to Music." *Emotion* 7, no. 4 (2007): 774–788.

Guillory, John. *Cultural Capital*. Chicago: University of Chicago Press, 1993.

Gusnard, Debra A., and Marcus E. Raichle. "Searching for a Baseline: Functional Imaging and the Resting Human Brain." *Nature Reviews: Neuroscience* 2 (2001): 685–694.

Guyer, Paul. "The Origins of Modern Aesthetics: 1711–35." In *The Blackwell Guide to Aesthetics*, ed. Peter Kivy, 15–44. London: Blackwell, 2004.

Hagendoorn, Ivar G. "Some Speculative Hypotheses About the Nature and Perception of Dance and Choreography." *Journal of Consciousness Studies* 11, nos. 3–4 (2005): 79–110.

Hagstrum, Jean H. *The Sister Arts: The Tradition of Literary Pictorialism and English Poetry from Dryden to Gray*. Chicago: University of Chicago Press, 1975.

Halpern, Andrea R. "Mental Scanning in Auditory Imagery for Songs." *Journal of Experimental Psychology: Learning, Memory, and Cognition* 14, no. 3 (1988): 434–443.

Halpern, Andrea R., and Robert Zatorre. "Mental Concerts: Musical Imagery and Auditory Cortex." *Neuron* 47 (2005): 9–12.

Halpern, Andrea R., and Robert Zatorre. "When That Tune Runs through Your Head: A PET Investigation of Auditory Imagery for Familiar Melodies." *Cerebral Cortex* 9 (7) (1999): 697–704.

Halpern, Andrea R., Robert J. Zatorre, Marc Bouffard, and Jennifer A. Johnson. "Behavioral and Neural Correlates of Perceived and Imagined Musical Timbre." *Neuropsychologia* 42 (2004): 1281–1292.

Hamilton, Ross. *Accident: A Philosophical and Literary History*. Chicago: University of Chicago Press, 2008.

Hanslick, Eduard. *The Beautiful in Music*. Trans. Gustav Cohen. New York: Da Capo Press, 1974.

Hargreaves, David J., and Adrian C. North. "Experimental Aesthetics and Liking for Music." In *Handbook of Music and Emotion: Theory, Research, Applications*, ed. Patrik N. Juslin and John A. Sloboda, 532–541. New York: Oxford University Press, 2010.

Hari, R., N. Forss, S. Avikainen, E. Kirveskari, S. Salenius, and Giacomo Rizzolatti. "Activation of Human Primary Motor Cortex During Action Observation: A Neuromagnetic Study." *Proceedings of the National Academy of Sciences of the United States of America* 95 (1998): 15061–15065.

Harrington, Deborah L., Kathleen Y. Haaland, and Neal Hermanowicz. "Temporal Processing in the Basal Ganglia." *Neuropsychology* 12, no. 1 (1998): 3–12.

Hart, Allen J., Paul J. Whalen, Lisa M. Shin, Sean C. McInerney, Hakan Fischer, and Scott L. Rauch. "Differential Response in the Human Amygdala to Racial Outgroup vs. Ingroup Face Stimuli." *NeuroReport* 11, no. 11 (2000): 2351–2354.

Hartman, Geoffrey. *The Fate of Reading*. Chicago: University of Chicago Press, 1975.

Hashimoto, R., and J. C. Rothwell. "Dynamic Changes in Corticospinal Excitability during Motor Imagery." *Experimental Brain Research* 125 (1999): 75–81.

Hassabis, Demis, Dharshan Kumaran, and Eleanor A. Maguire. "Using Imagination to Understand the Neural Basis of Episodic Memory." *Journal of Neuroscience* 27 (52) (2007): 24365–24374.

Hassabis, Demis, Dharshan Kumaran, Serralynne D. Vann, and Eleanor A. Maguire. "Patients with Hippocampal Amnesia Cannot Imagine New Experiences." *Proceedings of the National Academy of Sciences of the United States of America* 105, no. 5 (2007): 1726–1731.

Hasson, U., O. Landesman, B. Knappmeyer, I. Vallines, N. Rubin, and D. Heeger. "Neurocinematics: The Neuroscience of Films." *Projections: The Journal for Movies and Mind* 2 (2008): 1–26.

Heaney, Seamus, and Ted Hughes, eds. *The Rattle Bag*. Boston: Faber and Faber, 1982.

Heath, Malcolm. *Unity in Greek Poetics*. Oxford: Clarendon Press, 1989.

Hegel, Georg. *Introductory Lectures on Aesthetics*. Trans. Bernard Bonsanquet, ed. Michael Inwood. New York: Penguin, 1993.

Hickok, Gregory. "Eight Problems for the Mirror Neuron Theory of Action Understanding in Monkeys and Humans." *Journal of Cognitive Neuroscience* 21, no. 7 (2009): 1229–1243.

Hjort, Mette, and Sue Laver, eds. *Emotion and the Arts*. New York: Oxford University Press, 1997.

Hogan, Patrick Colm. *Cognitive Science, Literature, and the Arts: A Guide for Humanists*. New York: Routledge, 2003.

Hogan, Patrick Colm. *The Mind and Its Stories: Narrative Universals and Human Emotion*. Cambridge: Cambridge University Press, 2003.

Hogan, Patrick Colm. *What Literature Teaches Us about Emotion*. Cambridge: Cambridge University Press, 2011.

Hogarth, William. In *The Analysis of Beauty*. Ed. Ronald Paulson. New Haven: Yale University Press, 1997.

Holden, Clare, and Ruth Mace. "Phylogenetic Analysis of the Evolution of Lactose Digestion in Adults." *Human Biology* 81, nos. 5–6 (2009): 597–619.

Holmes, Emily A., Anna E. Coughtrey, and Abigail Connor. "Looking at or through Rose-Tinted Glasses? Imagery Perspective and Positive Mood." *Emotion* 8, no. 6 (2008): 875–879.

Holmes, Emily A., Andrew Mathews, Bundy Mackintosh, and Tim Dalgleish. "The Causal Effect of Mental Imagery on Emotion Assessed Using Picture-Word Cues." *Emotion* 8, no. 3 (2008): 395–409.

Hopkins, Gerard Manley. *The Major Works*. Ed. Catherine Phillips. New York: Oxford University Press, 2002.

Horace. *Ars Poetica*. In *Satires, Epistles, Ars Poetica*. Trans. H. Ruston Fairclough, 450–489. Cambridge, MA: Harvard University Press, 2005.

Hsu, Ming, Cedric Anen, and Steven R. Quartz. "The Right and the Good: Distributive Justice and Neural Encoding of Equity and Efficiency." *Science* 320, no. 5879 (2008): 1092–1095.

Hubbard, E. M., and V. S. Ramachandran. "Refining the Experimental Lever: A Reply to Shanon and Pribram." *Journal of Consciousness Studies* 10, no. 3 (2003): 77–84.

Huettel, Scott A., C. Jill Stowe, Evan M. Gordon, Brent T. Warner, and Michael L. Platt. "Neural Signatures of Economic Preferences for Risk and Ambiguity." *Neuron* 49 (2006): 765–775.

Hume, David. "Of the Standard of Taste." In *Eighteenth-Century British Aesthetics*, ed. Dabney Townsend, 230–241. Amityville, NY: Baywood, 1999.

Huron, David. *Sweet Anticipation: Music and the Psychology of Expectation*. Cambridge, MA: MIT Press, 2006.

Husted, D. S., N. A. Shapira, and W. K. Goodman. "The Neurocircuitry of Obsessive-Compulsive Disorder and Disgust." *Progress in Neuro-Psychopharmacology & Biological Psychiatry* 30 (2006): 389–399.

Hutcheson, Francis. In *An Inquiry into the Original of our Ideas of Beauty and Virtue*. Ed. Wolfgang Leidhold. Indianapolis: Liberty Fund, 2004. First published London, 1725.

Hutcheson, Francis. "To the Author of the Dublin Journal." In *Eighteenth-Century British Aesthetics*, ed. Dabney Townsend, 142–150. Amityville, NY: Baywood, 1999.

Iacoboni, Marco, Istvan Molnar-Szakacs, Vittorio Gallese, G. Buccino, John C. Mazziotta, and Giacomo Rizzolatti. "Grasping the Intentions of Others with One's Own Mirror Neuron System." *PLoS Biology* 3 (2005): e79.

Iacoboni, Marco, R. P. Woods, M. Brass, H. Bekkering, and John C. Mazziotta. "Cortical Mechanisms of Human Imitation." *Science* 286 (1999): 2526–2528.

Isaac, A., D. F. Marks, and D. G. Russell. "An Instrument for Assessing Imagery for Movement: The Vividness of Movement Imagery Questionnaire." *Journal of Mental Imagery* 10 (1986): 23–30.

Iser, Wolfgang. *The Act of Reading*. Baltimore, MD: Johns Hopkins University Press, 1980.

Ishizu, Tomohiro, and Semir Zeki. "Toward a Brain-Based Theory of Beauty." *PLoS ONE* 6, no. 7 (2011): e21852.

Jacobsen, Thomas, Ricarda I. Schubotz, Lea Höfel, and D. Yves von Cramon. "Brain Correlates of Aesthetic Judgment of Beauty." *NeuroImage* 29 (2006): 276–285.

Johnson, James H. *Listening in Paris: A Cultural History*. Berkeley: University of California Press, 1996.

Johnson-Frey, S. H., F. R. Maloof, R. Newman-Norlund, C. Farrer, Souheil Inati, and S. T. Grafton. "Actions or Hand-Object Interactions? Human Inferior Frontal Cortex and Action Observation." *Neuron* 39 (2003): 1053–1058.

Johnson-Laird, P. N., and Keith Oatley. "Emotions, Music, and Literature." In *Handbook of Emotions*. 3rd ed., ed. Michael Lewis, Jeannette M.

Haviland-Jones, and Lisa Feldman Barrett, 102–113. New York: Guilford Press, 2008.

Jones, Robert W. *Gender and the Formation of Taste in Eighteenth-Century Britain: The Analysis of Beauty*. Cambridge: Cambridge University Press, 1998.

Juslin, Patrik N., and Petri Lauuka. "Expression, Perception, and Induction of Musical Emotions: A Review and a Questionnaire Study of Everyday Listening." *Journal of New Music Research* 33 (2004): 217–238.

Juslin, Patrik N., Simon Liljeström, Daniel Västfjäll, and Lars-Olov Lundqvist. "How Does Music Evoke Emotions? Exploring the Underlying Mechanisms." In *Handbook of Music and Emotions: Theory, Research and Applications*, ed. Patrik N. Juslin and John A. Sloboda. New York: Oxford University Press, 2010.

Kandel, Eric R. *The Age of Insight: The Quest to Understand the Unconscious in Art, Mind, and Brain, from Vienna 1900 to the Present*. New York: Random House, 2012.

Kant, Immanuel. *Critique of Judgment*. Trans. Werner S. Pluhar. Indianapolis: Hackett, 1987.

Kawabata, Hideaki, and Semir Zeki. "Neural Correlates of Beauty." *Journal of Neurophysiology* 91 (2004): 1699–1705.

Kearney, Richard. *The Wake of Imagination: Toward a Postmodern Culture*. Minneapolis: University of Minnesota Press, 1988.

Keats, John. *The Complete Poems*. Ed. Jack Stillinger. Cambridge, MA: Belknap Press of Harvard University Press, 1982.

Kelley, Ann E. "Memory and Addiction: Shared Neural Circuitry and Molecular Mechanisms." *Neuron* 44 (2004): 169–171.

Kelley, W. M., C. N. Macrae, C. L. Wyland, S. Caglar, Souheil Inati, and T. F. Heatherton. "Finding the Self? An Event-Related fMRI Study." *Journal of Cognitive Neuroscience* 14, no. 5 (2002): 785–794.

Kilner, James M., Karl J. Friston, and Chris D. Frith. "The Mirror-Neuron System: A Bayesian Perspective." *NeuroReport* 18, no. 6 (2007): 619–623.

Kinderman, William. *Beethoven's Diabelli Variations*. New York: Oxford University Press, 1999.

Kim, Hackjin, Ralph Adolphs, John P. O'Doherty, and Shinsuke Shimojo. "Temporal Isolation of Neural Processes Underlying Face Preference Decisions." *Proceedings of the National Academy of Sciences of the United States of America* 104, no. 46 (2007): 18253–18258.

Kirk, U., M. Skov, M. S. Christensen, and N. Nygaard. "Brain Correlates of Aesthetic Expertise: A Parametric fMRI Study." *Brain and Cognition* 69 (2009): 306–315.

Kitayama, Shinobu, and Jiyoung Park. "Cultural Neuroscience of the Self: Understanding the Social Grounding of the Brain." *SCAN* 5 (2010): 111–129.

Kivy, Peter. *Music Alone: Philosophical Reflections on the Purely Musical Experience*. Ithaca, NY: Cornell University Press, 1990.

Klein, Stanley B. The Cognitive Neuroscience of Knowing One's Self. In *The Cognitive Neurosciences*. 3rd ed., ed. Michael S. Gazzaniga, 1077–1089. Cambridge, MA: MIT Press, 2004.

Knittel, K. M. "Wagner, Deafness, and the Reception of Beethoven's Late Style." *Journal of the American Musicological Society* 51, no. 1 (1998): 49–82.

Knutson, Brian, and Jeffrey C. Cooper. "Functional Magnetic Resonance Imaging of Reward Prediction." *Current Opinion in Neurology* 18 (2005): 411–417.

Koelsch, Stefan, Thomas Fritz, D. Yves Von Cramon, Karsten Müller, and Angela Friederici. "Investigating Emotion with Music: An fMRI Study." *Human Brain Mapping* 27 (2006): 239–250.

Kosslyn, Stephen. "Aspects of a Cognitive Neuroscience of Mental Imagery." In *Essential Sources in the Scientific Study of Consciousness*, ed. Bernard J. Baars, William P. Banks, and James B. Newman, 457–468. Cambridge, MA: MIT Press, 2003.

Kosslyn, Stephen. *Image and Mind*. Cambridge, MA: Harvard University Press, 1980.

Kosslyn, Stephen. Mental Imagery. In *Conversations in the Cognitive Neurosciences*, ed. Michael S. Gazzaniga, 155–174. Cambridge, MA: MIT Press, 1997.

Kosslyn, Stephen, W. L. Thompson, and G. Ganis. *The Case for Mental Imagery*. New York: Oxford University Press, 2006.

Kosslyn, Stephen, William L. Thompson, Mary J. Wraga, and Nathaniel M. Alpert. "Imagining Rotation by Endogenous Versus Exogenous Forces: Distinct Neural Mechanisms." *NeuroReport* 12 (2001): 2519–2525.

Kramnick, Jonathan. "Against Literary Darwinism." *Critical Inquiry* 37, no. 2 (2011): 315–347.

Krieger, Murray. *The Play and Place of Criticism*. Baltimore, MD: Johns Hopkins University Press, 1959.

Kroll, Richard. *The Material Word: Literate Culture in the Restoration and Early Eighteenth Century*. Baltimore, MD: Johns Hopkins University Press, 1991.

Kuhnen, Camelia M., and Brian Knutson. "The Neural Basis of Financial Risk Taking." *Neuron* 47 (2005): 763–770.

Lacey, S., H. Hagtvedt, V. M. Patrick, A. Anderson, R. Stilla, G. Deshpande, X. Hu, J. R. Sato, S. Reddy, and K. Sathian. "Art for Reward's Sake: Visual Art Recruits the Ventral Striatum." *NeuroImage* 55 (2011): 420–433. doi:10.1016/j.neuroimage.2010.11.027.

Lamarque, Peter. "How Can We Fear and Pity Fictions?" *British Journal of Aesthetics* 21, no. 4 (1981): 291–304.

Lamarque, Peter. "Learning from Literature." *Dalhousie Review* 77 (1997): 7–21.

Lane, Richard D., Eric. M. Reiman, Margaret M. Bradley, Peter J. Lang, Geoffrey L. Ahern, R. J. Davidson, and Gary E. Schwartz. "Neuroanatomical Correlates of Pleasant and Unpleasant Emotion." *Neuropsychologia* 35, no. 11 (1997): 1437–1444.

Laufs, H., K. Krakow, P. Sterzer, E. Eger, A. Beyerle, A. Salek-Haddadi, and A. Kleinschmidt. "Electroencephalographic Signatures of Attentional and Cognitive Default Modes in Spontaneous Brain Activity Fluctuations at Rest." *Proceedings of the National Academy of Sciences of the United States of America* 100, no. 19 (2003): 11053–11058.

LeDoux, Joseph E. *The Emotional Brain: The Mysterious Underpinnings of Emotional Life*. New York: Simon and Schuster, 1998.

LeDoux, Joseph E., and Elizabeth A. Phelps. "Emotional Networks in the Brain." In *Handbook of Emotions*. 3rd ed., ed. Michael Lewis, Jeannette

M. Haviland-Jones, and Lisa Feldman Barrett, 159–177. New York: Guilford, 2008.

Leppert, Richard. "The Social Discipline of Listening." In *Aural Cultures,* ed. Jim Drobnik, 19–36. Toronto: YYZ Books, 2004.

Levelt, Wilem J. M. "The Architecture of Normal Spoken Language Use." In *Linguistics Disorders and Pathologies: An International Handbook,* ed. Gerhard Blanken et al., 1–15. Berlin: de Gruyter, 1993.

Levine, Joseph M. *Between the Ancients and Moderns: Baroque Culture in Restoration England.* New Haven, CT: Yale University Press, 1999.

Levinson, Jerrold. "Emotion in Response to Art: A Survey of the Terrain." In *Emotion and the Arts,* ed. Mette Hjort and Sue Laver, 20–34. New York: Oxford University Press, 1997.

Levitin, Daniel. "The Neural Correlates of Temporal Structure in Music." *Music and Medicine* 1, no. 1 (2009): 9–13.

Levitin, Daniel. *This Is Your Brain on Music: The Science of a Human Obsession.* New York: Penguin, 2007.

Levitin, Daniel. *The World in Six Songs: How the Musical Brain Created Human Nature.* New York: Dutton, 2008.

Lipking, Lawrence I. *The Ordering of the Arts in Eighteenth-Century England.* Princeton, NJ: Princeton University Press, 1970.

Lippman, Edward A. *Musical Thought in Ancient Greece.* New York: Columbia University Press, 1964.

Liu, Alan. *Wordsworth: The Sense of History.* Stanford: Stanford University Press, 1989.

Locher, Paul J., Jeffrey K. Smith, and Lisa F. Smith. "The Influence of Presentation Format and Viewer Training in the Visual Arts on the Perception of Pictorial and Aesthetic Qualities of Paintings." *Perception* 30 (2001): 449–465.

Lomax, A. "The Cross-Cultural Variation of Rhythmic Style." In *Interaction Rhythms: Periodicity in Human Behavior,* ed. M. Davis. New York: Human Sciences Press, 1982.

Lyons, Michael, Ruth Campbell, Andre Plante, Mike Coleman, Miyuki Kamachi, and Shigeru Agamatsu. "The Noh Mask Effect: Vertical Viewpoint Dependence of Facial Expression Perception." *Proceedings: Biological Sciences* 267, no. 1459 (2000): 2239–2245.

Macrae, C. N., T. F. Heatherton, and W. M. Kelley. "A Self Less Ordinary: The Medial Prefrontal Cortex and You." In *The Cognitive Neurosciences*. 3rd ed., ed. Michael S. Gazzaniga, 1067–1075. Cambridge, MA: MIT Press, 2004.

Maia, Tiago V. "Reinforcement Learning, Conditioning, and the Brain: Successes and Challenges." *Cognitive, Affective, & Behavioral Neuroscience* 9, no. 4 (2009): 243–264.

Manilli, Giacomo. *Villa Borghese: Fuori di Porta Pinciana*. Rome, 1650.

Marks, D. F. "Visual Imagery Differences in the Recall of Pictures." *British Journal of Psychology* 64 (1973): 17–24.

Marshall, David. *The Frame of Art: Fictions of Aesthetic Experience, 1750–1815*. Baltimore, MD: Johns Hopkins University Press, 2005.

Martindale, Colin. "The Pleasures of Thought: A Theory of Cognitive Hedonics." *Journal of Mind and Behavior* 5, no. 1 (1984): 49–80.

Maslow, Abraham. *Toward a Psychology of Being*. 3rd ed. New York: Wiley, 1999.

Menon, V., and J. Daniel Levitin. "The Rewards of Music Listening: Response and Physiological Connectivity of the Mesolimbic System." *NeuroImage* 28 (2005): 175–184.

Merleau-Ponty, Maurice. *Phenomenology of Perception*. Trans. Colin Smith. New York: Routledge, 2002.

Middleton, F. A., and P. L. Strick. "Basal-Ganglia 'Projections' to the Prefrontal Cortex of the Primate." *Cerebral Cortex* 12 (2002): 926–935.

Miller, Christopher R. "Jane Austen's Aesthetics and Ethics of Surprise." *Narrative* 13, no. 3 (2005): 238–260.

Miller, Christopher R. *Surprise: The Poetics of the Unexpected from Milton to Austen*. Ithaca, NY: Cornell University Press, forthcoming.

Miller, Christopher R. "Wordsworth's Anatomies of Surprise." *Studies in Romanticism* 46 (Winter 2007): 409–431.

Miller, Mara. *The Garden as an Art*. Albany: State University of New York Press, 1993.

Mitchell, W.J.T. *Iconology: Image, Text, Ideology*. Chicago: University of Chicago Press, 1987.

Molnar-Szakacs, Istvan, and Katie Overy. "Music and Mirror Neurons: From Motion to 'E'motion." *SCAN* 1 (2006): 234–241.

Monk, Samuel Holt. *The Sublime: A Study of Critical Theories in XVIII-Century England*. Ann Arbor: University of Michigan Press, 1960.

Moran, J. M., C. N. Macrae, T. F. Heatherton, C. L. Wyland, and W. M. Kelley. "Neuroanatomical Evidence for Distinct Cognitive and Affective Components of Self." *Journal of Cognitive Neuroscience* 18, no. 9 (2006): 1586–1594.

Moulton, Samuel T, and Stephen Kosslyn. "Imagining Predictions: Mental Imagery as Mental Emulation." *Philosophical Transactions of the Royal Society of London, Series B, Biological Sciences* 264 (2009): 1273–1280.

Murry, John Middleton. *Keats*. New York: Noonday, 1955.

Nagel, Thomas. "What Is It Like to Be a Bat?" *Philosophical Review* 83, no. 4 (1974): 435–450.

Nalbantian, Suzanne, Paul M. Matthews, and James L. McClelland, eds. *Memory Process: Neuroscientific and Humanistic Perspectives*. Cambridge, MA: MIT Press, 2011.

Ngai, Sianne. "The Cuteness of the Avant Garde." *Critical Inquiry* 31 (Summer 2005): 811–847.

Ngai, Sianne. "Stuplimity: Shock and Boredom in Twentieth-Century Aesthetics." *Postmodern Culture* 10, no. 2 (2000).

Nicholson, Marjorie Hope. *Newton Demands the Muse: Newton's "Opticks" and the Eighteenth Century Poets*. Princeton, NJ: Princeton University Press, 1946.

Norman, Kenneth A., Sean M. Polyn, Greg J. Detre, and James V. Haxby. "Beyond Mind-Reading: Multi-Voxel Pattern Analysis of fMRI Data." *Trends in Cognitive Sciences* 10, no. 9 (2006): 424–430.

Novitz, David. *Knowledge, Fiction, and Imagination*. Philadelphia: Temple University Press, 1987.

Nussbaum, Charles O. *The Musical Representation: Meaning, Ontology, and Emotion*. Cambridge, MA: MIT Press, 2007.

Nussbaum, Martha. *Love's Knowledge: Essays on Philosophy and Literature*. New York: Oxford University Press, 1992.

Nyklicek, I., J. F. Thayer, and L. J. P. Van Doornen. "Cardiorespiratory Differentiation of Musically Induced Emotions." *Journal of Psychophysiology* 11 (1997): 304–321.

Oatley, Keith. "Emotions and the Story Worlds of Fiction." In *Narrative Impact: Social and Cognitive Foundations*, ed. M. C. Green, J. J. Strange, and T. C. Brock, 39–69. Mahwah, NJ: Erlbaum, 2002.

Oatley, Keith. "A Taxonomy of the Emotions of Literary Responses and a Theory of Identification in Fictional Narrative." *Poetics* 23 (1994): 53–74.

Oatley, Keith, and P. N. Johnson-Laird. "The Communicative Theory of Emotions: Empirical Tests, Mental Models, and Implications for Social Interaction." In *Striving and Feeling: Interactions among Goals, Affect, and Self-Regulation*, ed. Leonard L. Martin and Abraham Tesser, 363–393. Hillsdale, NJ: Erlbaum, 1996.

Okada, Hitoshi, Kazuo Matsuoka, and Takeo Hatakeyama. "Individual Differences in the Range of Sensory Modalities Experienced in Dreams." *Dreaming* 15, no. 2 (2005): 106–115.

Olkkonen, Maria, Thorsten Hansen, and Karl R. Gegenfurtner. "Color Appearance of Familiar Objects: Effects of Object Shape, Texture, and Illumination Changes." *Journal of Vision* 8, no. 5 (2008): 13–16.

O'Regan, J. Kevin, and Alva Noë. "A Sensorimotor Account of Vision and Visual Consciousness." *Behavioral and Brain Sciences* 24 (2001): 939–1031.

Orians, G. H. "An Evolutionary Perspective on Aesthetics." *Bulletin of Psychology and the Arts* 2 (2001): 25–29.

O'Rourke, James L. *Keats's Odes and Contemporary Criticism*. Gainesville: University Press of Florida, 1998.

Østby, Y., K. B. Walhovd, C. K. Tamnes, H. Grydeland, L. T. Westlye, A. M. Fjell. "Mental Time Travel and Default-Mode Network Functional Connectivity in the Developing Brain." *Proceedings of the National Academy of Sciences* 109, no. 42 (2012): 16800–16804.

Ovid. *Metamorphoses*. Trans. A. D. Melville. New York: Oxford University Press, 2009.

Ovid. *Ovid's Metamorphoses in Fifteen Books, Translated by the Most Eminent Hands*, ed. Samuel Garth. London, 1717.

Palmer, Stephen. "Gestalt Perception." In *The MIT Encyclopedia of the Cognitive Sciences*, ed. Robert Wilson and Frank Keil, 344–346. Cambridge, MA: MIT Press, 1999.

Palmer, Stephen. *Vision Science: From Photons to Phenomenology*. Cambridge, MA: MIT Press, 1991.

Panksepp, Jaak. "The Affective Brain and Core Consciousness: How Does Neural Activity Generate Emotional Feelings?" In *Handbook of Emotions*, 3rd ed., ed. Michael Lewis, Jeannette M. Haviland-Jones, and Lisa Feldman Barrett. New York: Guilford Press, 2008.

Panksepp, Jaak. "The Emotional Sources of 'Chills' Induced by Music." *Music Perception* 13, no. 2 (1995): 171–207.

Pascal, Blaise. *Pensées*. Trans. Honor Levi. New York: Oxford University Press, 2008.

Paulson, Ronald. *The Beautiful, Novel, and Strange: Aesthetics and Heterodoxy*. Baltimore, MD: Johns Hopkins University Press, 1995.

Pearcy, Lee T. *The Mediated Muse: English Translations of Ovid 1560–1700*. Hamden, CT: Archon, 1984.

Peretz, Isabelle. "Listen to the Brain: A Biological Perspective on Musical Emotions." In *Music and Emotion: Theory and Research*, ed. Patrik N. Juslin and John A. Sloboda, 105–134. New York: Oxford University Press, 2001.

Peretz, Isabelle, and Lisa Gagnon. "Dissociation between Recognition and Emotional Judgements for Melodies." *Neurocase* 5 (1999): 21–30.

Peretz, Isabelle, and Robert J. Zatorre. "Brain Organization for Music Processing." *Annual Review of Psychology* 56 (2005): 89–114.

Phan, K. Luan, Tor D. Wager, S. F. Taylor, and I. Liberzon. "Functional Neuroimaging Studies of Human Emotions." *CNS Spectrums* 9, no. 4 (2004): 258–266.

Phelps, Elizabeth A. "Emotion and Cognition: Insights from Studies of the Human Amygdala." *Annual Review of Psychology* 527 (2006): 27–53.

Phelps, Elizabeth A., C. J. Cannaistraci, and W. A. Cunningham. "Intact Performance on an Indirect Measure of Race Bias Following Amygdala Damage." *Neuropsychologia* 41 (2003): 203–208.

Phillips, M. L., A. W. Young, C. Senior, M. Brammer, C. Andrew, S.C.R. Williams, J. A. Gray, and A. S. David. "A Specific Neural Substrate for Perceiving Facial Expressions of Disgust." *Nature* 389 (1997): 495–498.

Phinney, A. W. "Keats in the Museum: Between Aesthetics and History." *Journal of English and Germanic Philology* 90, no. 2 (1991): 208–229.

Pinker, Steven. *How the Mind Works*. New York: Norton, 1999.

Plato. "Laws II." In *Musical Aesthetics: A Historical Reader*. Ed. Edward A. Lippman, vol. 1, 5–24. New York: Pendragon Press, 1986.

Plato. *Phaedrus*. Trans. Alexander Nehamas and Paul Woodruff. Indianapolis: Hackett, 1995.

Plato. *Republic*. Trans. Robin Waterfield. New York: Oxford University Press, 1994.

Plato. *Symposium*. Trans. Alexander Nehamas and Paul Woodruff. Indianapolis: Hackett, 1989.

Platt, Michael L., and A. Scott Huettel. "Risky Business: The Neuroeconomics of Decision Making under Uncertainty." *Nature Neuroscience* 11, no. 4 (2008): 398–403.

Porro, Carlo A., Maria Pia Francescato, Valentina Cettolo, Mathew E. Diamond, Patrizia Baraldi, Chiava Zuiani, Massimo Bazzocchi, and Pietro E. di Prampero. "Primary Motor and Sensory Cortex Activation during Motor Performance and Motor Imagery: A Functional Magnetic Resonance Imaging Study." *Journal of Neuroscience* 16, no. 23 (1996): 7688–7698.

Prather, S. C., R. John Votaw, and K. Sathian. "Task-Specific Recruitment of Dorsal and Ventral Visual Areas during Tactile Perception." *Neuropsychologia* 42 (2004): 1079–1087.

Pratt, Carroll. *The Meaning of Music*. New York: McGraw-Hill, 1931.

Preminger, Son. "Transformative Art: Art as Means for Long-term Neurocognitive Change." *Frontiers in Human Neuroscience* 6 (2012): 96. doi:10.3389/fnhum.2012.00096.

Pribram, Karl. "Commentary on 'Synaesthesia' by Ramachandran and Hubbard." *Journal of Consciousness Studies* 10, no. 3 (2003): 75–76.

Prinz, Jesse. "Can Critics Be Dispassionate? The Role of Emotion in Aesthetic Judgment." Paper presented at a meeting of the American Society for Aesthetics, Houston, 2004.

Prinz, Jesse. "Emotion and Aesthetic Value." Paper presented at a meeting of the American Philosophical Association, Pacific Division, San Francisco, 2007.

Prinz, Jesse. *Gut Reactions: A Perceptual Theory of Emotion.* New York: Oxford University Press, 2006.

Puce, A., T. Allison, J. C. Gore, and G. McCarthy. "Face-Sensitive Regions in Human Extrastriate Cortex Studied by Functional MRI." *Journal of Neurophysiology* 74 (1995): 1192–1199.

Pylyshyn, Zenon. "Is the Imagery Debate Over? If So, What Was It About?" In *Language, Brain, and Cognitive Development: Essays in Honor of Jacques Mehler*, ed. Emmanuel Dupoux, 59–82. Cambridge, MA: MIT Press, 2001.

Pylyshyn, Zenon. "Return of the Mental Image: Are There Really Pictures in the Brain?" *Trends in Cognitive Sciences* 7, no. 3 (2003): 113–118.

Quartz, Steven R. "Reason, Emotion and Decision-Making: Risk and Reward Computation with Feeling." *Trends in Cognitive Sciences* 13, no. 5 (2009): 209–214.

Quintilian. *The Orator's Education.* Trans. Donald A. Russell. 5 vols. Cambridge, MA: Harvard University Press, 2001.

Raichle, Marcus E., and Abraham Z. Snyder. "A Default Mode of Brain Function: A Brief History of an Evolving Idea." *NeuroImage* 37 (2007): 1083–1090.

Raichle, Marcus E., Mary Ann MacLeod, Abraham Z. Snyder, William J. Powers, Debra A. Gusnard, and Gordon L. Shulman. "A Default Mode of Brain Function." *Proceedings of the National Academy of Sciences of the United States of America* 98 (2) (2001): 676–682.

Ramachandran, V. S. *The Tell-Tale Brain: A Neuroscientist's Quest for What Makes Us Human.* New York: Norton, 2011.

Ramachandran, V. S., and E. M. Hubbard. "Synaesthesia: A Window into Perception, Thought and Language." *Journal of Consciousness Studies* 8, no. 12 (2001): 3–34.

Reber, Rolf, Norbert Schwarz, and Piotr Winkielman. "Processing Fluency and Aesthetic Pleasure: Is Beauty in the Perceiver's Processing Experience?" *Personality and Social Psychology Review* 8, no. 4 (2004): 364–382.

Rentschler, Ingo, Martin Jüttner, Alexander Unzicker, and Theodor Landis. "Innate and Learned Components of Human Visual Preference." *Current Biology* 9 (1999): 665–671.

Richards, I. A. *Principles of Literary Criticism*. New York: Routledge, 2001.

Richardson, A. *Mental Imagery*. New York: Springer, 1969.

Richardson, Alan. *The Neural Sublime*. Baltimore, MD: Johns Hopkins University Press, 2010.

Richardson, Alan, and Francis F. Steen. "Literature and the Cognitive Revolution: An Introduction." *Poetics Today* 23, no. 1 (2002): 1–8.

Rickard, Nikki S. "Intense Emotional Responses to Music: A Test of the Physiological Arousal Hypothesis." *Psychology of Music* 32 (2004): 371–388.

Ridley, Aaron. *Music, Value and the Passions*. Ithaca, NY: Cornell University Press, 1995.

Riffaterre, Michel. "The Stylistic Approach to Literary History." *New Literary History* 2, no. 1 (1970): 39–55.

Rizzolatti, Giacomo, and Laila Craighero. "The Mirror-Neuron System." *Annual Review of Neuroscience* 27 (2004): 169–192.

Robinson, Jenefer. *Deeper Than Reason: Emotion and Its Role in Literature, Music, and Art*. New York: Oxford University Press, 2005.

Rockwell, Joti. "Banjo Transformation and Bluegrass Rhythm." *Journal of Music Therapy* 53, no. 1 (2009): 137–162.

Rockwell, Joti. "Time on the Crooked Road: Isochrony, Meter, and Disruption in Old-Time Country and Bluegrass Music." *Ethnomusicology* 55, no. 1 (2011): 55–76.

Rolls, Edmund T. *Emotion Explained*. New York: Oxford University Press, 2005.

Rosen, Charles. *The Classical Style: Haydn, Mozart, Beethoven*. Expanded ed. New York: W. W. Norton, 1997.

Rosenbert, Neil V. *Bluegrass: A History*. Champaign: University of Illinois Press, 2005.

Rossini, Paolo M., Simone Rossi, Patrizio Pasqualetti, and Franca Tecchio. "Corticospinal Excitability Modulation to Hand Muscles during Movement Imagery." *Cerebral Cortex* 9 (1999): 161–167.

Sabatinelli, Dean, Peter J. Lang, Margaret M. Bradley, and Tobias Flaisch. "The Neural Basis of Narrative Imagery: Emotion and Action." *Progress in Brain Research* 156 (2006): 93–103.

Sacks, Oliver. *Musicophilia*. New York: Knopf, 2007.

Salimpoor, Valorie N., Mitchel Benovoy, Gregory Longo, Jeremy R. Cooperstock, and Robert J. Zatorre. "The Rewarding Aspects of Music Listening Are Related to Degree of Emotional Arousal." *PLos ONE* 4, no. 10 (2009).

Salimpoor, Valorie N., Mitchel Benovoy, Kevin Larcher, Alain Dagher, and Robert J. Zatorre,. "Anatomically Distinct Dopamine Release during Anticipation and Experience of Peak Emotion to Music." *Nature Neuroscience* 14, no. 2 (2011): 257–262.

Sandys, George. *Ovid's Metamorphoses Englished by G.S.* London, 1628.

Sathian, K. "Visual Cortical Activity during Tactile Perception in the Sighted and the Visually Deprived." *Developmental Psychobiology* 46 (2005): 279–286.

Saxe, Rebecca, and Nancy Kanwisher. "People Thinking about Thinking People: The Role of the Temporo-parietal Junction in 'Theory of Mind.'" *NeuroImage* 19 (2003): 1835–1842.

Scarry, Elaine. *Dreaming by the Book*. New York: Farrar, Straus and Giroux, 1999.

Scarry, Elaine. *On Beauty and Being Just*. Princeton, NJ: Princeton University Press, 1999.

Scherer, Klaus R. "Appraisal Theory." In *Handbook of Cognition and Emotion*, ed. Tim Dalgleish and Mick Power, 637–663. New York: Wiley, 1999.

Scherer, Klaus R. "Toward a Concept of 'Modal Emotions." In *The Nature of Emotion*, ed. P. Ekman and R. J. Davidson, 25–31. New York: Oxford University Press, 1994.

Schopenhauer, Arthur. *The World as Will and Representation*. New York, New York: Dover, 1966.

Shaftesbury, Anthony Cooper. In *Characteristics of Men, Manners, Opinions, Times*. Ed. Lawrence E. Klein. New York: Cambridge University Press, 1999.

Sheehan, P. W. "A Shortened Form of Betts' Questionnaire upon Mental Imagery." *Journal of Clinical Psychology* 23 (1967): 386–389.

Shelley, Percy Bysshe. In *The Complete Poetry of Percy Bysshe Shelley*. vol. 3. Ed. Donald H. Reiman, Neil Fraistat, and Nora Crook. Baltimore, MD: Johns Hopkins University Press, 2012.

Shiner, Larry. *The Invention of Art: A Cultural History*. Chicago: University of Chicago Press, 2001.

Sibley, Frank. "Aesthetic and Nonaesthetic." *Philosophical Review* 74, no. 2 (1965): 135–159.

Sibley, Frank. "Aesthetic Concepts." *Philosophical Review* 68 (1959): 421–450.

Sibley, Frank. "Particularity, Art and Evaluation." *Aristotelian Society Supplementary Volume* 48 (1974): 1–21.

Sidney, Philip. "The Defence of Poesy." In *Sidney's "The Defence of Poesy" and Selected Renaissance Literary Criticism*, ed. Gavin Alexandar. New York: Penguin, 2004.

Siegel, Jonah. *Desire and Excess: The Nineteenth-Century Culture of Art*. Princeton: Princeton University Press, 2000.

Simpson, J. R., A. Z. Snyder, D. A. Gusnard, and M. E. Raichle. "Emotion-Induced Changes in Human Medial Prefrontal Cortex: I. During Cognitive Task Performance." *Proceedings of the National Academy of Sciences of the United States of America* 93 (2001): 683–687.

Simpson, J. R., A. Z. Snyder, D. A. Gusnard, and M. E. Raichle. "Emotion-Induced Changes in Human Medial Prefrontal Cortex: II. During Anticipatory Anxiety." *Proceedings of the National Academy of Sciences of the United States of America* 93 (2001): 688–693.

Siskin, Clifford. *The Historicity of Romantic Discourse*. New York: Oxford University Press, 1988.

Siskin, Clifford. *The Work of Writing: Literature and Social Change in Britain, 1700–1830*. Baltimore, MD: Johns Hopkins University Press, 1998.

Sitter, John. "Touching Satire." Paper presented at a meeting of the American Society for Eighteenth-Century Studies, Montreal, 2006.

Sloboda, John A. "Music in Everyday Life: The Role of Emotions." In *Handbook of Music and Emotion: Theory, Research, Applications*, ed. Patrik N. Juslin and John A. Sloboda, 493–514. New York: Oxford University Press, 2010.

Smith, Adam. In *The Theory of Moral Sentiments*. Ed. D. D. Raphael and A. L. Macfie. Indianapolis: Liberty Fund, 1984.

Smith, Barbara Herrnstein. *Poetic Closure: A Study of How Poems End*. Chicago: University of Chicago Press, 1968.

Smith, Stephen M., Peter T. Fox, Karla L. Miller, David C. Glahn, P. Mickle Fox, Clare E. Mackay, Nicola Filippini, Kate E. Watkins, Roberto Toro, Angela R. Laird, and Christian F. Beckmann. "Correspondence of the Brain's Functional Architecture during Activation and Rest." *Proceedings of the National Academy of Sciences of the United States of America* 106, no. 31 (2009): 13040–13045.

Sohn, Young H., Nguyet Dang, and Mark Hallett. "Suppression of Corticospinal Excitability during Negative Motor Imagery." *Journal of Neurophysiology* 90 (2003): 2303–2309.

Solomon, Maynard. *Late Beethoven: Music, Thought, Imagination*. Berkeley: University of California, 2003.

Solomon, Robert C. *The Passions: Emotions and the Meaning of Life*. Indianapolis: Hackett, 1993.

Solso, Robert L. *Cognition and the Visual Arts*. Cambridge, MA: MIT Press, 1996.

Spinoza, Baruch. *Ethics, Treatise on the Emendation of the Intellect, and Selected Letters*. Trans. Samuel Shirley, ed. Seymour Feldman. Indianapolis: Hackett, 1991.

Spitzer, Michael. *Music as Philosophy: Adorno and Beethoven's Late Style*. Bloomington: Indiana University Press, 2006.

Spolsky, Ellen. "Making 'Quite Anew': Brain Modularity and Creativity." In *Introduction to Cognitive Cultural Studies*, ed. Lisa Zunshine, 84–102. Baltimore, MD: Johns Hopkins University Press, 2010.

Spreng, R. Nathan, Raymond A. Mar, and Alice S. N. Kim. "The Common Neural Basis of Autobiographical Memory, Prospection, Navigation, Theory of Mind and the Default Mode: A Quantitative Meta-Analysis." *Journal of Cognitive Neuroscience* 21, no. 3 (2008): 489–510.

St. Clair, William. *Lord Elgin and the Marbles: The Controversial History of the Parthenon Sculptures*. New York: Oxford University Press, 1998.

Stafford, Barbara Maria. "Beauty of the Invisible: Winckelmann and the Aesthetics of Imperceptibility." *Zeitschrift für Kunstgeschichte* 43, no. 1 (1980): 65–80.

Starr, G. Gabrielle. "Burney, Ovid and the Value of the Beautiful." *Eighteenth-Century Fiction* 24, no. 1 (2012): 77–104.

Starr, G. Gabrielle. "Cavendish, Aesthetics, and the Anti-Platonic Line." *Eighteenth-Century Studies* 29, no. 3 (2006): 295–308.

Starr, G. Gabrielle. "Ethics, Meaning and the Work of Beauty." *Eighteenth-Century Studies* 35, no. 3 (2002): 361–378.

Starr, G. Gabrielle. "Multi-Sensory Imagery." In *Introduction to Cognitive Cultural Studies*, ed. Lisa Zunshine, 275–291. Baltimore, MD: Johns Hopkins University Press, 2010.

Steen, Francis F. "A Cognitive Account of Aesthetics." In *The Artful Mind*, ed. Mark Turner. New York: Oxford University Press, 2006.

Stefan, Katja, Leonard G. Cohen, Julie Duque, Riccardo Mazzochio, Pablo Celnik, Lumi Sawaki, Leslie Ungerleider, and Joseph Classen. "Formation of a Motor Memory by Action Observation." *Journal of Neuroscience* 25, no. 41 (2005): 9339–9346.

Steriade, M., and R. R. Llinás. "The Functional States of the Thalamus and the Associated Neuronal Interplay." *Physiological Reviews* 68 (1988): 649–742.

Stevens, Catherine, and Shirley McKechnie. "Thinking in Action: Thought Made Visible in Contemporary Dance." *Cognitive Processing* 6 (2005): 243–252.

Stevens, J. A. "Interference Effects Demonstrate Distinct Roles for Visual and Motor Imagery during the Mental Representation of Human Action." *Cognition* 95 (2005): 329–350.

Stevens, J. A. "Olfactory Dreams: Phenomenology, Relationship to Volitional Imagery and Odor Identification." *Imagination, Cognition and Personality* 24, no. 1 (2005): 69–90.

Stevenson, Richard J., and Trevor I. Case. "Olfactory Imagery: A Review." *Psychonomic Bulletin & Review* 12, no. 2 (2005): 244–264.

Stolnitz, Jerome. "On the Cognitive Triviality of Art." *British Journal of Aesthetics* 32 (1992): 191–200.

Stolnitz, Jerome. "On the Origins of 'Aesthetic Disinterestedness'." *Journal of Aesthetics and Art Criticism* 20 (1961): 131–144.

Stuckey, Charles. "Rhythmic Lines: Van Gogh's Drawings." *Art in America* 94, no. 3 (2006): 112–117.

Swift, Jonathan. *The Complete Poems.* Ed. Pat Rogers. New York: Penguin, 1989.

Talairach, J., and P. Tournoux. *Co-planar Sterotaxic Atlas of the Human Brain: 3-Dimensional Proportional System—An Approach to Cerebral Imaging.* New York: Thieme Medical Publishers, 1988.

Teasdale, John D., Robert J. Howard, Sally G. Cox, Yvonne Ha, M. Brammer, S.C.R. Williams, and Stuart A. Checkley. "Functional MRI Study of the Cognitive Generation of Affect." *American Journal of Psychiatry* 156, no. 2 (1999): 209–215.

Temperley, David. *Music and Probability.* Cambridge, MA: MIT Press, 2007.

Terwogt, Mark Meerum, and Flora Van Grinsven. "Musical Expression of Moodstates." *Psychology of Music* 19 (1991): 99–109.

Thompson, William Forde, E. Glenn Schellenberg, and Gabriela Husain. "Arousal, Mood, and the Mozart Effect." *Psychological Science* 12, no. 3 (2001): 248–251.

Tobias, T. J. "Afferents to Prefrontal Cortex from the Thalamic Mediodorsal Nucleus in the Rhesus Monkey." *Brain Research* 83 (1975): 191–212.

Trainor, Laurel J., and L. A. Schmidt. "Processing Emotions Induced by Music." In *The Cognitive Neuroscience of Music*, ed. Isabelle Peretz and Robert Zatorre, 310–324. New York: Oxford University Press, 2004.

Trainor, Laurel J., and Sandra E. Trehub. "The Development of Referential Meaning in Music." *Music Perception* 9 (1992): 455–470.

Tramo, Mark J., Peter A. Carani, Bertrande Delgutte, and Louis D. Braida. "Neurobiological Foundations for the Theory of Harmony in Western Tonal Music." *Annals of the New York Academy of Sciences* 930 (2001): 92–116.

Tramo, Mark J., Peter A. Carani, Christine K. Koh, Nikos Makris, and Louis D. Braida. "Neurophysiology and Neuroanatomy of Pitch Perception: Auditory Cortex." *Annals of the New York Academy of Sciences* 1060 (2005): 148–174.

Tschacher, Wolfgang, Steven Greenwood, Volker Kirchberg, Stéphanie Wintzerith, Karen van Den Berg, and Martin Tröndle. "Physiological Correlates of Aesthetic Perception of Artworks in a Museum." *Psychology of Aesthetics, Creativity, and the Arts* 6, no. 1 (2012): 96–103.

Tsur, Reuven. "Some Cognitive Foundations of 'Cultural Programs.'" *Poetics Today* 23, no. 1 (2002): 63–89.

Turner, Mark. *The Literary Mind*. New York: Oxford University Press, 1997.

Tye, Michael. "The Subjective Qualities of Experience." *Mind* 95, no. 377 (1986): 1–17.

Urry, H. L., J. B. Nitschke, I. Dolksi, D. C. Jackson, K. M. Dalton, C. J. Mueller, M. A. Rosenkranc, C. D. Ryff, B. H. Singer and R. J. Davidson, et al. "Making a Life Worth Living: Neural Correlates of Well-Being." *Psychological Science* 15, no. 6 (2004): 367–372.

Vartanian, Oshin. "Conscious Experience of Pleasure in Art." In *Neuroaesthetics*, ed. Martin Skov and Oshin Vartanian, 261–273. Amityville, NY: Baywood, 2009.

Vartanian, Oshin, and V. Goel. "Neuroanatomical Correlates of Aesthetic Preference for Paintings." *NeuroReport* 15:893–897 (2004).

Vendler, Helen H. *The Odes of John Keats*. Cambridge, MA: Belknap Press of Harvard University Press, 1983.

Verdejo-Garcia, A., M. Perez-Garcia, and Antoine Bechara. "Emotion, Decision-Making and Substance Dependence: A Somatic-Marker Model of Addiction." *Current Neuropharmacology* 4 (2006): 17–31.

Vermeule, Blakey. *Why Do We Care about Literary Characters?* Baltimore, MD: Johns Hopkins University Press, 2009.

Vessel, Edward A., and Nava Rubin. "Beauty and the Beholder: Highly Individual Taste for Abstract, but Not Real-World Images." *Journal of Vision* 10, no. 2 (2010): 1–14.

Vessel, Edward A., G. Gabrielle Starr, and Nava Rubin. "The Brain on Art: Intense Aesthetic Experience Activates the Default Mode Network." *Frontiers in Human Neuroscience* 6, no. 66 (2012). doi:10.3389/fnhum.2012.00066.

Vianna, Eduardo Paulo Morawski, Nasir Naqvi, Antoine Bechara, and Daniel Tranel. "Does Vivid Emotional Imagery Depend on Body Signals?" *International Journal of Psychophysiology* 72 (2009): 46–50.

von Helmholtz, Hermann. "On the Physiological Causes of Harmony in Music." In *Science and Culture*, ed. David Cahan. Chicago: University of Chicago Press, 1995.

von Helmholtz, Hermann. "On the Relation of Optics to Painting." In *Science and Culture*, ed. David Cahan, 279–309. Chicago: University of Chicago Press, 1995.

Wager, Tor D., Lisa Feldman Barrett, Eliza Bliss-Moreau, Kristen A. Lindquist, Seth Duncan, Hedy Kober, Josh Joseph, Matthew Davidson, and Jennifer Mize. "The Neuroimaging of Emotion." In *Handbook of Emotions*. 3rd ed., ed. Michael Lewis, Jeannette M. Haviland-Jones, and Lisa Feldman Barrett, 249–271. New York: Guilford Press, 2008.

Walton, Kendall. *Mimesis and Make-Believe*. Cambridge, MA: Harvard University Press, 1990.

Wasserman, Earl. *The Finer Tone*. Baltimore, MD: Johns Hopkins University Press, 1967.

Watson, Charles S. "Uncertainty, Informational Masking, and the Capacity of Immediate Auditory Memory." In *Auditory Processing of Complex Sounds*, ed. William A. Yost and Charles S. Watson, 368–379. Hillsdale, NJ: Erlbaum, 1987.

Watson, D., L. A. Clark, and A. Tellegen. "Development and Validation of Brief Measures of Positive and Negative Affect: The PANAS Scales." *Journal of Personality and Social Psychology* 54 (1988): 1063–1070.

Weber, William. "Did People Listen in the 18th Century?" *Early Music* 25 (1997): 678–691.

Weinbrot, Howard. *The Formal Strain: Studies in Augustan Imitation and Satire*. Chicago: University of Chicago Press, 1969.

Wimsatt, W. K., and Monroe Beardsley. *The Verbal Icon*. Lexington: University of Kentucky Press, 1954.

Winckelmann, Johann. "On the Imitation of the Painting and Sculpture of the Greeks." In *German Essays on Art History*. Trans. Henry Fuseli, ed. Gert Schiff, 1–17. New York: Continuum, 1988.

Wittkower, Rudolf. *Bernini*. New York: Phaidon, 1997.

Yates, Frances. *The Art of Memory*. Chicago: University of Chicago Press, 1966.

Young, Edward. *Conjectures on Original Composition*. London, 1759.

Young, Kay. *Imagining Minds: The Neuro-Aesthetics of Austen, Eliot, and Hardy*. Columbus: Ohio State University Press, 2010.

Zajonc, Robert B. "Attitudinal Effects of Mere Exposure." *Journal of Personality and Social Psychology* 9, no. 2 (1968): 1–27.

Zatorre, Robert. "Music, the Food of Neuroscience?" *Nature* 434, no. 7031 (2005): 312–315.

Zeki, Semir. *Inner Vision: An Exploration of Art and the Brain.* New York: Oxford University Press, 2000.

Zentner, Marcel, Didier Grandjean, and Klaus R. Scherer. "Emotions Evoked by the Sound of Music: Characterization, Classification, and Measurement." *Emotion* 8, no. 4 (2008): 494–521.

Zhang, Minming, Valerie D. Weisser, Randall Stilla, S. C. Prather, and K. Sathian. "Multisensory Cortical Processing of Object Shape and Its Relation to Mental Imagery." *Cognitive, Affective, & Behavioral Neuroscience* 4, no. 2 (2004): 251–259.

Zunshine, Lisa. *Why We Read Fiction: Theory of Mind and the Novel.* Columbus: Ohio State University Press, 2006.

Zunshine, Lisa. *Strange Concepts and the Stories They Make Possible.* Baltimore, MD: Johns Hopkins University Press, 2009.

Index

Addison, Joseph, 70, 121
Aesthetic computational value, 50
Aesthetic experience, xv, 24–27, 51–53, 54–67, 119–120
 and knowledge, xv–xvi, 11–25, 49–52, 65–67, 72, 76–78, 96–100, 118–127
Aesthetic terminology, 2, 4, 39, 45
Aesthetic value, 48–49
Affordances, 80, 87
Anterior medial prefrontal cortex, 42, 60–63, 156
Aristotle, 8, 13, 26, 117
Augustine, Saint, 43

Basal ganglia, 24, 61, 88. *See also* Striatum; Substantia nigra
Beauty, xii–xiii, 5–7, 12, 15–19, 21, 24, 34, 39, 45, 48, 50, 56, 64–66, 71–72, 81–82, 84, 91–93, 100, 103–108, 112–113, 117–118, 119, 121, 123–127, 138–142, 145, 147–149. *See also* Aesthetic terminology
Beethoven, Ludwig von, 132–137
Bernini, Gian Lorenzo, 19, 121–127
Bishop, Elizabeth, 94–100
Bluegrass, 128–132
Burke, Edmund, 10, 39, 123

Chills effect (music), 43–44, 48, 51, 54
Cicero, 1
Close reading and individual differences, 111–118

Dance, 5, 10, 52, 86, 99, 134, 140, 148
Default mode network, xv, 21, 23–25, 34, 46, 50–51, 57–67, 97–100
Dryden, John, 118–124

Emotion, 21–23, 40–41, 46–48
 and action tendencies, 36–38
 and aesthetic response, 4–7,
  9–10, 13, 17, 18–20, 23–28,
  33–34, 38–40, 41–46,
  55–59, 83, 87, 88, 92–94,
  96–97, 113, 120–122, 125–
  128, 128–132, 136, 146–
  147, 163–167
 basic, 38–40
Empathy, 83–84, 94
Epistemology and aesthetics,
  13–17, 18–20, 118–127
Evolutionary psychology, 26–28,
  49–51

Faces, 49–51
fMRI, 23, 42, 44–46, 57, 59, 83,
  151–157
Frijda, Nico, 21, 37, 39–40
Fulton, Alice, 124–127

Glass, Philip, 146
Gogh, Vincent van, 138–144
Gombrich, E. H., 99, 132–134,
  137–138

Hemispheric lateralization, 41, 43
Hippocampus, 24, 61, 63, 146,
  155
Hogarth, William, 70–72,
  139–141
Hopkins, Gerard Manley, 89–90,
  96
Horace, 5, 90
Hume, David, 19, 39
Hutcheson, Francis, 15–18

Imagery, xv, 7–11, 23, 69–72. *See also* Imagination

 auditory, 78, 86–91
 centrality of motor, 82–91,
  93–97, 130–132, 133–134,
  139–142
 and default mode network,
  81–83, 97–100
 and epistemology, 76–81
 haptic, 75, 79–80, 96
 limits of sensory, 102–118
 multisensory/multimodal,
  78–81, 91, 93–97
 olfactory, 74, 77–78
 and reward, 92–93
 visual, 72–81
Imagination, 3, 7–11, 17–19,
  24–26, 58, 64–66. *See also* Imagery
 and knowledge, 14–17
Individual differences, 54–67,
  72–73, 77–78, 93, 102–103,
  115–117
Inferior frontal gyrus, pars triangularis, 42

Kant, Immanuel, xiv, 35, 49,
  64–65
Keats, John, 11–14, 43, 77–78,
  102–118
Kivy, Peter, 39

Landscape, 27, 49–51, 148

Memory, xv, 24, 26, 40, 46, 48,
  51, 60–63, 93, 127, 144–149
Mirror neurons, 82–83
Music, 3, 5–7, 9–10, 13, 20, 39,
  41–44, 46, 48, 53, 54–67,
  72, 77–79, 86–88, 93–94,
  98–100, 107, 128–137

Novelty, 119–122, 128–137

Orbitofrontal cortex, 24, 26, 41, 48
Ovid, 19, 25, 43, 76–79, 118–127, 144–148

Painting. *See* Visual art
Plato, 5–6, 7–8, 13–14, 104, 106–107, 117
Poetry, 2, 5–8, 10, 12–16, 43–44, 52–53, 69–70, 89–91, 97–100, 102–103, 107–113, 114–118, 118–127, 144–146
Pollock, Jasper, 85–86
Pontine reticular formation, 56
Posterior cingulate cortex, 61–63, 155
Prinz, Jesse, 19, 36

Reward, 46–53, 122–124, 128–137
Rubin, Nava, 23, 41, 44, 55, 59, 64, 151

Shelley, Percy Bysshe, 107–108
Sister arts, theory of, 2–13, 17, 21–22, 33–35, 48, 50–53, 69–70, 86, 93, 99–100, 108, 116–118, 123, 144–149
Smith, Adam, 83–84
Smith, Barbara Herrnstein, 110–111
Spinoza, Baruch, 65–67
Stanley, Ralph, 130–132
Striatum, 26, 42, 51, 61
Sublime, 64–65. *See also* Aesthetic terminology

Substantia nigra, 26, 42, 61, 63, 155
Superior frontal gyrus, 42
Swift, Jonathan, 84

Temporo-parietal junction, 60
Translation, 119–127

Vessel, Edward A., 23, 41, 44, 49, 55, 59, 63, 151
Visual art, 18, 23, 41–46, 48, 55, 58–60, 70–72, 81–82, 84–86, 94, 104–107, 121–127, 138–144

Walton, Kendall, 6–7, 37
Waltz, 86, 132–137
Weissberg, Eric, 119–124
Winckelmann, Johann, 104–106, 117, 137, 140

Zeki, Semir, 41, 48